After Aquinas

AFTER AQUINAS

Versions of Thomism

Fergus Kerr

350 Main Street, Malden, MA 02148-5018, USA
108 Cowley Road, Oxford OX4 1JF, UK
550 Swanston Street, Carlton, Victoria 3053, Australia
Kurfürstendamm 57, 10707 Berlin, Germany

First published 2002 by Blackwell Publishers Ltd, a Blackwell
Publishing company

Library of Congress Cataloguing-in-Publication Data has been applied for.

ISBN 0-631-21312-0 (hbk); ISBN 0-631-21313-9 (pbk)

A catalogue record for this title is available from the British Library.

Set in 10 on 12 pt Sabon
by SNP Best-set Typesetter Ltd., Hong Kong
Printed and bound in the United Kingdom by T. J. International,
Padstow, Cornwall

For further information on
Blackwell Publishing, visit our website:
http://www.blackwellpublishing.com

CONTENTS

PREFACE

Curricula determine that most students of Christian theology, in the English-speaking world, and not excluding Roman Catholic ordinands, never need read deeply in the writings of Thomas Aquinas. They will hear, in the Philosophy of Religion course, that he opened his most famous book, the *Summa Theologiae*, with five proofs from features of the world that there is a First Cause. They may read that the God whose existence he has thus demonstrated is the unmoved mover of Mediterranean antiquity, with little if anything to do with the God of Christian revelation. His works will not appear among books recommended for courses on the Trinity or Christology. In Christian ethics, on the other hand, they will hear that Thomas is the classical exponent of a system of morals based on natural law.[1]

That is, roughly, the standard conception of Thomas's thought, which the following chapters are intended to destabilize.

In the first place, a great deal of interesting work on Thomas, particularly by North American scholars, deserves to be better known. Without attempting a comprehensive survey, I highlight work which opens alternatives to the standard account.

A bibliography necessarily discloses elements of autobiography. I am not a medievalist: I barely touch on the immense amount of research on thirteenth-century thought. Nor am I competent to discuss the history of the reception of Thomas's work: by his immediate successors; by the generation affected by John Duns Scotus; by sixteenth-century expositors such as Suárez, Cajetan and Bañes; by those, like Las Casas and Vitoria, who used his teaching about natural law to develop a doctrine of human rights to defend the indigenous peoples of Latin America – to mention only the salient phases in the story.

I start with the revival of interest in Thomas, influentially endorsed in 1879 by Pope Leo XIII. Created primarily to resist the influence in Roman Catholic theology of modern philosophy (Descartes, Kant, and Hegel), Leonine Thomism spawned a vast literature but, in the 1920s, split into rival and conflicting understandings of Thomas's work. The most contentious issue was whether modern philosophy must simply be rejected or might to some extent be integrated with Thomas's philosophy. Those who took the latter course, like Joseph Maréchal, Bernard Lonergan and Karl Rahner, came to be known as Transcendental Thomists. Others, like Etienne Gilson and Jacques Maritain, thought any compromise with modern philosophy inevitably bred misconceptions of Thomas's work. On the other hand, obviously stimulated by reading Bergson, Blondel and others, they focused on Thomas's identification of God as 'subsistent existence' to such an extent that their contribution is known as Existential Thomism. Many went on reading Thomas as an Aristotelian (and therefore anti-idealist), while others, by the 1950s, reconstructed his debts to Christian Platonism. Some, in Britain particularly, saw Thomas as a precursor in elucidating problems set by modern philosophy.

I first studied philosophy under Donald MacKinnon and A.G.N. Flew at the University of Aberdeen. Some years later, I came to Thomas Aquinas, guided principally by Cornelius Ernst, in the light of Heidegger and Wittgenstein as well as of Aristotle. I then studied Thomas's theology at Le Saulchoir, the theological faculty of the Dominican friars in Paris, in the historical style represented by M.-D. Chenu. Finally, I had a year in Munich, spending much less time (as it turned out) listening to Karl Rahner than working through Heidegger with Adolf Darlap.

In one way or another, as readers familiar with these names would realize, my understanding of Thomas has always been affected by several different, conflicting and incommensurable approaches to his work. All along, for most of my teachers, Karl Barth loomed in the background, an admirer of Thomas and a ferocious critic of Thomism. Now that I come to spell out some (only some!) of the interpretations of Thomas's work that should be allowed to unsettle the standard account, I find it impossible to leave Barth and some of his recent interpreters out of the conversation.

In chapter 1 I outline Thomas's biography, highlighting the conflicts by which his work is marked. In chapter 2 I discuss how Thomas's view of the self and his account of knowledge played an important part, and perhaps should still do so, in philosophical attempts to overcome the Cartesian legacy of solipsism and scepticism in modern philosophy. In

chapters 3 and 4, in connection with natural theology, I outline prelim-
inaries that need to be taken into account, some of which cast a non-
standard light on the subject. Chapter 5 deals with the question of
existence or 'being' – briefly in the English-language tradition, mostly in
a post-Heideggerian context. Chapter 6 sets out contrasting views about
Thomas's natural law theory. In chapter 7, I discuss Thomas's theological ethics; in chapter 8 the great dispute about nature and grace; and in
chapter 9 his concept of sanctification as deified creaturehood. In the
next two chapters I outline what Thomas says, in the *Summa Theologiae*, first about Christ and then about God, in the hope that, inadequate
as any Christology must now be that antedates modern biblical studies,
Thomas's is not quite so barren as is often supposed; and, in the hope
that, whatever we are to make of this, Thomas's God, far from being the
static entity of classical theism, is so 'dynamic' as to be describable primarily with verbs. Finally I suggest that, while the irreducibly diverse
interpretations of Thomas reflect readers' often radically different philosophical and confessional presuppositions, his thought oscillates so much
between originality and tradition that no single account could ever be
unchallengeable.

These chapters started as lectures or seminar papers, delivered over
many years. I have Alex Wright to thank for persuading me to write them
up as a book. Among friends who read the draft and did their best to
save me from the results of my ignorance and prejudice, it is a pleasure
to thank Vivian Boland, Mark Edney and Laurence Paul Hemming. For
help in preparing the manuscript for publication I am grateful to Jacinta
O'Driscoll, as well as to Laura Barry, Alison Dunnett and especially
Jenny Roberts.

I dedicate the book to the memory of Cornelius Ernst (1924–77) and
Herbert McCabe (1926–2001): differing greatly in their approach to
reading Saint Thomas, undivided in their admiration for his work.

Chapter 1

LIFE AND TIMES

Thinkers as great as Thomas Aquinas are much more than the product of circumstances. On the other hand, his work needs to be read with some knowledge of the many conflicts – political, ecclesiastical and intellectual – in which he was involved all his life. Otherwise, his thought, detached from history, becomes a closed system which, while it attracts some readers and repels others, has nothing to do with the very diversified, often contentious and (obviously) unfinished work that he left behind.[1]

Biography

Tommaso di Aquino died on 7 March 1274 at Fossanova (then a Cistercian monastery, now a national monument). He was born no great distance away, between 1224 and 1226, at Roccasecca, the family castle (now ruined), midway between Rome and Naples, in what was then the farthest northwestern province of the Kingdom of Sicily. He became a friar of the Order of Preachers in 1244, studied in Paris and Cologne 1245–52, lectured in Paris 1252–9, in Italy 1259–68, back in Paris 1268–72, before returning to Naples to set up a house of studies, with the choice of site, curriculum, and so on, left to him.

After celebrating the eucharist on 6 December 1273 Thomas ceased to do theology: 'I cannot do any more. Everything I have written seems to me so much straw compared with what I have seen'. To interpret this as meaning that he regarded his writings as entirely worthless would be absurd. It is an expression of the tension throughout his theological work between the labour of reasoning about Christian revelation and the longing for the promised face-to-face vision of God by which his whole life was shaped.

In February 1274 Thomas set out to attend the Council of Lyons, convoked by Pope Gregory X with the aim of restoring communion with the Eastern Orthodox Church. Unwell, he diverted to his niece's house, where he dictated the last of his compositions, a letter to the abbot of Monte Cassino in response to a problem the monks had about the relationship between the infallibility of divine foreknowledge and the freedom of the human creature. It shows no falling off in intellectual powers. Indeed, it expresses what is perhaps Thomas's most characteristic insight: to put it in modern terms, that theories purporting to reconcile human autonomy and divine freedom are superfluous since, properly understood, there is no competition between divine and creaturely causalities.

While the treasured anecdotes make him out to be absent-minded, Thomas's unworldliness should not be exaggerated. He was no impractical academic. Twice his colleagues entrusted him with founding and administering study centres. More significantly, as we shall see, his life was marked by one conflict after another.

Readers familiar only with the *Summa Theologiae* are not to be blamed if they find the prose style colourless and impersonal. His treatment of views which he rejects is (almost) always polite. His work seems objective and dispassionate. Even in the *Summa*, however, one can find diverting cameos that show another side to Thomas's character, or at least disclose something of the turbulence he witnessed around him – perhaps every day.

Consider, for example, his account of how rage may deprive one of the use of speech. Typically, in a culture delighting in citing authoritative precedents for everything, he quotes Gregory the Great (c.540–604): 'the tongue stammers, the countenance takes fire, the eyes grow fierce' (ST 1–2.48.4).[2] One need not assume that he never saw men in a rage. Indeed, Thomas writes a good deal about the range of emotion. In the *Summa*, for example, 24 of the 42 questions dealing with our psychological make-up as moral agents are devoted to the *passiones animae* (ST 1–2.6–48). The 'passion' of the soul which attracts most attention is delight and its opposite, depression (1–2.31–9). Thomas's list of remedies to mitigate depression is quite unoriginal: do something pleasurable, have a good cry, get a friend's sympathy, think about divine and future happiness, take a nap or a hot bath (1–2.38): unoriginal but humane and practical.

Above all, however, the imperturbable Buddha-like serenity attributed to him in the standard iconography is belied by the surviving manuscripts in his own hand: physical evidence of raw intellectual energy and passion.[3]

Family: Between Pope and Emperor

The Aquino family, Normans settled south of Naples since the end of the tenth century, lived on the strife-ridden border between the Papal states and the Kingdom of Sicily. In 1208 Pope Innocent III installed the 13-year-old son of the Emperor Henry VI (dead since 1197) as Frederick II, Holy Roman Emperor.[4] By the time Thomas was born, Pope and Emperor had fallen out irretrievably. Frederick's ambitions to reunite the Holy Roman Empire kept bringing him up against papal determination to thwart him. By 1239, for example, Pope Gregory IX was denouncing him as a Muslim who kept a harem guarded by eunuchs (which was true). He retaliated by deriding the Pope as Antichrist (a common charge in these pre-Reformation days). In 1241, when Frederick called on the princes of Christendom to unite against the papacy, Gregory convoked a general council. Frederick prevented it from taking place by kidnapping about a hundred of the bishops.

Thus, from his earliest days until he got to Paris in 1245 as a young Dominican friar, Thomas lived at the cusp of this unceasing and increasingly ferocious contest between the King and one pope after another (Frederick saw off three popes, not counting Celestine IV who lasted only three weeks, nor Innocent IV who survived him).

The Aquino family were heavily involved in this conflict. Thomas's father was one of Frederick II's barons. Aimo, his eldest brother, took part in the Emperor's expedition to the Holy Land (the fifth crusade); taken prisoner, he was ransomed through Pope Gregory's intercession, and remained loyal to the papal side for the rest of his life. Rinaldo, another brother, at first on Frederick II's side, deserted him when he was deposed by Pope Innocent IV in 1245; he was put to death the following year, allegedly for being involved in a plot to assassinate the Emperor.

School and University

In 1231 Thomas was sent to school at the nearby Benedictine abbey of Monte Cassino, aged at most seven, apparently with his own servants. For the best part of the next ten years he was immersed in the liturgical and biblical-patristic culture of the Latin Church. Very different from what his own style of doing theology would be, he was brought up in the monastic tradition of meditative reading of Scripture, *lectio divina*, with study and prayer almost inseparable.[5]

When Frederick II's troops reoccupied Monte Cassino, the monks were expelled and Thomas sent home. The youngest son of a military family, educated so far in a monastery founded by Benedict himself, he now got the opportunity to continue his education as a student at the university of Naples. This was the first university founded independently of the Church, as recently as 1224, as part of Frederick's campaign to outmanoeuvre the dominance of the papacy in the education of the ruling elites. Naples, at the time, was an outpost of the exotic culture that flourished at Frederick's court in Palermo. In the course of studying the seven liberal arts, Thomas had at least one teacher, Peter of Ireland, who had a particular interest in Aristotle.

Thus, by the time he was 20, Thomas had been exposed to two radically different cultures: the age-old tradition of Latin monasticism, richly indebted to Augustine and Christian neo-Platonism, and, on the other hand, the pagan philosophy of Aristotle, brought to the West by Jewish and especially Muslim scholars. The tension between what seemed at the time two apparently incommensurable traditions was to dominate Thomas's intellectual work.

Cathars

Thomas's work was shadowed throughout by the long and extremely violent struggle in Western Christendom between Cathars and Catholics. When he was about 20, Thomas decided to join the Dominican friars: a contemplative way of life that issues in preaching and teaching, half monastic, so to speak, and half in the world of the new universities. Founded by Dominic Guzman, they had been present in Naples for 20 years or so.[6] Their origins lie in the resolve of the ecclesiastical authorities to eliminate Catharism.

By the middle of the twelfth century the perennial call for reform in the Church began to consolidate, especially in France, the Rhineland and Lombardy, into a movement of clergy and laity out to restore the 'purity' of early Christianity as they conceived it. In their day they were known as Cathars (Greek *katharos*: 'pure'), Albigensians (though Toulouse was more the centre of the movement than Albi), or Manichees, as Thomas usually calls them.[7] According to their teachings, the body and the material creation are evil; they rejected infant baptism, the Eucharist, marriage, meat eating, the doctrines of hell, purgatory and the resurrection of the body, and much else.

To some extent, the Church authorities sought to engage with the 'heretics' through preaching and missionary work, as well as by the internal reforms decreed at the Lateran Council in 1215. The ascetical ideals of the friars, for example, were shaped largely in response to the Cathars' desire to see evangelical simplicity among Christ's disciples.

In 1252 Pope Innocent IV decreed severe measures against those suspected of sympathy with Catharist doctrines. The surrender of Montségur in 1244 and the fall of Quéribus in 1255 may have looked like the end, but, as always, dissenters in the Church proved difficult to silence. In the early fourteenth century, after a century of ferocious repression, there were still surviving Catharist congregations (a Catharist bishop in northern Italy was arrested in 1321; the last Cathar was burnt in Languedoc in 1330).[8]

Thomas probably never met a Cathar. Nevertheless, his frequent allusions to Manicheanism should not be regarded as referring only to the past, or to heresies he regarded as purely hypothetical. For one thing, he was in no position, even in the 1270s, let alone when he started teaching in the 1250s, to think that Catharism had been eradicated. For another, as a young friar he must have been well aware of the role of the Dominicans in the struggle against Catharism. He may have met friars who were, or had been, employed as inquisitors (even though only a handful of them were, at the time). It makes better sense to regard his theology as seriously engaging with Catharism. For example, his repeated emphasis on the goodness of created nature, pervading his work, is best understood in this light.

Conflict in the Paris Faculty

Thomas had a struggle with his family before they allowed him to join the friars: he was abducted by his brother Rinaldo, still with Frederick II's army, and held under house arrest for nearly two years. He then went to Paris to study for ordination, where he attended lectures by his older confrère Albert the Great.[9] In June 1248 the Order founded an international college for Dominican friars and others who might attend their courses in Cologne. Albert took Thomas with him to set up the new venture. He continued to work as assistant to Albert; transcripts he made of courses by Albert survive.

These years of apprenticeship in Cologne were the final stage in Thomas's formation as a theologian (he must have been ordained priest in 1250/51 though no record survives).

In September 1252 he returned to Paris to lecture. He immediately found himself in the middle of an often extremely nasty power struggle. The secular masters, the diocesan clergy who occupied the principal chairs in the theology faculty, resented the arrival of the Franciscan and Dominican friars. Being clergy mostly from dioceses in northern France and Belgium, they disliked the increasing influence of the friars, parachuted into the faculty for a few years, with allegiances elsewhere and particularly to the papacy. The French bishops wanted the friars curbed. Initially, although already giving lectures, Thomas and Bonaventure, his Franciscan colleague, were refused membership of the theology faculty; they were admitted only at the command of Pope Alexander IV.

The conflict was not only literary. In 1253 the faculty twice suspended classes, to put pressure on the friars, who, however, refused to stop teaching. In 1255, hostility to the friars reached such a pitch that King Louis IX sent in the royal archers to guard the Dominican priory against the hooligan element in the divinity faculty.

Thomas's first publications are vigorously expressed defences of the vocation and ascetical practices of the friars.[10] In 1254, the Franciscan friar Gerard de Borgo San Donnino published a book proclaiming that the third age of the world had begun around 1200. He was taken to mean – and probably did mean – that the recently founded friars were the first fruits of this 'new age'. Thomas's allusions, as usual, are discreet but he cannot have been indifferent to this episode. Writing much later, he states that the New Law (of the Gospel) is already nothing less than 'the grace of the Holy Spirit given inwardly to Christ's faithful', thus ruling out the idea of any further 'dispensation of the Holy Spirit when spiritual men will reign' – certainly a response to the apocalypticism of Joachim of Fiore (c.1135–1202) as reformulated and exaggerated by Gerard (cf. ST 1–2.106).[11]

All this the secular masters exploited delightedly, even launching the canard that the book was written by certain Dominican friars. Gerard refused to retract his doctrines, was dismissed from teaching and imprisoned on the orders of Bonaventure, Minister General of the Franciscans since 1257.[12] These were hectic times.

Principal Works

In 1252/5, the arts faculty in Paris began to teach all of Aristotle's work, after years of resistance by church authorities. For the rest of Thomas's career the theology faculty remained deeply suspicious of how the new ideas were being handled in the arts faculty. While always a member of the theology faculty, when teaching at Paris, Thomas was interested in developments in the philosophy faculty and composed works which some readers at least regard as straightforwardly philosophical. His first composition, the short treatise *De ente et essentia*, is heavily indebted to Ibn Sina, the Muslim thinker whose work he had no doubt met at university in Naples. Here, in what was to be a widely read treatise, Thomas expounds the metaphysical doctrines held in common by Christians, Jews and Muslims at the time. It is more a glossary of common terms, such as 'being', 'nature', 'essence', and so on, than an argument. But we get the first exposition of Thomas's most characteristic thesis: in created beings, there is a real distinction between their nature (essence) and their existence – in God, however, there is no such distinction.[13]

Thomas's inaugural lecture, showing his debt to Denys's neo-Platonic Christianity, speaks of the theologian's place, relatively minor and yet honourable, in the descent of divine wisdom.[14] The accompanying lecture is in praise of Holy Scripture. It is as if, as he came into his maturity as a teacher, he wanted to signal his debt to the traditional biblical-patristic culture which he inherited.[15]

More personal exploration of theological method is to be found in his incomplete commentaries on works by Boethius. As he reads him, Boethius is taking divine revelation for granted and testing how far philosophical reasoning can bring the believer to deeper understanding of the Christian faith. Here, the young professor was verifying the legitimacy of using logic to display the coherence of revelation. Indeed, at the point where Boethius applies his method to the study of the doctrine of the Trinity, Thomas abandons his exposition, as if he now felt free to go his own way.[16]

About this time, he started to write the exposition of 'the truth of the Catholic faith' that would be known as the *Summa Contra Gentiles*. Whether or not composed for missionaries in Muslim Spain (as tradition says), this book reads more like an experiment to see how near the ancient Mediterranean world's search for wisdom might come to the brink of biblical revelation. The first three of the four books investigate how far the truths of the Christian faith can be expounded on the basis of principles available to non-believers; only in the fourth do the arguments depend on specifically Christian revelation. 'Although the truth of the Christian faith . . . surpasses the capacity of the reason, nevertheless the truth that the human reason is naturally endowed to know cannot be opposed to the truth of the Christian faith', Thomas contends, the implication of which is that for us 'to be able to see something of the loftiest realities, however thin and weak the sight may be, is a cause of the greatest joy' (*Contra Gentiles* I. 7–8).[17]

Much of Thomas's literary production takes the form of transcripts of disputations in which he participated. From his first years of teaching, we have the greater part of the disputed questions *De Veritate* in a version dictated by Thomas himself. This collection of 29 disputations deals with truth, divine knowledge, divine ideas, the Word, providence, predestination, the Book of Life, angelic knowledge, the human mind as locus of the image of the Trinity, teaching and learning, prophecy, ecstasy, faith, inferior and superior reason, synderesis, conscience, Adam's knowledge of God before the Fall, the soul's knowledge after death, Christ's knowledge, as well as the good, the will, free will, our sensual nature, the emotions, grace, the justification of the unrighteous and the grace of Christ. Not the ragbag this may seem, these transcripts are the equivalent of a theologian's working papers, offering privileged access to the problems of the day and Thomas's approach to dealing with them.[18]

There are two later collections: *De Potentia*, six questions on the theme of divine power and six on the Trinity; and *De Malo*, 16 questions on evil, sin, the cause of sin, original sin, the punishment of original sin, human choice, venial sin, the capital vices, vainglory, envy, acedia, anger, avarice, gluttony, lust and demons.[19]

Face-to-face argument was an essential part of medieval pedagogy. Most of the teaching in theology took the form of line-by-line exposition of Scripture, with an assistant reading out the text and the professor paraphrasing, citing parallels, and commenting. The doctrinal questions that naturally arose were kept for the regular disputations, when the class, or sometimes the entire faculty, gathered, sometimes for the whole day, to argue over these and any other questions students raised.

Disputation as a method assumes there will be conflicting interpretations of texts and doctrines that need to be exposed, explored and resolved. As a glance at these disputations would confirm, Thomas proceeds by reformulating a thesis as a question; then setting out a number of arguments, citing authoritative texts (Scripture, Augustine, Denys, Gregory and suchlike) that seem to run against the thesis; next expounding his preferred answer to the question (using logic much more frequently than invoking knockdown proof texts); and finally going through the initial objections, admitting them, suitably qualified, or simply refuting them, one by one. Thomas's mind (but in this he was no different from his contemporaries) worked argumentatively, dialectically: reaching a view by considering, often rejecting, sometimes refining, alternative views. The method was not intended to reach a compromise or supposed consensus, by splitting the difference between the conflicting interpretations. It allowed the disputants to discover the strengths as well as the weaknesses of opposing views; but the aim was to work out the truth by considering and eliminating error, however common or plausible or seemingly supported by authority.

The purpose of Thomas's most famous work, the *Summa Theologiae*, was, as he says in the prologue, to set out Christian doctrine in an orderly way, considering how 'newcomers to this teaching are greatly hindered by various writings on the subject, partly because of the swarm of pointless questions, articles, and arguments, partly because essential information is given according to the requirements of textual commentary or the occasions of academic debate, partly because repetitiousness has bred boredom and muddle in their thinking' (ST 1. Foreword).[20] Thomas did not abandon exposition of Scripture nor participation in disputations. On the other hand, seeing the defects of both practices, one text-bound, the other problem-dominated, he evidently wanted to provide an overview of the Christian doctrine with which he wanted future preachers and pastors to be familiar.

Aristotle

On the standard interpretation, Thomas is an 'Aristotelian'. This requires nuancing, in the light of recent scholarship, even if it is plausible at all.[21]

While familiar with Aristotle's works since his student days, Thomas undertook what looks like an attempt to work his way through all the writings of Aristotle, beginning at the end of 1267 with the *De anima*, and continuing into the last year of his life. This was personal study; he never lectured on Aristotle. No doubt he thought that professors in the arts faculty (clergy, of course), too much influenced by Muslim interpretations, misunderstood Aristotle. Perhaps he felt obliged to ensure that Islam should not win by philosophy the hegemony it had quite recently lost in battle. As he read, also, he came to think that some of Aristotle's ideas helped to elucidate Christian doctrine.

Of the 12 commentaries Thomas embarked upon, he left seven unfinished. He completed the *De anima* contemporaneously with dictating the questions on the human soul in the *Summa Theologiae*.[22]

Similarly, he completed an exposition of the *Ethics* as he was composing the lengthy analyses of the cardinal virtues in the *Summa*.[23] Whether this is an original and important work or not is much disputed. Some regard it as half-baked; others think it is an over-theological reading; others again think it is a serious attempt to expound a moral philosophy complete in itself, bracketing out Christian revelation. In this last case, Thomas would not just be trawling Aristotle's *Ethics* for material he could use in his own account of Christian ethics, but experimenting to see how far a coherent ethics could be developed independently of Christian beliefs. What reading Aristotle enabled Thomas to do, anyway, was to rethink the standard moral theology treatises on virtue and vice in a much wider context.

About the same time, Thomas started a commentary on Aristotle's *Metaphysics*. Here, too, there is much dispute over whether it is a serious work of metaphysics or merely a pedestrian exposition. It comes much too late in his career to have any influence on his writing. His metaphysical positions had been established years before.[24]

In the letter of condolence sent by the masters in the arts faculty in Paris to the Dominican friars in May 1274 – 'For news has come to us which floods us with grief and amazement, bewilders our understanding, transfixes our very vitals, and well-nigh breaks our hearts' (there was no such letter from the theology faculty!) – they asked for Thomas's bones for interment in Paris but also for 'some writings of a philosophical nature, begun by him at Paris, left unfinished at his departure, but completed, we have reason to believe, in the place to which he was transferred': translations that he promised to send them, Simplicius on Aristotle's *De anima*, Proclus on Plato's *Timaeus*, and the *De aquarum conductibus et ingeniis erigendis*[25]; and finally 'any new writings of his own on logic, such as, when he was about to leave us, we took the liberty of asking him to write'. Thomas's commentary on the *Posterior Analytics*, begun in Paris and completed in Naples, was sent to Paris, together with his commentary on the *Peri hermenias*, started in Paris but never finished.

We need a full-scale study of Thomas's work on Aristotle, assessing the content as well as establishing the ways in which the various texts interweave with concerns in the arts faculty and with Thomas's other works. At present, the purpose, status and value of Thomas's work on Aristotle remain in dispute.[26]

In 1272, Thomas composed (as it turned out) his last non-biblical commentary – on the *Liber de causis*, long attributed to Aristotle but, as Thomas suspected, a neo-Platonic work heavily indebted to Proclus and Denys (compiled, so scholars now think, by an unknown Muslim philosopher). Some readers would regard this venture into neo-Platonism as a sideline; others would think that, for all the importance of his uses of Aristotle, specifically as regards the soul and virtue, Thomas remained always far more deeply neo-Platonist than Aristotelian.[27]

Confrontations

Thomas was involved in several tense confrontations. The most influential exponent of Aristotle at the time – known indeed as 'The Commentator' – was Ibn Rushd, whose theories reached Paris about 1230.[28] In

1270 Thomas wrote his *De unitate intellectus, contra Averroistas Parisienses*, arguing that certain masters in the arts faculty were mistaken in thinking that Aristotle lent them any support in denying the existence of a mind in each human being and positing instead some kind of super mind in which human minds were mere participations.[29]

Probably in the same year, Thomas composed his *De aeternitate mundi contra murmurantes*: the thesis here is that, contrary to what eminent theologians of the day believed, it cannot be proved by reason alone that the world did not exist from eternity.[30] On the contrary, Thomas contends, the idea that the world had a beginning is solely a matter of faith. For him, the concept of being created has to do with ontological dependence on God as first cause of all things and is not to be equated with having a beginning. All one can do philosophically, then, is to show that the world is dependent for its existence on the first cause, but this would be true even if it had always existed.

Even more problematic theologically, indeed dividing him from many of his colleagues, Thomas defended the doctrine of the unicity of substantial form in corporeal creatures. Controversy had raged for decades. Roughly, adopting the Aristotelian thesis that it is the soul that makes the human body what it is, Thomas argued that a human being is a unity. The alternative view, held by the majority, was that human beings are made up of three substantial forms: vegetative, sensible and intellectual. In brief, we are not rational all the way down, so to speak. In 1270, when Thomas debated the question before the theology faculty, he was in the minority, perhaps even on his own. His unitary concept of the human creature seemed to verge on heresy. Most worryingly, he seemed to mean that the body of Christ in the tomb was not the same as the body that hung on the cross (e.g. ST 3.50.5). Assuming that Christ really died, and thus that his body was separated from his soul, then, if the rational soul is the unique form of the body, it looked as if the body in the tomb was not the same as the body of the living Christ. On the other hand, if we were to allow for a body-giving form really distinct from the rationality-giving form, that would ensure the requisite identity.

Thomas's view dispensed with a form supplying the human being's bodiliness independently of rationality. Of course, the man Jesus Christ was really and truly dead, his soul's being separated from his body; yet, since his dead body remained united to the Person of the Son (the Son of God did not die), there was no problem about its remaining the same body. Aristotle's philosophical conception of the human being cleared away the fanciful philosophy the theologians thought they needed, in order to allow the doctrine of the hypostatic union to show up more clearly. The question no doubt seems arcane: how many theologians today would even be interested in the status of Christ's body after his death? On the other hand, Thomas's thesis, updated no doubt, that the 'lower' forms, say at the levels of growth and sensitivity, are annihilated or integrated by the advent or emergence in the human creature of rationality, might give rise to considerable discussion still.

The 219 Propositions

Three years after Thomas's death, a number of theories were condemned by the theology faculty in Oxford at the behest of the archbishop of Canterbury, Robert Kilwardby, himself a Dominican friar, not of course involving Thomas by name, but plainly alluding to some of his 'Aristotelian' positions.[31]

Much more importantly, a couple of weeks previously, on 7 March 1277, the anniversary of Thomas's death, the bishop of Paris censured a list of 219 theses, allegedly being taught in the university and 'prejudicial to faith', a list cobbled together in a hurry, at the behest of Pope John XXI.[32]

The significance of the 219 propositions, and whether Thomas is envisaged in any of them, are matters of considerable controversy. According to Edward Grant, for example, the 'most significant outcome' of the condemnation in 1277 was 'an emphasis on the reality and importance of God's absolute power to do whatever He pleases short of bringing about a logical contradiction'.[33] He allows that the topics covered range widely but, on his reading, they mostly bear, implicitly if not always explicitly, on a certain determinism introduced into natural philosophy by Greco-Arabic physics, in response to which it seemed necessary to insist on God's infinite and absolute creative and causative power.

According to Etienne Gilson, on the other hand, the 219 propositions amount more broadly to 'a sort of polymorphic naturalism stressing the rights of pagan nature against Christian nature, of philosophy against theology, of reason against faith'.[34]

Several of the theses come from the treatise on courtly love by Andreas Capellanus, mentioned in the bishop's letter introducing the Condemnation. While it is true that the third part of this then popular book is the highly critical response of the orthodox Christian moralist to the extremely colourful exposition in the first two parts of what we might call 'free love', it looks as if the compilers of the 219 propositions suspected that it was the first two parts that attracted members of the university (clerics mostly, of course). One might cite such doctrines as the following: there cannot be sin in the higher powers of the soul, thus sin is never a matter of will but only of emotion; the sin against nature, such as *abusus in coitu*, though contrary to the nature of the species is not contrary to the nature of the individual; refraining completely from sexual intercourse damages the individual's moral development as well as the continuity of the human species; fornication, as between an unmarried man and an unmarried woman, is not a sin; and much else in the same vein.

As Gilson concludes, and as David Piché has worked out in convincing detail, the main thrust of the 219 propositions is to the effect that the philosophical way of life is vastly superior to that of theologians.[35]

Consider propositions such as these: we know no more by knowing theology (that is to say, than by doing philosophy); what a theologian says is based on myths (*sermones theologi fundati sunt in fabulis*); the only true wisdom is the wisdom of the *philosophi*; there is no way of life superior to the practice of philosophy (*vacare philosophiae*); the poor cannot be virtuous (perhaps alluding to the controversies about evangelical poverty); there are no virtues other than those that are either taught or innate (i.e. no 'infused' grace-given virtues); happiness (*felicitas*) is accessible in this life, not in any other; and so on.

It may seem a hotchpotch. Yet, in the claim that 'chastity is not a greater value than perfect abstinence', we surely have the key. That is to say, as Piché suggests, celibates in the arts faculty were saying, or being reported as saying, that their choice of *abstinentia perfecta* was superior to the *castitas* to which the clergy, the monks and the friars, in the theology faculty were vowed.

In brief, some of the clergy in the arts faculty in Paris were perceived as being so seduced by Aristotle's *Ethics* that they believed that the study of wisdom to which the philosopher is dedicated, supported by a life of total asceticism, resulting in quasi-mathematical knowledge of the First Cause, would deliver all the happiness, the beatitude, available to human beings. To quote Boethius of Dacia, one of the most prominent of the masters: 'The philosopher is the man living according to the right order of nature and acquiring the highest and ultimate goal of human life'. In other words, these Catholic clergymen teaching in the arts faculty in the university of Paris in the 1270s either were, or were thought to be, so bewitched by their reading of Aristotle that they believed that knowledge of the First Cause was available now; as the exercise of our highest intellectual capacity it was the activity which already made us divine.

Thus, when Thomas asks at the beginning of the *Summa Theologiae* whether any teaching is required apart from the *philosophicae disciplinae*, it is not the abstract and hypothetical question it may seem (ST 1.1.1). On the contrary, the language is more or less the language we find in the 219 propositions: *scientia*, wisdom, reason, *philosophia*, theology, teaching, being, beatitude, causality, and so on. Coming to Thomas cold, so to speak, isolated from context, it is easy to assume, either delightedly or dismissively, that he has appropriated Aristotelian ideals of reasoning and systematic thought. If, on the other hand, we read Thomas in the light of the ideal of the philosophical life that seems to have caught the imagination of some of the leading masters in the arts faculty in his day, we begin to see how he distances himself from everything they say. Ironically, instead of almost replacing Christian doctrine by Aristotelianism, as critics sometimes say, Thomas was out, historically, to resist the 'wisdom-lovers' – the *philosophi* – in the arts faculty, by trying to transpose and integrate key Aristotelian terms into traditional Christianity.

Hermeneutic Conflict

However celebrated his reputation as the 'Angelic Doctor', as *doctor communis*, particularly since the revival of Thomism in the late nineteenth century, Thomas's theology has always been in contention. If his theology is 'angelic', it is not because it floats above and beyond history; if his teaching is 'common', it is not because it has always been accepted.

In the versions of Thomism current from the 1850s to the 1960s, Thomas's work, particularly his *Summa Theologiae*, was regarded as the high point of medieval Christianity, either a unique balance of faith and reason, a harmonizing of revealed theology and natural theology, an incomparable synthesis, or (by adversaries) as a singularly vicious corruption of Christian doctrine by Hellenistic paganism.

One admirer writes as follows:

> The genius for ordering which this greatest of Christian thinkers possessed is a genius of lay-out . . . all the questions have been resolved, as far as this is possible. In the genuinely supernatural serenity which remains the mystery of this great saint, there opens up before the eye, as a source of ever fresh wonder, a kind of heavenly world of wisdom in which everything that seems confused and hopeless on the murky earth clears away like clouds to give way to a radiant azure sky.

This over-ripe account of Thomas – dating from 1945 – leads the writer, Hans Urs von Balthasar, to the following bleak judgement:

> [W]here one can no longer presuppose the unity of such unique holiness with such unique prudence, where the supernatural gift of grace is

imitated only in an external fashion, as it were a technique that could be learned, this particular charism of the Angel of the Schools, this gift of clarification, of smoothing out and calming down ... can become a disaster for thought ...

In particular, the logic becomes 'not seldom the special art of evasion and of explaining things away.[36]

This harsh comment on some of his own 'Thomist' contemporaries prompts Balthasar to consider the tension in Thomas's thought: 'despite his will to clarify, he is a master in the art of leaving questions open', indeed he displays 'an astonishing breadth, flexibility, and mutability of perspectives which allow quite automatically the aporetic element in his thinking to emerge'. Compared with the modern Thomist, who evidently endorses only the 'will to clarify', often reducing it to an 'art of evasion', Thomas himself knows how to leave questions open – his thinking even includes an 'aporetic element'.

Henri de Lubac, Balthasar's friend and teacher, argued, about the same time, that the 'robust but a little static mass of his synthesis' is nonetheless somewhat unstable. Thomas is 'a transitional writer (*un auteur de transition*)'. In particular, thinking of the reception of his ideas, de Lubac goes on: 'the ambivalence of his thought in unstable equilibrium, ransom of its very richness, explains how it could afterwards be interpreted in such opposed senses (*l'ambivalence de sa pensée en équilibre instable, rançon de sa richesse même, explique qu'on ait pu dans la suite l'interpréter en des senses si opposés)'.[37]

In a letter to de Lubac in 1956, Gilson commented that, from the beginning, so-called Thomists have done nothing but make of Thomas's theology 'a brew of *philosophia aristotelico-thomistica* concocted to give off a vague deism fit only for the use of right-thinking candidates for high-school diplomas and Arts degrees'. Indeed, according to Gilson, obviously expecting de Lubac to agree with him, the Thomist theology established in Catholic seminaries and universities was seldom other than 'rationalism': pandering to the 'deism' that most Thomists – 'deep down' – prefer to teach.[38]

It would be easy to document equally angry comments on how to read Thomas. Much more recently, and very pacifically, Serge-Thomas Bonino speaks of a 'hermeneutic conflict, more or less hidden', in recent interpretations of Thomas's work: medievalists, philosophers and theologians focus on aspects of his work that give rise to somewhat divergent readings; a 'truly Thomist approach' ought to be 'catholic', 'integrating these diverse approaches'.[39]

Current readings of Thomas's work are so conflicting, and even incommensurable, that integrating them into a single interpretation seems impossible. Some readings are deeply misguided; but even these, since they issue from respectable theological and philosophical presuppositions, demand and deserve attention. We need to ask what it is, in Thomas's work, and in the uses to which it has been put by opponents as well as disciples, that makes certain misreadings attractive, and almost unavoidable.

Chapter 2

OVERCOMING EPISTEMOLOGY

In the last hundred years or so, Thomas Aquinas has been treated as a model of how to deal with modern philosophy – modern philosophy understood, since Descartes, as principally concerned with epistemology.[1] In short, so far as Christian theology goes, unless and until we have a philosophically acceptable account of how we know anything to be true or false, we cannot say what we know about the world, other people, or God.

Leonine Thomism

Whether Thomas should ever have been regarded as the prototype of the anti-Cartesian philosopher has been contested by Alasdair MacIntyre, in one of the most notable contributions to the renewal of interest in his work.[2]

For MacIntyre, the importance of Thomas as exemplar resides in the way that he integrated the contending traditions in his day at the university of Paris – Aristotelianism and Augustinianism – into a new dialectical synthesis with the capacity to direct enquiry still further beyond itself, particularly with respect to moral issues, virtue ethics, and so on.

More directly challenging, however, in terms of modern reception of Thomas's work, is MacIntyre's claim that the study of Thomas, 'by epistemologizing itself after *Aeterni Patris*, proceeded to reenact the disagreements of post-Cartesian philosophy'. That is to say, the study of Thomas prompted by Pope Leo XIII's endorsement in 1879 was hijacked,

MacIntyre would say, by its being drafted as the alternative to modern philosophy, indeed as therapy for Cartesianism.

In particular, MacIntyre picks out the version of Thomism that emerged from the history of philosophy published in 1853–60 by Joseph Kleutgen, who argued in favour of a rupture, dividing the philosophy of modern times from that of what he called *die Vorzeit* (pre-modernity as we might say).[3] While endorsing this account of the discontinuity in the history of Western philosophy, MacIntyre judges that Kleutgen – 'a thinker of outstanding philosophical ability and erudition' – should have located the rupture that brought to birth modernity much farther back, specifically in the failure of Thomas's immediate successors to appreciate and appropriate the aspects of his thought which transcended the limitations of the existing Augustinianism and Aristotelianism. More to the point here, however, Thomas was read through Suárez[4] – 'already a distinctively modern thinker, perhaps more authentically than Descartes the founder of modern philosophy' – the result of which was that Thomas became the answer to Descartes.

Epistemological questions are not mentioned in the encyclical *Aeterni Patris*, MacIntyre notes. Rather, the encyclical sees Thomas's achievement as 'the culmination of a tradition, to which both pre-Christian and patristic authors have contributed'. In Kleutgen's reading of the account of truth in the first question of the *De Veritate*, however, according to MacIntyre, what Thomas is doing is already distorted. He is engaged in integrating the various relevant considerations advanced by his predecessors in the rival Augustinian and Aristotelian traditions – two different understandings of truth, indeed two different epistemologies, one might say – but not a work of integration that amounts to 'epistemological justification' in the modern sense. As Thomism developed, Kleutgen's 'opening up a kind of epistemological question for which there is no place within Aquinas's own scheme of thought', and going on to 'supply an epistemological answer to that question by reading into texts in *De Veritate* an epistemological argument which is not in fact there', spilled out into a variety of anti-Cartesian Thomisms, all treating Thomas as an ally in an anachronistically conceived struggle to defeat modernity.

In the encyclical, which was probably drafted in consultation with Kleutgen, Leo XIII certainly addresses his fellow bishops in no uncertain terms, indeed flamboyantly and inflammatorily, on the importance of 'teaching philosophical studies in such a way as shall most fitly correspond with the blessing of faith and be consonant with the respect due to the human sciences themselves'.[5] He notes that much error has crept into theology through theories originally propounded in philosophical schools. He insists on the value of the 'sound use of philosophy': 'God has not endowed the human mind with reason to no purpose; and the added light of faith, so far from extinguishing or diminishing the vigour of the mind, rather on the contrary perfects it'. Philosophy, 'rightly practised', is 'a means of preparing and smoothing the way, as it were, to the true faith and suitably disposing the minds of its disciples for the reception of revelation'. The Pope cites Clement of Alexandria: philosophy as 'preparatory education for the Christian faith', Origen: 'a prelude to and auxiliary of Christianity', and Clement again: 'the guide to the Gospel'. He celebrates the patristic and medieval conceptions of the relationship between reason and faith. Principally, his concern is that there is no 'real conflict' between modern physics and Scholastic philosophy. In its way, the revival of Thomas's 'philosophy' is envisaged as the Roman Catholic Church's recipe for dealing with the 'science versus religion' controversies of the day.

On the other hand, precisely in this connection, Leo XIII claims that the Schoolmen, 'following the common tradition of the holy Fathers', taught that the mind cannot attain to knowledge of immaterial things except by sensible things – which looks like a certain reserve about idealist and intuitionist epistemologies; though it is true, as MacIntyre says, that overcoming post-Cartesian epistemology is not the dominant theme in the encyclical.

There is, anyway, no doubt that the return to Thomas recommended by Leo XIII, was a return to 'sound philosophy'. Christian doctrine (it is assumed) is never isolated from contemporary philosophical theories but always liable to be undermined by them as well as likely to be helped. In the letter *Cum hoc sit* (4 August 1880), in which the Pope fatefully declared Thomas to be patron saint of Catholic 'schools' (seminaries, colleges and university faculties), he refers to the 'restoration' of 'Christian philosophy' 'according to the mind of the Angelic Doctor'.

The Sceptical Problem

A glance at the history of Catholic theology prior to Kleutgen suggests that, if he saw the problem residing not so much in conflict between science and religion (Leo XIII's concern) but in the effects of Cartesian/Kantian philosophy, his view was not unjustifiable. The story of the outburst of theological activity in the first half of the nineteenth century, as Catholic theologians sought to rethink Christianity in response to modern philosophy, is largely unfamiliar, mainly because it has not yet been told.

Georg Hermes (1775–1831), for example, very influential at the time, held the Cartesian view that our only certain knowledge was of ideas actually present in the mind, yet that, while the criterion of objective truth lies in our subjective beliefs, it is still possible to prove the existence of God by reason, and then to demonstrate the possibility of supernatural revelation. Anton Günther (1783–1863) held that the mysteries of the Trinity and the Incarnation could be demonstrated by rational argument; that there was no real gap between natural and revealed truth; and that the existence of God could be deduced from analysis of self-consciousness. Antonio Rosmini-Serbati (1797–1855) sought to finesse Enlightenment rationalism and what he (already) regarded as an over-Aristotelianizing Thomism, by maintaining that all human knowledge implies an immediate intuition of divine truth.

Against such speculations, theologians such as Kleutgen turned to pre-Cartesian philosophy, seeking to recreate Catholic theology as it supposedly was before the late-medieval developments which gave rise not only to the Reformation but (more importantly, for Catholic theologians, at this stage) to philosophy as an autonomous and methodologically sceptical discipline.

The rise of modern Thomism is only fully intelligible as the Roman Catholic Church's repeated rejection of attempts by distinguished Catholic theologians to rethink Christian doctrine in terms of post-Cartesian philosophy.[6]

Well into the 1960s it was standard practice in seminary courses to introduce students to theology by way of two or three years studying metaphysics and natural theology, as for example by R.P. Phillips.[7]

The 'first part of metaphysics' according to Phillips, is epistemology. The problem is to 'see whether we can have knowledge of any being other than our own minds'. If we decide in advance of any examination of the capacity of the mind for giving us knowledge of real being, we effectively assume that 'the mind can know only its own ideas and processes', so Phillips assumes. The 'fundamental dogma' of Descartes, Hobbes and Locke, is that 'the mind only knows its own ideas'. We have to be convinced that this cannot be right, 'since a dogmatic religion which did not presuppose this capacity would be a mere fatuity'.

Clearly, Phillips takes it as obvious that seminarians come to theological studies with idealist/empiricist philosophical prejudices which they need to expose and disown.

Phillips then considers 'the sceptical problem'. He discusses the ontological value of our knowledge of concrete things, idealism and realism, the existence of the individual thinking subject, the existence of the extra-mental and corporeal world, and the intuitive character of sense knowledge.

Phillips's following section tackles the ontological value of our knowledge of abstract things: the problem of universals, theories of truth and the nature of science. That leads into general metaphysics: being in general, the unity and analogy of being, the properties of being, potency and act, essence and existence, substance, subsistence and personality, accidental being, the nature of causality, the principle of finality, and the co-ordination of causes.

That in turn leads into natural theology: the demonstrability of the existence of God, the demonstration of the existence of God, the nature of God, God's knowledge, the divine will and its effects, the divine motion, the divine omnipotence and miracles, and finally providence and the problem of evil. (All of this, it may be noted, counts as 'natural theology'.)

Wittgensteinian Thomism

R.P. Phillips's book first appeared in 1935. Twenty years later, when I came to study Thomas Aquinas, taught by Cornelius Ernst,[8] we began with Thomas's commentary on Aristotle's *De Anima*, in conjunction with the questions about the soul in the *Summa Theologiae*. In retrospect, indeed even at the time, the course was obviously designed to overcome the Cartesian/empiricist inheritance with which budding theologians were assumed to be burdened; explicitly, Ernst sought to retrieve the pre-modern understanding of the soul to be found in Thomas.

We were invited, at the start, to write an essay on 'the visibility of the soul'. This trapped us into arguing, on introspectionist grounds, that a human being's soul is naturally invisible – visible only to God. We were to be brought to see that what Thomas meant by saying that the soul is the form of the body is pretty much what Wittgenstein meant: 'The human body is the best picture of the human soul'.[9] In short, it would take the discipline of being subjected to Wittgenstein's exposure of the absurdities of assuming that the interior life is radically private to prepare us to understand Thomas Aquinas's pre-Cartesian account of the human mind and will.

Quite independently, the anti-Cartesian potential in Thomas's account of mind and will was being introduced into academic philosophy by students of Wittgenstein who were themselves to become important philosophers. In his recent study of what he calls 'Wittgensteinian Thomism', Roger Pouivet discusses two remarkable studies by young Catholic philosophers that appeared in 1957: G.E.M. Anscombe's *Intention*, demythologizing modern notions of will, and now regarded as a classic in analytic philosophy which completely revolutionized the philosophy of intentionality and action, with deep implications for moral philosophy; and P.T. Geach's *Mental Acts*, drawing openly on Thomas, and doing the same for notions of mental states, explicit in its hostility to 'decadent Scholasticism', which means 'many of [Thomas's] professed followers'.[10]

Cartesianism

On the face of it, scepticism about the existence of the world outside our minds, or about our power to know other people's minds, may seem to those of a common sense disposition to be a typical philosophical pseudo-problem. In fact, of course, the challenge of scepticism has dominated philosophy since the discovery, in the sixteenth century, of Sextus Empiricus's manuscripts – a discovery that influenced Descartes; but, arguably anyway, epistemological scepticism has constituted the matrix of philosophy ever since Socrates, Plato and Aristotle resisted the Sophists.

It is easy to see why. To be sceptical about how far our cognitive powers extend is to be sceptical about how much we can know about the world, about other people, about ourselves, about society and morality – and about any transcendent reality.[11]

Common sense suspicions of pseudo-problems do not break the hold on the Western imagination of the idealist/empiricist picture of the radical solitude of the modern self. The 'Cartesian' myth of the 'ghost in the machine' (Gilbert Ryle's phrase) takes its origin and authority from something much deeper than any philosopher's theorizing. For Stanley Cavell, for example, the set of problems which philosophers know as 'Cartesianism' – how much we can know of the world or of other people's minds or of anything transcendent – is only an intellectually refined expression of an age-old desire to escape the contingencies of history and limits of language. In short, the threat of scepticism is the flip side of the longing for immortality.[12]

For Kant, as Donald MacKinnon emphasized, human beings, 'inherently metaphysical animals', have a 'continuing metaphysical malaise' which is 'at once the surest index of men's worth, and of their poverty':

> The restless dissatisfaction with relatively unsystematised description of the world around them, which drove men on to simpler, more economical and more comprehensive orderings of their explanatory concepts was, on Kant's view, only one fruitful manifestation of this besetting nisus towards the unconditioned; but what was a matter of pride was also a profound occasion of temptation, and here the issue was one which ranged beyond the mere threat of intellectual error in a limited sense; the suggestion that our concepts could somehow be enlarged so as to capture the unconditioned was an illusion, and it was an illusion which was most dangerous

in that it obscured from us the actual commerce with the unconditioned we continually enjoy.[13]

Kant was concerned to lay bare some, at least, of the sources of the 'ambivalence of the metaphysical pursuit'. By introducing 'metaphysical agnosticism', he transformed the very idea of agnosticism: it is 'no more the name of a kind of wistful straining after the unattainable, of a kind of regret that we cannot, to speak crudely, jump out of our cognitive skins'. On the contrary: 'It is a something which . . . has a certain kinship with the *via negativa* of the classical theology, a purification of our concepts from every taint of anthropomorphism, to the intent that we may at least see what it is that, in our attempted use of these concepts to scrutinise the unconditioned, we are attempting.'

As a matter of historical fact, so MacKinnon claims, the modern preoccupation with the problem of knowledge 'had its remoter background in the rich profusion of works of medieval spirituality which took self-knowledge as their theme'. Whether or not he was right to trace Cartesian Scepticism to late-medieval religious practices, MacKinnon was well aware of the appeal of Thomism as an antidote to idealist/empiricist epistemologies. He must have been amused at being regarded as at the forefront of a generation of Oxford theologians who were in a position to bring Karl Barth and Thomas Aquinas together to outflank 'Liberal Protestantism'.

According to R. Cant, the Church of England stood, in 1946, between 'the conflicting dogmatisms' of Barthian neo-Calvinism and neo-Thomist Catholicism. Referring to Edwyn Hoskyns, translator of Barth's second exposition of the Epistle to the Romans, Cant sees 'the spectacular return of Thomism in the theological field'[14] as moving in the same direction as Barthianism – 'away from Liberalism'. He claims that already, in 1928, Hoskyns had seen Barth and Maritain as 'moving along the same lines'. Looking forward, he names F.L. Cross and A.M. Farrer, as well as MacKinnon, as promisingly likely to integrate post-Hoskyns Barth with more traditional metaphysically grounded theology.[15]

Barth on Cartesianism

The comparison between Maritain and Barth might not occur to many Thomists or any Barthians. Whether they read much of each other's work seems unlikely. On the other hand, they certainly met, in March 1934, under the auspices of the Dominican friars in Paris, when Barth was introduced to Gilson and Gabriel Marcel as well – 'the well-known spokesmen of the academic revival movement in French Catholicism'.[16]

If they discussed Descartes, Barth and Maritain (and indeed Gilson and Marcel) would have agreed. Maritain's studies of Descartes, dating back to 1920, and in particular his contention that there can be no useful work in philosophy until reason 'first of all cures itself of Cartesian errors', amount to a much less complicated attitude than Barth's to Cartesianism. For Maritain, Descartes was just wrong; for Barth, as we shall see, Descartes was wrong but only because he was not right enough.

The historical significance of Descartes was incalculable, Maritain thought: three centuries of rationalism (as he regarded Cartesianism) was a 'tragic experience'. The 'sin' of Descartes is 'a sin of angelism'. By this Maritain means that Descartes conceived human thought on the model of angelic thought: thought was now regarded as intuitive, and thus freed from the burden of discursive reasoning; innate, as to its origin, and thus independent of material things. What this 'angelist psychology' introduces is nothing less than a revolution in the very idea of mind, and thus of intelligibility, scientific understanding and explanation: 'Henceforth, to understand is to separate; to be intelligible is to be capable of mathematical reconstruction'.[17]

The first volume of *Church Dogmatics* came out in 1932. It seems likely that Maritain at least must have known something of Barth's attack on 'indirect Christian Cartesianism'. At one level, we might say, Descartes is Barth's principal target: he ascribes the liberal-modernism in Protestant theology, to which he was so deeply opposed, to the grip of Cartesian epistemology on theological methodology since the Enlightenment. Barth quotes Protestant theologians incautious enough to appeal to Descartes: 'The I-experience establishes for man the surest certainty for reality that he can conceive of or that is possible for him at all. It is the presupposition . . . of all validation of reality with reference to the external world', and suchlike.[18]

This Cartesianism is not as impregnable as it purports to be, Barth says, even philosophically. On the other hand, we must be careful not to get so impatient with Descartes that we 'throw ourselves into the arms of e.g. Aristotle or Thomas [!] . . . Suspicious of the other side too, we shall simply make the point that at any rate in theology one cannot think along Cartesian lines'.

It is not Barth's business, as a theologian, to discuss whether there is a better philosophy than the Cartesian way. Doing philosophy, even working at de-Cartesianizing therapy, will not get us far: 'Theologians with Cartesian inclinations cannot be directly and strictly reduced *ad absurdum* and overturned'. On the contrary, God alone can cure them: 'The power with which their mouth must be stopped is not under our control'.

Much later, in his treatment of the doctrine of creation, Barth has a lengthy discussion of the 'radical question of the reality of that which is' – the question that 'stands at the very beginning of modern philosophy'.[19] Here he concludes that, although neither the question as raised by Descartes nor the answer given by him can be regarded as 'serious', nevertheless his philosophy is 'a good example of the fact that we cannot with impunity seek the reality of the created world anywhere but at the point where it is undoubtedly given, namely, in the revelation of God the Creator'.

Cartesian scepticism about the reality of the world outside our heads is not an illusion that philosophical work can destroy: 'Our consciousness of ourselves and the world, i.e. our awareness and conception of our ego, and of people and things existing outside ourselves, might well be a matter of mere supposition, of pure appearance, a form of nothingness, and our step from consciousness to being a hollow fiction'. We do have to step from inside our heads towards the reality outside, Barth seems to assume. Indeed, we have no direct and unmediated awareness of our own or any other reality: 'It is only true that we immediately *suppose* that we have such an awareness' (my emphasis). Again: 'It is only true that we instinctively suppose that we and other beings exist, and that our consciousness *implies* actual existence, that of ourselves and of others' (my emphasis).

It does not seem to Barth that we could dispose of this mere hypothesis that the world exists by philosophical reflection. 'How can we be sure that supposed reality is real?', he asks – and turns to revelation, not reason, for the answer: 'To affirm that we are, that something is, with any sense of security, we have not merely to say this, but to be authorised and inescapably compelled to say it . . . we say it because it has first been said to us'.

In short, we are right to say that we exist because God has told us so: 'A higher Judge must have intervened between our consciousness and our supposed intrinsic [internal] and extrinsic [external] being, and decided that our consciousness does not deceive us, and that our being is no imaginary being'.

In other words, Barth seems to think, we need God to step in between our minds and the external world, indeed between our minds and themselves, to fill the gap, to guarantee that what seems to be really is: 'it is only because God has informed us that we are real that our I-consciousness and world-consciousness is then removed from the sphere of appearance' – now, indeed, 'we are forbidden to doubt existence and ourselves'.

Barth goes on to write of our having to 'cross the bridge from mere consciousness . . . to the recognition of existence': displaying the hold on his mind of the Cartesian picture of the human mind as trapped on one side of a chasm, with getting to know anything as a perilous leap across.

Rather than Cartesian reliance on the certainty of self-consciousness, Barth proposes sheer obedience to the authority of divine revelation. It is 'as and because we believe in God' that 'we believe . . . that we are . . . and that the world which surrounds us also is'. In other words, it is because we believe in God that we believe in the existence of the world and of ourselves. Descartes did not go nearly far enough. We can be certain of the 'presupposition' that we are real only because God has been revealed to us as our Creator. Neither Cartesian doubt nor Cartesian certainty goes anything like deep enough. But the question is whether by accepting the problem of the existence of the external world in these terms (presupposition, hypothesis, consciousness, the first person viewpoint, certainty and all the rest) – without the slightest protest or even under erasure – Barth has not conceded everything to Descartes already.

Kant, famously, declared that the 'scandal of philosophy' was that no proof had yet been given for the reality of the world outside the subject's consciousness. Heidegger, almost as famously, contended that the scandal is not that no such proof has been provided but that such a proof was ever expected and attempted. It is no better, in Heidegger's view, to suggest that, since the existence of things outside the mind is impossible to prove, it must therefore be 'taken on faith', Kant's phrase. Even if talking of 'faith in the reality of the external world' did not assume that at bottom and ideally something stronger should be available, one would still be trying to satisfy the demand for such a proof; one would still be presupposing the construct of an isolated subject. To have faith in the reality of the 'external world', as Heidegger contends, rests on the picture of the subject who is 'worldless or unsure of its world' – who must 'at bottom, first assure itself of a world'.[20]

One need not be a Heideggerian to think that Barth's appeal to faith in God's word as alone answering the demand for certainty about the existence of the external world remains locked into a Cartesian scepticism which needs philosophical treatment.

Objective-participation

Wherever one came from, then, in the heyday of Thomism, budding theologians had 'Cartesian inclinations' (Barth's phrase), and needed to be 'cured' (as Maritain put it).

As regards the Thomist agenda, there were two questions: first, do we need this Cartesian conception of the self; and second, do we need to posit intervening entities of some kind between our minds and objects in the world out there if we are to have knowledge?

On the Cartesian view we think of having a mind and being a person very much in terms of the 'subject', the 'I' as privileged and unified locus of self-consciousness, facing an array of objects out there (including other human beings) which one apprehends initially in the images, impressions, sense data, or other representations of them which we make, or they force on us. In contrast, Thomas Aquinas has a non-subject-centred conception of the self: the objects out there in the world become intelligible in the act of awakening the intellectual acts on our part which manifest our intelligence.

Instead of being objects out there, either opposing us blankly or inertly waiting for us to look at them, so to speak, in our first-person perspective, it is the world that has priority, in the sense that objects elicit and configure the powers of the soul (as Thomas would say): 'With us, to understand is in a way to be passive' (ST 1.79.2). Indeed, citing Aristotle, Thomas contends that the human mind is 'at first like a clean tablet (*tabula rasa*) on which nothing is written'. Certainly, we have to 'assign on the part of the intellect some power to make things actually intelligible'; but this capacity, which we are inclined to regard as primary or all-important, since it seems to fall to us to impose intelligibility on things, is, according to Thomas (as to Aristotle before him), secondary. The intellect is a 'passive force' (ST 1.79.2).

In short, the difference between the prevailing modern conception of the self and that which we find in Thomas may be put in terms of a contrast between a 'subjectivist-observing' perspective and an 'objective-participant' one.

The contrast between a 'subjective-individualist' conception of persons and an 'objective-participant' conception is drawn by Christopher Gill.[21] He finds the latter in ancient Greek philosophy and literature; but, citing MacIntyre, Gill allows that 'medieval Christianity' can be seen as embodying one version of an objective-participant conception of human persons, in contrast with the 'more familiar type of Christian theorizing about personal identity' that he finds in the post-Cartesian soul–body dualism of Richard Swinburne. However that may be, it seems justifiable to suggest that Thomas has a 'non-subject-centred' approach to human experience, in the sense that he never pictures the mind as projecting significance on intrinsically unintelligible and valueless objects but always rather as the actualization of intellectual capacities by potentially significant objects, according to the axiom '*intellectus in actu est intelligibile in actu*': our intellectual capacities actualized *are* the world's intelligibility realized.

Here, not for the last time, we see Thomas appealing to Aristotle, not succumbing to the charms of a naturalism that would in due course generate a Christ-free theology, and a theology-free philosophy, as is often supposed on the standard reading, but rather securing the specificity of Christian doctrine over against neo-Platonic (or, we might as well say, Cartesian) temptations.

Thomas seems to fear that the introspectionist and illuminationist philosophy of mind of his day, which he attributed to the *platonici* but found much more pertinently in the hugely influential theology of Augustine, was tacitly dominated by an ideal of knowledge which could be instantiated only by the divine mind.

The ultimate perfection of mind is indeed its own immanent activity, Thomas contends, 'not the sort of activity that goes out to something else and to the completion of that, say the constructing of a building, but remaining in the agent as its actuality and perfection'. In other words, the mind is aware of its own act of knowing – but the only mind that is identical with its own mental act is the divine mind: 'for God to understand his own understanding is the same thing as to understand his own essence, for his essence is his understanding' (ST 1.79.1). While Thomas has a proto-Wittgensteinian conception of how subjective experience depends on our engagement with objects in the public world,[22] his 'theory of knowledge' is very much in aid of acknowledging the radical difference between our minds and the divine mind. The proto-'Cartesian' self-transparent subject whom he finds in Augustine's introspectionist doctrine seemed dangerously close to an idolatrous displacement of the divine subject's self-awareness.[23]

In other words, if we characterize scepticism, with MacKinnon, as perpetual dissatisfaction with the cognitive situation of the human mind, as in effect a demand for divine knowledge, it is not implausible to suggest that Thomas was well aware of this temptation.

Mind/World Identity

While certainly discussed by 'Wittgenstein Thomists', the principle that mind and world coincide in the act of meaning is a central plank in what John Haldane has recently labelled 'Analytical Thomism'.[24]

It would be an exaggeration to claim that this recourse to Thomas Aquinas is transforming current debates in analytic philosophy about the mind/world relationship, yet there is a significant appeal to Aristotle which now sometimes includes Thomas also.

Consider the following examples. Charles Taylor argues against 'representationalist' theories of the mind/world relationship: views that presuppose a gap between our minds and things in the world and seek to bridge it by positing intermediate entities such as mental images, sense data, raw feels, and so on. Sometimes he appeals to the pre-modern view, thinking of Aristotle, not explicitly of Thomas, according to which one comes to know something by the mind's becoming one with the object of thought. Thought and thing collaborate, so to speak, rather than confront each other, with the mind's having to impose intelligibility on inherently unintelligible objects. Aristotle sometimes sounds as though he is supporting representationalism, Taylor says; but, on the contrary, his model of how knowledge happens is participational: 'being informed by the same *eidos*, the mind participates in the being of the object known rather than simply depicting it'. However, Taylor concludes, this philosophy of mind depends totally on the philosophy of forms, and once that has collapsed, as he seems to assume it has, the account becomes 'untenable' and 'almost unintelligible'.[25]

Similarly, Hilary Putnam speaks, not of representationalism, but of the 'tempting idea that there has to be an "interface" between our conceptual powers and the external world'. In modern philosophy, and when we begin to think about these questions, it seems overwhelmingly obvious that what goes on in our heads is separated by a chasm from what is there in the world outside. We are strongly tempted to think that 'our conceptual powers cannot reach all the way to the objects themselves'. Looking for a way out of this 'egocentric predicament', Putnam appeals to a statement by John McDowell: 'We need to stand firm on the idea that the structure of elements that constitutes a thought, and the structure of elements that constitutes something that is the case, can be the very same thing'. This claim, John Haldane says, comes 'as close as makes no substantial difference to the old orthodoxy of Thomist metaphysical realism'.[26]

Our access to the world, for Thomas, as Norman Kretzmann says, 'is utterly direct, to the point of formal identity between the extra-mental object and the actually cognizing faculty'.[27]

Many others speak in similar terms. Long ago, in a pioneering and now classic study, Bernard Lonergan spoke of 'knowing by identity' as the 'theorem of immaterial assimilation'. He focused on Thomas's rejection of what he thought of as the Platonist conception of knowledge on the model of confrontation (*Summa Contra Gentiles* 2.98). On the contrary, knowledge is a kind of assimilation: the object (world) made known or becoming intelligible is one's mind actually knowing or understanding.[28]

G.E.M. Anscombe, maintaining that, since Frege, we have come to see that 'thoughts are characterized by what they are of, with no substantive being of their own' (thus rejecting Descartes's 'angelism', no doubt unwittingly), argues that the medieval concept of intentional existence, brought to the fore by Brentano,[29] 'may even be making a come-back, a reappearance in modern dress' – but, she warns, 'these matters are still very dark'.[30]

In brief, looking for an alternative to modern philosophical claims to the effect that we never see the world immediately but always through intervenient entities of some kind (thus opening scepticism about whether things really are as they appear to us), these philosophers look to the natural or naive realism which sees no need for any such intermediaries between us and the world.

For the 'naive' realist the world (reality) is altogether independent of our knowledge of it, in the sense that our minds simply reflect things just as they are, over against us, in a wholly passive way. Against this view the Thomist wants to say that knowledge is the product of a collaboration between the object known and the subject who knows: the knower enables the thing known to become intelligible, thus to enter the domain of meaning, while the thing's becoming intelligible activates the mind's capacities. Knowing is a new way of being on the knower's part; being known is a new way of being on the part of the object known. For Thomas, meaning is the mind's perfection, the coming to fulfilment of the human being's intellectual powers; simultaneously, it is the world's intelligibility being realized.

Doctrine of Creation

Of course, it is one thing to see mind/world identity theory as the alternative to scepticism-vulnerable representationalism; it is quite another to make it stand up as a worked-out philosophical account. Philosophers are not likely to be persuaded by mantra-like repetitions of the axiom: '*Anima est quodammodo omnia*' – the human mind is in a certain way identical with the world, as the world is in a certain way identical with the human mind. Thomas likes to cite this axiom, from Aristotle (though no doubt the picture of the human being as microcosm lies somewhere in the remote background). Then again, though one might like to think that the 'subjective-individualist' view of the human person and 'representationalist' theories of knowledge should yield to better philosophy, Thomas's preference for the 'objective-participant' and 'mind/world identity' views are clearly grounded in theological considerations: specifically in the doctrine of creation.

Thomas sees no gap between mind and world, thought and things, that needs to be bridged, either by idealist/empiricist representations or (as with Barth) by divine intervention. His view of how our minds are related to the world is interwoven with his doctrine of God: no epistemology without theology. But his (perhaps naive) confidence that things are indeed as they seem, that there is no veil between the world and our minds, springs from, indeed is identical with, his belief in the world's belonging to God.

In the end, as at the outset, unity, truth, goodness and beauty coincide, Thomas thinks, in being: in particular, *ens et verum convertuntur*: what is, is the case. The word 'true' expresses a certain fittingness of world to mind (*convenientia entis ad intellectum*). This world/mind *convenientia* comes about by there being something 'born to be attuned to everything' (*natum . . . convenire cum omni ente*), which is, in turn, the human 'soul' (*anima*). And Thomas quotes Aristotle: 'the soul, in a way, is everything' – a neat paraphrase, he no doubt thought, of the doctrine of creation and, specifically, of the human being as created in the image and likeness of God (*De veritate*, 1).

Our experience of things is not a confrontation with something utterly alien, but a way of absorbing, and being absorbed by, the world to which we naturally belong. The mind does not primarily depict, reflect or mirror the world; rather, it assimilates the world as it is assimilated to the world. That is an easy claim to make but, of course, very hard to credit as a philosophical account of our way of knowing, and thus of actually *being* the world. Much else perhaps needs to be in place. Thomas takes for granted this non-subject-centred way of being in the world. We are inclined to begin with the mind, asking how our mental acts relate to the world; he begins on the contrary with the external objects which evoke intellectual activity on our part, and thus bring to fulfilment the capacities with which we are endowed.

We are inclined to assume that the objects of our knowledge remain totally unaffected. To be known, for an object unaware of it, is as if nothing had happened. This surely misses something. On Thomas's view, articulating as it does the doctrine of creation in terms of the metaphysics of participation, the object, in being known by the subject, is brought more clearly into the light and to that extent its nature and destiny are fulfilled.

It is easy to see how our minds are affected, changed, enriched and so on, by absorbing what comes to view in the world. But for Thomas it makes sense to hold that, even if there were no human minds, things would still be 'true' – in relation, that is, to God's mind (*De veritate*). He does not look at the world and see it as simply all that is the case, in itself; rather, he sees the world, and things in it, as destined to a certain fulfilment, with appointed ends, modes and opportunities. It is perhaps not too much to say that Thomas sees the way that things are in terms of the way that they ought to be. Certainly, he does not picture knowing as the subject's projecting value and intelligibility upon raw data. Rather, we exist at all only by participation in being (the doctrine of creation), and, since minds are what we are, we participate, by exercising our intellectual capacities, and of course to a very limited extent, in God's own knowledge of the world.

Not Without Theology

One way of engaging with the work of Thomas Aquinas, then, is to explore (1) his non-Cartesian approach to self-knowledge and (2) his mind/world identity view of knowledge as possible ways of recovering from what are perceived as still deeply entrenched and widely influential modern philosophical myths about the self and about our cognitive situation in the world.

Thus, in Wittgensteinian Thomism and Analytical Thomism, as more widely, if variously, in the Thomist tradition represented by R.P. Phillips, Thomas is appealed to as a source of good philosophy; as a resource in identifying, exposing and overcoming the Cartesian/empiricist presuppositions about self and world that are not difficult to find at work in much modern Christian theology. But, though these are philosophical considerations, the options that he adopted have a significant bearing on his theology and (one may say) the spirituality inscribed in his theology. In particular, the non-interiorist account of the self with its insistence on the engagement of the self in public social practices is precisely the account of the moral agent as a rational and social animal which is explored at great length in the *secunda pars* of the *Summa Theologiae*, commonly regarded as the most personally original and innovative of all his works. When he discusses the notion of conscience, for example, Thomas denies that it is, properly speaking, a faculty, such as we tend to think today; rather, conscience is 'applying our knowledge to what we do' (ST 1.79.13) – indeed, as the etymology suggests, he thinks it is 'knowledge with another' – in principle, that is to say, a shareable act of applying experience to what we do.

Secondly, the mind/world identity theory, the thought that I am so much at home in the world that, in a certain way, in the event of meaning, I may be said to be the world, and the world to be in me, is a thought that fits perfectly with Thomas's characteristic emphasis on the doctrine of creation.

Many people, certainly philosophers, regard the world as inherently hostile or at least indifferent to human beings: unsurprisingly they have no difficulty in postulating some kind of screen between the mind and the world, a confrontation, perhaps a voluntaristic imposition of concepts on raw and hopelessly unreachable objects. Others, with a naturalistic epistemology rooted in evolutionary theory, might argue that, biologically, we are animals in tune with the surrounding environment and it is not at all odd that our minds and the objects with which we deal ordinarily match perfectly. There need be no kind of theism in the background to make some such view plausible. Others, in certain non-Christian religious traditions, which for Aquinas would have been represented typically by the Manicheanism against which he developed his theology of the goodness of being, might be inclined to posit some kind of veil between the mind and the world. Indeed, they might be inclined to say that the real world is radically inaccessible to the human mind.

For Thomas, in contrast to such views, human beings are created in God's image and likeness, and, more particularly, are born such that our minds are connaturally open to the world that reveals itself to us and even reveals itself as created. Well aware of alternative epistemologies, and never denouncing representationalist ones as 'heretical', Thomas probably saw the mind/world identity theory, not as an isolated instance of good philosophy, but as a philosophical conception that confirmed his perhaps optimistic and anthropocentric sense of how creatures of every kind, and certainly creatures of the human kind, are at home as participants in the world that is God's creation.

In the end, as always, Thomas relates everything back to God: as the image of God we too are each the source of our actions, as having free will and control of our actions (ST 1–2. prologue). 'We receive knowledge from natural things', Thomas says (e.g. ST 1.14), 'of which God, by his knowledge, is the cause': unsurprisingly, since we are born to know what there is and to love its goodness, on Thomas's view, our relationship with what there is – 'being' – would seem to him better expressed as identity than as either confrontation or inference from intervening entities.

In short, epistemology is not separable from theology. Thomas's conceptions of the self and of knowledge were – perhaps still should be – invoked as paradigmatic alternatives to modern subjective individualism and epistemological representationalism. But he was not conducting a speculative inquiry into human understanding either for its own sake or as polemics against rival theories. He is interested in the activity of the human mind only in order to elucidate the way in which human beings imitate God.

Imitating God

Since physical objects cannot represent God our understanding anything about them cannot be a way of imitating God. The type of knowledge on which philosophers interested in epistemology have often focused, as it happens, is knowledge of objects ('middle-sized dry goods'). In the *Summa Theologiae*, Thomas opens his discussion of human understanding of material objects (ST 1.84–6) by saying that he will, as a theologian, discuss only the intellectual and appetitive powers in which the virtues are found (ST 1.78): in short, his interest is in the moral dimension of knowledge, in moral epistemology so to speak. The discussion goes even more deeply into darker matters than modern epistemology ever reaches. It is true, Thomas maintains, that we understand and judge everything in the light of the First Truth, in the sense that the light of the mind, whether natural or grace-given, is nothing other than an impact, so to speak, of the First Truth (referring us back to ST 1.12.2), yet that is how something is known; it does not mean that God, as First Truth, is that which is known by our minds (ST 1.88.3). On the contrary, citing John 1:18, 'no one has ever seen God', Thomas insists that it is the physical world – *quidditas rei materialis* – of which we have knowledge, not God.

The whole series of questions on the nature of the human being (qq 75–89) culminates by considering the cognitive situation, so to speak, of the 'separated soul' (*anima separata*), before moving on to consider the creation of Adam and Eve as bodily beings (ST 1.90–2) and then the human being as 'made in God's image and likeness' (ST 1.93). It then turns out that the image of God is to be found in a human being as he or she is 'carried towards God', specifically by actively knowing and loving God (ST 1.93.8).

Assuming we have read his account of God's knowing and loving (ST 1.14–17), Thomas mines Aristotle's *de Anima*, certainly, but his account of mind and will, conducted as an exercise in negative theology ('This is how we know; that is how God must know'), preparing the way for the account to come of the moral and sacramental movement of human beings to God (in the *secunda pars*), is finally focused on the human creature as 'image of God' – as 'imaging' the triune Godhead (*secundum verbum conceptum de Dei notitia et amorem exinde derivatum*) (ST 1.93.8).

Thomas's treatise on human understanding is not only never independent of a theological interest in creation as flowing from and being drawn back into God as *principium et finis* but, in this consideration of the human being as *imago Dei*, the epistemology is always already a contribution to the doctrine of God as Trinity.

Chapter 3

PROLEGOMENA
TO NATURAL
THEOLOGY

Long after Thomas Aquinas's day, religious people and Christians in general take it for granted that the world is caused. Even in secularized British culture, many would think that the world has 'something behind it', as they might rather vaguely say. Most would, of course, doubt that Jesus Christ might have anything to do with this. On the other hand, in the Psalms, the Wisdom books of the Greek Old Testament, the patristic tradition, and so on, in which Thomas was immersed from an early age, the assumption is that the world reveals the glory of God: the divine presence is more or less evident.

The Invention of Antichrist

Nevertheless, one of the most intractable differences between admirers and adversaries of Thomas (including Catholics among the latter) centres on his supposed commitment to natural theology, understood as purely philosophical arguments to prove God's existence as the preamble to and foundation of Christian faith.

Karl Barth quotes Gottlieb Söhngen (1892–1971), a fine theologian, almost unknown outside Germany, to the effect that, even on the narrowest interpretation of Roman Catholic doctrine, 'there is no *theologia naturalis* that can be unmoored from salvation history'.[1] If this were true, Barth goes on to say, he would have to withdraw his famous remark that the notion of *analogia entis* is 'the invention of anti-Christ' and the root of all Roman Catholic deviations from true Christian doctrine. He concludes, however, that Söhngen's views could not be 'authentically Roman Catholic'.

For Barth, at that stage anyway, to be 'authentically Roman Catholic', one had to hold to the view that there is a philosophically obtainable knowledge of God 'superordinated' to biblically revealed knowledge of God – a knowledge of God acquired by arguing by analogy from the existence and nature of beings to the existence and nature of the Supreme Being. Created beings and the divine being are considered together under the description of being, a master concept supposedly developed prior to and independently of any theological considerations. Christian doctrine of God is thus subordinated to naturalistic metaphysics. This is what Roman Catholics have to believe, in order for Barth to be in a position to attack them.

The question of the role of reasoning as regards knowledge of God certainly divides Protestants and Catholics, in particular Barthians and Thomists; but, to some extent at least, the division is sustained by what look like incompatible understandings of some of the basic concepts.

In an important book on alternatives to 'classical theism', Colin Gunton argues that the decline of belief in God in the Western world is related almost entirely to the 'classical concept of God'. By and large, 'in most secular writing, and certainly in the mainstream of philosophy since Descartes', there has been only one concept of God at issue: the 'pattern of most discussion of the nature and existence of God was laid down in the Middle Ages, classically in the *Summa Theologica* of St Thomas Aquinas'. Indeed: 'Modern philosophy of religion in the Anglo-Saxon world is still conducted largely against a background of Aquinas's concept and the great critiques of its central doctrines and assumptions in Descartes, Spinoza, Hume, and Kant'.[2]

That is one way of reading Thomas Aquinas, by no means uncommon. If not the originator, then he is the prototype of modern philosophical theologians who argue about the existence of the first cause of the world, bracketing out the God revealed in the Christian or any other specific historical religion.

There is a much darker version of the story. According to T.F. Torrance, the 'Latin heresy', already evident in Augustine, culminated in Thomas's elaboration of an autonomous natural theology, dealing with the being of God in general and in abstraction from the God self-revealed historically in the Christian dispensation.[3] Down the line, in liberal Protestantism as well as in neo-Thomist theology, the Christian message was interpreted in terms of a philosophy of religion reached before and apart from the only real knowledge of God exclusively given historically through his self-revelation in Christ. With Kant, 'God was held to be really unknowable as he is in himself, so that divine revelation was regarded as having no objective truth or informational content'. With Schleiermacher we have 'the idea of a deep-seated kinship between the divine Spirit and the human spirit, in virtue of which epistemic contact might be made with God in the depths of the religious consciousness or through the kind of self-understanding generated in human beings by the personality of Jesus'. It is no surprise, indeed it was inevitable, that this dualism would lead to 'a naturalisation and cultural secularisation of the Gospel', and eventually to 'the strange natural theology' of the German Christians, for whom the national folk-consciousness awaked by Hitler was held to be a revelation of the Spirit of God.

It was no surprise either, then, that we find Barth raging against Roman Catholic theologians who cited the Thomist axiom 'grace does not destroy but perfects nature' in order to justify the Concordat between the Vatican and Nazi Germany. Torrance, with Barth, denounces the 'Thomist' doctrine of *analogia entis*: 'an inherent kinship of analogy of being between man and God', a 'continuity of the uncreated Spirit with man's created spirit' – 'the sweet but insidious effect of Augustinian thought in western theology' – all of which displays 'the subtle work-righteousness of Tridentine Roman theology'.[4]

Vatican I

The success of agnosticism since the Enlightenment has been accompanied by much debate about the viability of arguments that proceed from the existence of the world to the existence of the cause to which the world owes its existence.

Mainstream Christian theology in Protestant traditions accepts Kant's 'Copernican revolution in philosophy', the reversal of earlier views of knowledge as our minds conforming to objects, in favour of the view that objects conform to our ways of knowing. Since knowledge is thus limited to what appears to us in sensory experience, metaphysical arguments for the existence of God, the immortality of the soul, and the freedom of the will, are revealed as illusory. In particular, as Kant argues, we must accept the impossibility of knowing anything of the supersensible realm. Thus, for theologians, God's existence is either provided by God's self-revelation or disclosed through reflection on the ethical imperatives inscribed in our rationality. On the one hand, we have fideism (God's existence as purely a matter of revelation) and, on the other, we have a sense of duty (inferences from the existence of conscience) that can only be divinely implanted; and suchlike.

Reacting against such epistemological scepticism, Leonine Thomists developed an increasingly determined and sophisticated tradition of theistic proofs. The First Vatican Council (1870) sought to steer a way between the twin errors of fideism and rationalism in Roman Catholic theologians, but is better remembered for anathematizing those who hold that 'the one, true God, our creator and lord, cannot be known with certainty from the things that have been made, by the natural light of human reason'.[5]

Among other things, the decree declares that natural knowledge about God and moral matters is to be distinguished from divine faith; that assent to Christian faith is not produced by reasoning; and that Catholics do not have to suspend their faith until they have verified the credibility of revelation. The chief anxiety, however, is that we might be tempted to think that people ought to be moved to faith only by each one's 'internal experience or private inspiration'.

Read in context, the claim for the possibility of knowing God with certainty from the world, by the natural light of reason, is not as ambitious as Roman Catholic apologists have often hoped and Barthian theologians always feared. As far as the fears of the latter are concerned, the idea that anyone might be coerced into faith by metaphysical arguments, or be expected to found faith in Christ on rationalist apologetics, is excluded. Perhaps surprisingly, no examples are offered of what sort of reasoning from the world to knowledge of God would be appropriate. The emphasis is entirely on the claim that reasoning of some kind from the existence of the world to the existence of God is possible, without appealing to faith – in opposition to the view, that is to say, that knowledge of God's existence is either solely the result of faith or dependent on subjective experience. The decree even states quite explicitly that 'the doctrine of the faith which God has revealed is put forward not as some philosophical discovery capable of being perfected by human intelligence, but as a divine deposit committed to the spouse of Christ to be faithfully protected and infallibly promulgated'.

Thus, if anything, far from encouraging foundationalist rationalism in natural theology, Vatican I was explicitly suspicious of anything of the kind.

It is a moot point whether it was ever justifiable, in the return to Thomas which gathered strength after 1870, to extract his arguments for the existence of a first cause and set them out in the context of post-Kantian agnosticism.

Indisputably, anyway, there is a wide range of judgements within the field of Thomist studies about the theistic proofs with which the *Summa Theologiae* opens (ST 1.2.3). Perhaps some of the conflicting interpretations may be illuminated by first taking a fresh look at some of the basic concepts and assumptions.

Contamination by Causalism

Obviously, Thomas takes it for granted that the world has been created, which, in the established language of the day, he equates with saying that the world is an 'effect' of God as 'cause'. The exploration of the properties which may or may not be attributed to this first cause is Thomas's way of elucidating the implications of the doctrine of creation as he inherits it from the biblico-patristic tradition. His main interest in doing so is to expose and exclude what he regards as conceptions of how God and the world are related which are incompatible with authentic Christian doctrine.

The principal motive on God's part for revealing himself as Trinity, so Thomas contends, is to enable a correct perception of the salvation of the human race, accomplished as this is by the incarnate Son and by the gift of the Holy Spirit; but, secondarily, it allows a correct understanding of the creation of the world:

> When we affirm that God created all things by his Word we exclude the error of those who claim that God produced things *ex necessitate naturae* – by postulating a procession of love it is shown that God did not produce creatures in virtue of any neediness on his part nor because of any alien cause extrinsic to him, but on account of love of his own goodness. (ST 1.32.1, citing Genesis 1:3–4 as so often)

Thomas repeatedly insists on the goodness of the created order. Again and again, he resists views which he suspects of Catharist dualism. His insistence that the aptitude for receiving divine grace is a good on the part of a creature with a human nature, which sin can never totally destroy, is another illustration of his determination to head off any temptation to succumb to Manichean dualism (ST 1.48.4; 1–2.85.2). If Thomas is celebrated as the theologian of the doctrine of creation, this is because of his commitment to curing Christians of the temptation to think that the world (as he would put it) might be the result of some external pressure on the creator or some compensatory expression of the creator's need. The world, for Thomas, much against what was quite widely believed in his time, is simply the expression of divine bounty: freely shared, entirely unforced, 'unnecessary' – simply an expression of love.

Beyond this, when we look at his discussions, the challenge for Thomas is never to prove God's existence, as if there is any doubt about that. His main concern is to disprove polytheism (ST 1.11.3, citing Deuteronomy 6:4: 'Behold, Israel, the Lord thy God is one God') and to deal with the perennial temptations, for Christians also, of thinking of

God as a special sort of creature (ST 1.3), emphasizing divine immanence at the expense of transcendence, or vice versa (ST 1.8–9). The question was not whether there is a god; it was about which god, and whose god, once it was clear that there is only one.

Consider, however, the anxieties that one modern theologian (by no means unrepresentative) has about Thomas's doctrine of creation in terms of causality. The story goes like this. A theological account of the world as created which would count as Christian must involve a conception of God as a personal agent: the existence of the world has to be attributed not to chance or necessity but to some form of intentional action.[6] This might seem very much what Thomas keeps insisting: the world is not the result of chance or necessity, but the creation of the First Cause to which must be attributed knowledge and will (cf. ST 1.2–26) – a self-conscious and intentional agent, as it would seem. The history of the theology of creation, however, so Colin Gunton avers, shows that the concept of God's personal agency has suffered 'contamination', as he puts it, 'by notions of emanation and causality'.

Leaving aside emanation, let us consider this understanding of causality.[7] First, 'causalism' – 'as scarcely needs to be said' – is 'characteristic of the Aristotelian forms of expression which still mark theology indelibly'. Note, however, that it is a 'polymorphic concept'. Indeed, Gunton allows, it may once have been a personal notion, as in Greek patristic talk of God the Father as *aitia*. Since the Enlightenment, however, as for example in the work of the Dutch Jewish philosopher Baruch Spinoza (1632–77), causality is construed on a mechanistic model: a development in which 'he was given encouragement by some of his mediaeval predecessors'.

That is to say, the Enlightenment paradigm of causing, taken from physics, originated in medieval conceptions of causing.

Turning to Thomas explicitly, Gunton allows – indeed 'must emphasise' – that 'personal or trinitarianly conceived agency in creation' is not 'completely lacking from his thought'. On the contrary, Thomas holds that 'creation is the outcome of the free, personal willing of the creator'. Nevertheless, the act of divine willing of creation is 'rather monistically conceived': the doctrine of God as Trinity 'plays little or no constitutive part' in Thomas's theology of creation.

The evidence for this defect is that, after considering the processions within the Godhead (ST 1.27–42) and the divine missions (1.43), Thomas turns to the procession of creatures from God (1.44), where he at once reverts to the God who is 'sheer existence subsisting in his very nature', 'the all-embracing cause of beings', 'the first exemplar cause of all things', and 'the final cause of all things' (1.44.1–4) – 'a chiefly abstract and merely "monotheistic" treatment of the status of God as first cause'.

In short, even after expounding his doctrine of God as Trinity, Thomas goes back to God as First Cause, as if nothing significant had happened in between.

One possibility, one might think, is that he might have assumed all along that the self-conscious and intentional agent causing the world as originating it *ex nihilo* and as attracting it as *telos*, is none other than the triune God: the God whom Thomas worshipped every day. But of course he does not spell this out. Thus, for the modern reader, the division between considering the unity of the divine nature and considering the distinction of persons in the Godhead is perceived as a gap, bridged at question 44 only by a leap back into what is taken to be purely philosophical theology.

What we find in question 44, according to Gunton, is 'a fairly strong conception of divine omnicausality' – only 'fairly strong', it is true; but the fear clearly is that, for Thomas, there is only one real cause and all other 'causes' are spurious. 'Omnicausality', here, means that there is no cause of anything that happens in the world but God alone.

It is 'symptomatic', for example, that Thomas rejects the view of the twelfth-century theologian Peter the Lombard, according to which God can share the divine creative power with creatures, so that they too may really create, not of course by their own authority, but ministerially (ST 1.45.5). This Gunton takes to be evidence of Thomas's consistent undermining of the independent and substantial reality of created beings.

This certainly conflicts with readings dear to a variety of other interpreters. The point Thomas makes, in rejecting the thesis that creating can be delegated, they would say, is that, whatever Lombard says about creating as the action proper to God alone, he believed that this is perfectly compatible with the view that created causes might be able also to create as acting in the power of the First Cause. For Thomas, deeply imbued with Christian neo-Platonism as his theology obviously is, this is nevertheless an unacceptable form of hierarchically descending emanation 'from above'. In the context of his time, he could only resist a doctrine of mediated creation which seemed inextricable from a picture of the cosmos as created by created intelligences (such as angels), delegated by, and suspiciously close to substituting for, the First Cause. Parting here from Lombard's view of the matter, Thomas wants to protect the singularity of divine creation: God alone creates, in the proper sense.

The Purpose of Creation

Gunton's discussion is extremely interesting, for several reasons. While his worries about the impersonality of Thomas's first cause are to the fore, and most require our attention, he has a number of related concerns.

Gunton rejects Thomas's thesis (ST 1.44.4) that it would not be appropriate for God to create 'only to communicate his own completeness, which is his goodness' (*solum communicare suam perfectionem, quae est ejus bonitas*) rather than 'to achieve some purpose' (*propter acquisitionem alicujus finis*). For Gunton, it seems, surprisingly, that it makes good sense, indeed it is even required, that God creates the world, in Thomas's phrase, 'to achieve some purpose'. This is the thought that above all horrifies Thomas. For him, this amounts to saying that God gains in some way from the existence of the world.

Here, it seems to me, we have conflicting appreciations of Thomas's view which are rooted in radically different theological expectations and suspicions.

Thomas is well aware that he is taking a stand. On the view with which he is obviously familiar but which he firmly rejects, God creates in order to get something he does not have. God creates 'for his own benefit' (*ad suam utilitatem*). Indeed, God creates because he needs to do so – 'out of lack' (*propter indigentiam*). For Thomas, on the other hand, 'God alone is supremely generous' (*ipse solus est maxime liberalis*), God acts 'not for any advantage but out of sheer bounty' (*non propter utilitatem sed solum propter suam bonitatem*).

Here, we may say, Thomas sounds quite 'Barthian':

> God has no need of us, He has no need of the world and heaven and earth at all. He is rich in Himself. He has fullness of life. All glory, all beauty, all goodness and holiness reside in Him. He is sufficient unto Himself, he is God, blessed in Himself. To what end, then, the world? Here in fact there is everything, here in the living God. How can there be something alongside God, of which he has no need? This is the riddle of creation.[8]

On this point, Gunton's reading of Thomas's text is perfectly accurate; it is just that he disagrees with Thomas's understanding of creation as simply the expression of sheer divine generosity.

Creatures as Causes

It is less surprising that Gunton rejects Thomas's view that creatures are really dependent on God but God has no real relationship with creatures (ST 1.45.3). Here, readers usually get what Thomas is saying right; it is just that they think he is wrong.

Being created, Thomas thinks, means that there is nothing in the creature other than a relationship to the creator; and since the divine creative act is nothing other than God with a relationship to the created, the God–creature relationship is not a real relationship in God, whereas the creature–God relationship is a real relationship in the creature (Thomas refers us to ST 1.13.7).

Here we have another crux. To say that creating, 'creation in its active sense', is nothing other than God with a relation to the creature seems to deprive the creature of independent reality. If God is not really related to the world and in particular to us, then it looks as if God is outside the world and indifferent to us, as one of the standard views of 'classical theism' maintains. For Thomas, however, it was vital to head off the thought that was tempting in his day, and certainly is in ours, that God is an item in the world, on however grander a scale than the rest of us. That would be idolatry: equivalent to making God a creature. In the relationship between creatures and creator, Thomas wants to say, creatures are utterly and totally indebted to God for their existence, whereas God is in no way dependent on or indebted to creatures. For Gunton, again reading the text correctly, this denial that God has a real relationship to the created order leads Thomas to 'detract from the creature's value as creature'. It is to 'tie the creature too closely to God, and so fail to give it space to be'. It detracts from 'the proper substantiality of the creature'. Indeed, some commentators, Harnack for one, have noted how near Thomas comes here to pantheism.[9]

This is all very provocative for old-fashioned Thomists. For them, it is important, even wildly exciting, that Thomas's concept of God as First Cause, far from diminishing or annulling created agents as secondary causes, actually preserves and respects them.[10]

When Thomas considers what we now call the transcendence and immanence of God, he cites Isaiah 26:12, one of his favourite texts: 'Lord, thou wilt ordain peace for us: for thou also hast wrought all our works in us'. He understand this to mean that 'God is in every thing, not indeed as part of its nature or as a property, but as the agent is present in what he does' (ST 1.8.1). 'God is above all things by the transcendence of his nature and yet is in all things as causing their being' (1.8.1.1). God is in everything 'inwardly' (*intime*). Indeed, God is in things 'containing them'; we might even say that 'things are more in God than God is in things' (1.8.1.2 and 3.3). Moreover, God is in things 'as giving them being, power and activity' (1.8.2).

Thomas sees no conflict between God's working in everything and every being's doing its own thing, so to speak. Or rather: he is well aware of the temptations, common in his day as in ours, to see rivalry between God's sovereign freedom and human autonomy, either making God an item in the world or reducing creatures to puppets. 'It seems difficult for some people', he remarks, 'to understand how natural effects are attributed to both God and to a natural agent' (*Contra Gentiles* 3.70.1).

How much Thomas knew of the *Mutakallimun*, the 'exponents of the Law of the Moors' (*Contra Gentiles* 3:65:10) may well be doubted. His knowledge of these Muslim theologians seems to depend on the account given in Rabbi Moses ben Maimon's *Guide for the Perplexed* (which appeared in 1190). Perhaps he preferred to cite them rather than any of his Christian contemporaries. He devotes so much attention to their misguided emphasis (as he thinks it) on the 'omnicausality' of God that one suspects they are really a stand-in for Christian theologians whom he regards as only too likely to succumb to the temptation to set creatures and creator over against one another in some kind of competition, and then to invent reconciling theories.

For Thomas, God is the cause that enables all agents to cause what they do (ST 3.67.1). There is no problem. He cites Isaiah 26:12 again, together with John 15:5: 'Without me, you can do nothing'; and Philippians 2:13: 'It is God who worketh in us both to will and to accomplish according to his good will'. For Thomas, evidently, Scripture settles it; there is no need for theoretical explanations of how divine freedom and human freedom do not, or need not be thought to, encroach on each other.

Yet, after insisting on God's being the one who is the cause of action for all things (*Contra Gentiles* 3. 67.6), and that no creature 'can serve as a medium for the carrying out of whatever the divine power can do, for divine power infinitely surpasses every created thing' (68.5), Thomas sees that he may now be interpreted as encouraging some people to think that 'no creature has an active role in the production of natural effects' (69.1). It might be thought, for example, that it is not the flame that heats the pot of soup on the stove but God who causes heat on the occasion of the flame, so to speak.

Given that creation is an act of God alone, it might indeed seem that God alone does everything that happens in the world, with no real contribution from any created agent (69.2). Thomas seems to have in mind the *Mutakallimun*; but he refers also to Plato (69.3), Ibn Sina, the Muslim philosopher (69.4) and Solomon Ibn Gabirol, the Spanish Jewish philosopher (whom Thomas supposed to be an Arab Muslim) (69.10), as all maintaining some form of the doctrine that God operates alone in all created agents (69:12), treating them as proxies or stand-ins for direct divine intervention.

What Thomas wants to maintain here is the distinction between God's doing everything, omnicausality as we might say, and God's doing everything on his own: monocausality. This latter position, which

Gunton (like Harnack) finds in Thomas, is exactly the position Thomas consistently excludes. Above all, it is incompatible with his understanding of divine wisdom (*Contra Gentiles* 3.69.13): 'if created things could in no way operate to produce their effects, and if God alone worked all activities immediately, these other things would be employed in a useless way by him, for the production of these effects'. God, however, has communicated his likeness to things, not just in their existing at all, but, 'as far as acting is concerned', God creates 'so that created things may also have their own actions' (3.69.14). Indeed, if creatures have no active role in what they do, that reduces them to ciphers, and 'to detract from the perfection of creatures is to detract from the perfection of divine power', and thus, in the end, this exaltation of divine omnicausality only detracts from the sovereignty of God as Thomas conceives it (3.69.15).

If the action by which an effect is produced proceeds from a human agent (as one is tempted to think) it surely does not proceed from God. When a thing can be done adequately by one agent it is superfluous to posit another: either God or the human agent does whatever it is. On the other hand, if God produces the entire natural effect, nothing is left for the human agent to do. Again and again, against all such tempting thoughts, Thomas returns us to his doctrine of double agency. Without arguing or developing any explanatory theory, he merely notes that there is nothing to stop us from thinking that the same effect is produced by a lower agent and by God – thus by both immediately – though in different ways. It is always by divine agency that the human agent produces his or her proper effect. It is not superfluous for creatures to do things, even if God can by himself produce all natural effects, as happens (Thomas thinks) in the case of miracles. To say this is not to concede something inadequate about God's agency. On the contrary, it is a result of God's bountiful goodness that creatures are really and truly agents of their own activities. We do not live under a regime of endlessly repeated miracles.

This is, again, a very Barthian concern. We must have no truck with theological occasionalism, playing down or excluding genuine created efficacy. This would be to misunderstand the character of the transcendence and immanence implied by the sovereignty of God. God's greatness does not require any diminishment of the creature whose being is constituted by being related to God. The *concursus* is not a convergence or concord of independent lines of divine and created agency.

Yet, we may allow, Thomas only excludes certain tempting views: yes, God does everything, God is not a partner in the existence and activities of the world; God does everything, however, in such a way that the autonomy and reality of created agents is respected. Above all: the effect is not attributed to a human agent and to divine agency in such a way that it is partly done by God and partly by the human agent; rather, it is done wholly by both, according to a different way, just as the same effect is wholly attributed to the instrument and also wholly to the principal agent – but now Thomas is referring us to an analogy, and either we see it or we don't. In the end, he excludes certain views and leaves us simply with the mystery of the relationship between divine creativity and human autonomy. 'That is just what we are like – agents of our own return to God'; 'That is what God is like – the God who gives us being and the power to act'. Thomas has nothing more basic to offer than these observations.

Agent Causation

The very idea of God as the cause of the world is, however, the great problem for many modern theologians. By accepting the Enlightenment's mechanistic conception of causation, no doubt inadvertently, they have lost sight of Aristotle's much richer, anyway very different, sense of causality, let alone of Thomas's.

'God causes our will to move without prejudice to our freedom' (*Contra Gentiles* 3:89): this is a remark that many would find unintelligible. But, if so, is this not because they are in thrall to a mechanistic model of causality which prevents them from seeing that the relationship of divine and human causalities, as Thomas understands it, is always already the interplay of self-conscious and intentional agents?

As we have noted, for Colin Gunton at least, Thomas's conception of cause anticipates the modern conception of cause along mechanistic lines (not that he offers detailed evidence for this), whereas we might have assumed (without seeing any need to provide evidence!) that, as a premodern, Thomas took for granted the ancient understanding of cause on the analogy of personal agency.

This is an irresolvable conflict of interpretations. Thomas, in the second half of the thirteenth century, is a transitional figure. In the end, there will always be room for disagreement, depending on whether one sees his theological terminology in continuity with his inheritance or as a new departure, anticipating developments to come centuries later.

It seems arguable, indeed likely, that when Thomas speaks of causation his model (as with Aristotle) is what philosophers sometimes label 'agent-causation'. That is to say, causing, for Thomas, is pictured on analogy with a person's own experience of bringing things about.

Modern Thomists may well have helped to occlude Thomas's conception of causality. According to David Braine, some so emphasised the adequacy of our causal argumentation to God as to open the way to the modern deistic way of thinking according to which God is indeed cause of the Universe and reason may know Him as such, but, knowing Him in this way, it thereby knows Him in a way which makes Him like creatures, the very opposite of Jewish and Christian orthodoxy, and the opposite of Aquinas's opinion.[11]

However that may be, there is no need to accept the mechanistic notion of causation as the paradigm for us now, let alone in pre-modern thinking. This is a prime case of allowing ourselves to be mystified by a philosophical picture. Our ordinary workaday pre-philosophical concept of causing is occluded by the model of the interaction of impersonal forces. The model no doubt seems unavoidable, captivating, 'scientific', and so on. 'The received philosopher's picture of the supposedly pre-philosophical view of causation', Braine says, 'is that it consists of pushes and pulls whereby one tangible object exercises agency in regard to another' (p.78). Yet, as he insists, this is no more than an imposition on common sense of a seventeenth-century philosophical theory. The much older and richer pre-modern conception of irreducibly distinctive modes of agency 'has been lost sight of or repudiated in an attempt to reduce all agency to the material or mechanical model, or to mysterious mentalistic variants of this'.

Braine refers us to Anscombe's discussion of knowledge without observation, Hampshire's discussion of intentional knowledge, and the work of Ryle and Wittgenstein. Perhaps still a minority in the highly scientistic climate of Anglo-American philosophy, such philosophers are out to undermine, and relieve us of, the superstition that the only way to picture causality is on the model of billiard balls being knocked around the table.

We may add one more: 'Causing', as J.L. Austin reminds us, 'was a notion taken from a man's own experience of doing simple actions, and by primitive man every event was construed in terms of this model: every event has a cause, that is, every event is an action done by somebody – if not by a man, then by a quasi-man, a spirit'. When, at the Enlightenment, wanting to say that events which are clearly not any agent's actions may yet be said to be 'caused', philosophers forged a 'new, unanthropomorphic meaning'. In time, in a culture dominated by physics, this meaning is the one that takes over and dominates the notion of causing.[12]

Supposing, however, that Thomas doesn't have the 'new, unanthropomorphic' conception of causality, mesmerizingly current in modern culture, but simply, unquestioningly, retains the old fashioned pre-scientific idea, with a tendency towards a certain residual anthropomorphism, then is it not likely that, when he thinks of God as First Cause, he thinks at the same time of God as creator, and as such the God, origin and goal of his being, whom he is, even by nature, obliged to worship? Is there any reason to suppose that Thomas's talk of God as First Cause takes God to be some kind of non-personal object, a self-enclosed static entity? Suppose Thomas's First Cause is always already a self-conscious and intentional agent? Given that God is source and goal of rational creatures who are causes of their own activities, how could Thomas have conceived of God as anything other than a personal agent?

Substance-in-relation

So much for the concept of cause: either we take Thomas's use of the word as anticipating the prevalent modern mechanistic picture or we take it as coloured at least residually by the ancient anthropomorphic conception.

As far as Thomas's notion of substance is concerned, we have a similar option: either to assume that he means an unknowable static inert substratum, as John Locke is said to mean, or to assume that he means something more 'Aristotelian'. Unfortunately, Aristotle's paradigm of a substance is often supposed to be a rock or a bedstead. According to one recent scholar, however, the paradigm is natural objects: 'The first and plainest examples of substances are animals and plants' – 'horses and hydrangias, goats and geraniums, ducks and dahlias'. In short: 'Neither technical science nor subtle metaphysics is needed to answer the eternal question "What is substance?": the answer is in front of our noses'.[13]

The model substance is something that is alive. Indeed, for Aristotle, thinking of animals and plants, substances are 'animate' – with 'soul', psyche – the thesis Thomas of course adopts (cf ST 1.75.1). Far from being a physicalist picture, with middle-size dry goods as the analogue, the Aristotelian/Thomist understanding of substance is more open to the charge, at the other extreme, of being residually 'animistic'.

Far from being inert self-enclosed entities like rocks and bedsteads, substances, for Thomas, are always already about to impinge on something else. Existing, as he often says, is naturally followed by doing (*agere sequitur esse*). Action, activity, inward and external, is the normal manifestation of being. Far from having a 'substantialist' ontology of self-enclosed monadic objects, occasionally knocking up against one another, Thomas's cosmological picture is, rather, of a constantly reassembling network of transactions, beings becoming themselves in their doings. 'Things exist for the sake of what they do' (*omnes res [sunt] propter suam operationem*) (ST 1.105.5). More clearly still: 'each and every thing shows forth that it exists for the sake of its activity; indeed, doing is the ultimate perfection of each thing' (*operatio est ultima perfectio rei*) (*Contra Gentiles* 3.113).

'Doing is the ultimate realization of a reality'. It would be hard to conceive of a more dynamic conception of substance than this – at the other extreme from the static entity that philosophers such as A.N. Whitehead have criticized and that many readers of Thomas take for granted. Whitehead's attacks on the notion of substance ontology lie behind the development of process philosophy and hence process theology – the rejection of so-called classical theism on the grounds that its God is an inert and isolated self-enclosed substance. Over against such a substance it has been found important to insist on process: being is always already becoming. Ironically, however, the concept of substance in classical theism, certainly in Thomas, is an always already self-communicating being.

The idea that the concept of substance has to be understood in terms of beings fulfilling themselves in their doings, as entities always interacting with others, has been occluded by reading later and certainly alien interpretations of substance into Thomas's language.

The point is familiar to those brought up on classics of French Thomist scholarship.[14] More accessibly, and a good deal more lucidly, in essays dating back to the 1950s, the eminent American philosopher William Norris Clarke has insisted on the intimate connection between being and doing, existence and activity, in Thomas's ontology.[15]

What Thomas has done, Clarke argues, is incorporate into his understanding of being as actualization the deepest insight of the whole neo-Platonic tradition of the self-diffusiveness of the Good (*bonum est diffusivum sui*) – thus yielding an ontology of substance in terms of the self-sharing, self-communicating dynamism of being. Interpreting activity as both immanent and transient, Clarke sees Thomas's picture of the world as 'a vast communication system, linked together precisely as a universe by the universal dynamic bond of action and interaction, through which the inner act of presence of one being is made known, or makes a difference, to another while leaving intact the distinct identity of each'.

On this view, a substance is always already in relation, self-revealing in its own unique proper way, acting, reacting and interacting. Rocks, obviously, do not communicate much; but in a world fairly populated by animate beings it is perfectly natural to think of them as intrinsically and spontaneously self-communicating, self-revealing entities, and thus as substances always in relationship.

Paradoxically, when fairly understood, the concept of substance in Thomas and in Aristotle, far from being the inert and static entity denounced by Whitehead and process thinkers, is virtually identical with the concept of being as becoming which they seek to substitute.

Norris Clarke no doubt owes something to process philosophy and thus to Whitehead; but his work is rooted in the European and largely French Thomism of the 1950s: stimulated by Gilson's 'metaphysics of Exodus' perhaps, yet opting against his 'Aristotelian' Thomas for the neo-Platonic participation metaphysics highlighted in Thomas's work by such interpreters as de Finance, Geiger, Fabro, and De Raeymaker.

Thomas's 'supreme being', far from being the static deity of substantialist metaphysics, is the subsistent (i.e. underived) sheer Act of existence, identically Intelligence and Will. Far from being a self-enclosed isolated substance, this sheer Act is also the freely self-diffusing Good, in effect self-communicative love. As participating in the infinite goodness of the Act whose very being is identically self-communicative love, all beings, by the very fact that they are, possess natural dynamism towards action and self communication – so Clarke reads Thomas's conception of the relationship between creator and creatures. Action is the self-revelation of being; to be is to be substance-in-relation: these are Clarke's key theses for interpreting Thomas Aquinas.

Finally, Clarke argues that, since for Thomas a person is 'that which is most perfect in all of nature' (ST 1.29.3), we might even go so far as to say that if the intrinsically self-communicating and relational notion of being may be brought in, such that a person is its highest expression, then the way lies open to understanding Thomas's concept of the human person not as an isolated self-enclosed individual but as intrinsically ordered towards community, friendship, others – we might be in a position to reconsider the definition of a person that Thomas borrows from Boethius: *naturae rationalis individua substantia* (ST 1.29.2) – regarded by some readers as heading towards Cartesian solipsism but, after all, meaning something more like an intrinsically self-communicative individual naturally capable of discursive reasoning.

Summing-up

Much more evidently needs to be said in explanation of the very idea of natural theology; but so far as Thomas is concerned a proper understanding of what he means by basic concepts like cause and substance should open the way to seeing his account of primary and secondary causalities as an account of the entirely non-competitive relationship between uncreated/divine and created/human agencies. God as First Cause is always already God as freely self-communicating goodness, and as final cause attracting created agents to their proper end or *telos* (God as beatitude). Of this longed-for beatitude a certain knowledge is naturally implanted in us (ST 1.2.1), of course *sub quadam confusione* – so Thomas allows as he considers whether God's existence stands in need of logical argument at all.

It begins to look, then, as if Thomas's natural theology, once we remember the paradigms for cause and substance that he inherited and left uncontested, while it may not be moored in salvation history, as Gottlieb Söhngen suggested, is nevertheless embedded in a theology of God as creator and self-diffusive Good.

Chapter 4

WAYS OF READING
THE FIVE WAYS

The Five Ways – Thomas Aquinas's best known arguments for the existence of God (ST 1.2.3) – have given rise to so much debate, particularly since the 1920s, that it is almost a shock to return to the text and see how very little space they occupy in the vast expanse of the *Summa Theologiae*.[1]

French Ways

The surprise is, particularly, that, in the last 50 years, the amount of attention given to the Five Ways in English-language writing is proportionately much greater than in French, German, Italian and other languages.

Partly, no doubt, the disproportion may be traced to the fact that, in these language traditions, Thomas is regarded primarily as a theologian, whereas the approach in the English-speaking world emphasises his contribution to philosophical theology. Students in Britain are likely to have read little or nothing more than the Five Ways, whereas in western Europe more widely most will have grappled with Thomas's doctrine of the Trinity, creation, Christology, and so on.

Partly, perhaps, the British interest in Thomas's contribution to Christian apologetics marks a difference between those who studied his work in (until recently) closed and stable Catholic environments and those who, for one reason or another, have to try to provide reasons to justify believing in God's existence, in a much more agnostic and secular culture.

However that may be, questions about the intended function of the Five Ways in the *Summa Theologiae* have long been on the agenda, in European Catholic theology, rather than questions about the validity of the arguments in themselves. British readers, indeed, if they know anything about it, are inclined to find the Continental approach cavalier and even rather frivolous. For example, in the monograph-length article on 'Dieu' in the prestigious *Dictionnaire de Théologie Catholique*, we read as follows:

> As for the argument of the prime mover such as Saint Thomas understood it, it is a long time since it has been taught, even in the Thomist camp ... If the argument is taken in the sense in which Saint Thomas borrowed it historically from the Arabs, it is not conclusive, and the criticism offered by Scotus is decisive ... The Neo-Thomists, by adverting to metaphysical considerations ... actually abandon the physical argument of the prime mover, just as do all the other members of the Thomistic school ... [The argument has only] survived in the ranks of Protestant scholasticism, among certain philosophers and well-intentioned apologists'.[2]

Published in 1939, 13 years after his death, these remarks by the Jesuit theologian Marcel Chossat (1862–1926), are quoted approvingly by Henri de Lubac in his *Sur les chemins de Dieu*, published in 1956, a widely read book, and an excellent example of Christian apologetics in the French Catholic style.[3]

Chossat's reflections, de Lubac exclaims parenthetically, 'might be dubbed "historicist"!' – the code word at the time for the 'relativism' of which certain French Thomists (Dominican friars especially) accused de Lubac and other representatives of *la nouvelle théologie*.[4]

Presumably de Lubac's point was that, two decades before the controversy set off by his own famous book *Surnaturel* (1946), a mainstream theologian like Chossat could describe Thomas's theistic proofs as so culturally conditioned as now to be obsolete. Moreover, this view appeared in the most authoritative of the great French Catholic encyclopaedias.

No doubt, tweaking his adversaries' tails even further, de Lubac liked Chossat's assumption that Thomas's arguments from the world to the unmoved mover depend on medieval natural science, and have nothing to do with reformulations by modern Thomists in terms of metaphysics. Gleefully, he cites the following remark by Louis-Bertrand Geiger, reviewing a clutch of books on natural theology: these new books

> mark, at bottom, the abandonment of the Wolffian type of rationalism, in which metaphysical concepts must be separated as far as possible from all empirical data, and consequently also from the whole pre-philosophical life of the mind. On the contrary, it seems to us important to emphasize

the whole spontaneous movement by which man rises up to God. The truly philosophical ways have no need to fear recalling their humble origins.[5]

Wolffianism

The agenda here, not to mention the insults, are all rather arcane for British readers. For one thing, de Lubac was clearly endorsing Chossat's assumption that Thomas's Five Ways cannot be abstracted from his cosmology, particularly, no doubt, his physics and astronomy. Secondly, de Lubac obviously liked Geiger's deriding the then widely taught seminary courses in metaphysics that had lost all connection with the longing for the transcendent that precedes all such theorizing. Thirdly, the joke was that the metaphysics taught in Catholic seminaries was very largely the creation of Christian Wolff (1679–1754), the German Protestant philosopher and mathematician, remembered (if at all) as the predecessor whose Enlightenment rationalism was inherited by Immanuel Kant and radically surpassed in the *Critique of Pure Reason* (1781).

Few now attempt to read Wolff's prolific works. The textbooks which he published, in logic, ontology, cosmology, rational psychology, natural theology, and so on, created the disciplines, as well as much of the terminology, in modern philosophy. Wolff's conception of metaphysics as 'the science of being', along with his division of philosophy into these disciplines, survived in the neo-Thomist curriculum in Roman Catholic institutions, right into the 1960s.

When de Lubac, Geiger, and many others, rejected neo-Thomist natural theology, in the 1950s, it was what they took to be the underlying Wolffian rationalism that they rejected. In the book which came out of Etienne Gilson's William James Lectures at Harvard the fourth chapter is largely devoted to Wolff: 'an extremely versatile mind, and perhaps the most accomplished professor of philosophy of all times'. Wolff explicitly related his idea of metaphysics to the work of Francisco Suárez, contending that Suárez had given the correct account of what Thomas Aquinas meant by the concept of being. Instead of maintaining with Thomas that *operatio sequitur esse* Wolff followed Suárez in saying that *operatio sequitur essentiam*. That is to say, the actions that we see in the world and in which we engage issue not from the 'existence' but from the 'essence' of the agent in question. Here, according to Gilson, we are at the level of 'primitive philosophical options'. On the Suárezian–Wolffian interpretation, existence is identified with essence: actually existing beings are regarded as fully actualized essences. What makes the difference between an actual essence and a merely possible one is existence. The question arises as to what existence adds to essence. Down the line, Suárez decides that between an actualized essence and its existence there is no real distinction but only a conceptual one. What this leads to, Gilson contends, is what he calls 'essentialism': 'the irrepressible essentialism of the human mind', much more deeply seated than the philosophies of Suárez or Wolff or their modern followers. Such thinkers only articulate 'the overwhelming tendency of human understanding to sterilize being by reducing it to an abstract concept'. What is required, Gilson argues, is 'the restoring of being itself to its legitimate position as the first principle of metaphysics'. This would be to grant with Thomas Aquinas that 'existence happens to essence . . . not as some sort of accidental determination, but as its supreme act, that is, as the cause of its being as well as of its operation'. This, however, is extremely difficult to see. As Gilson says, of being: ' "to be" escapes all abstract representation', which is why (he thinks) philosophers, 'confronted with an element of reality for which no conceptual representation is available', ceaselessly turn attention to considering essences, bracketing out or ignoring the 'the true metaphysics of being'.[6]

Both Henri de Lubac and Marie-Dominique Chenu believed that aspersions of unorthodoxy were thrown on their work because of interventions by Réginald Garrigou-Lagrange. They were delighted by Gilson's note on the subterranean influence of Wolff on the exegesis of Thomas, naming Garrigou-Lagrange's major work *Dieu, son existence et sa nature. Solution Thomiste des antinomies agnostiques* (third edition of 1920).[7] Garrigou-Lagrange found the charge incomprehensible; his allies insisted that he had never read a word of Wolff. Years later, after Garrigou-Lagrange's death, Chenu published a savage attack on neo-Thomists, picking out Garrigou's work.[8] In effect, he maintained that what might seem an intramural squabble about how to read Thomas, or a much larger, even if equally esoteric, conflict between Suárezian Thomists and others, in fact touched one of the deepest issues at stake in the Second Vatican Council (1962–5). According to Chenu, the first drafts of texts offered to the bishops included one 'on knowing truth' (*De cognitione veritatis*) that attempted to establish the validity of the first principles of reason as indispensable to faith, appealing to the universal principles of identity, contradiction, sufficient reason, efficient and final causality, all (he claims) in Leibnizian–Wolffian language. His contention, briefly, is that, at Vatican II, the rationalistic natural theology taught in most Roman Catholic institutions for the previous hundred years was irreversibly rejected by the bishops, chiefly in their insistence on the priority of Scripture in the exposition of Catholic doctrine.

In fact, in his first major work *Le Sens Commun*, published in 1908 and frequently reissued over the years, Garrigou-Lagrange tells us in the preface that he owes a great deal to the work of a certain A. Spir: *Pensée et réalité* (1896). This is the translation of *Denken und Wirklichkeit* (1873), by Afrikan Alexandrovich Spir (1837–1890), a Russian naval officer who settled in Germany and published prolifically. On the evidence of this book, Spir seems to have been a Russian Orthodox with distinctly Cartesian inclinations in philosophy, certainly a strange inspiration for Garrigou-Lagrange's metaphysical defence of the principle of sufficient reason.

Years before, in 1937, in the pamphlet that annoyed Garrigou-Lagrange, Chenu accused the 'Thomist orthodoxy' of being 'contaminated by Wolffianism', naming the long dead Cardinal Zigliara (1833–93), responsible for inaugurating the (still far from complete) critical edition of Thomas's writings, as well as the author of a half dozen widely used textbooks of Thomist thought. In fact, no doubt, Garrigou-Lagrange was in Chenu's sights. We need to be disinfected of 'Baroque Scholasticism': 'the philosophy of the clerical functionaries at the court of the Emperor Joseph II'. The Augustinian 'sap' and the Dionysian 'mysticism' had been allowed to drain out of Thomas's thought, so that he seemed little more than a positivist. Natural theology was reduced to a set of cosmological proofs – 'with no more religious character than the arguments of eighteenth-century Deists'. With these and similar insults Chenu ridiculed the Thomists in Rome.[9]

Thomas's arguments for the existence of God, in short, read quite differently depending on whether one comes to them with the presuppositions of Thomists like Zigliara and Garrigou-Lagrange, or alternatively with the approach that we find in Thomists like Gilson and Chenu: 'Wolffian rationalists' or 'historicist Modernists', in the coded exchange of insults in the heyday of neo-Thomism.

What Thomas Writes

Turning to look at the text in which Thomas sets out the Five Ways of demonstrating that God exists, in the *Summa Theologiae* (ST 1.2.3), the first – banal – point to make is that we should read article 3 of question 2 ('whether God exists') in the context of the previous two articles ('whether God's existence is self-evident' and 'whether God's existence is demonstrable').

That God exists is not self-evident, Thomas contends. On the contrary, this is a truth that needs to be demonstrated (ST 1.2.1). That is to say, he finds himself in a Church, and no doubt in a theology faculty, in which some people – probably most people – regarded God's existence as self-evident. Obviously, in thirteenth-century Europe, people lived in a world in which the presence of the divine seemed all too palpable (as

it no doubt still is, in many regions of the world today, outside Europe).
Thomas begins by citing John of Damascus – for Thomas always the
most authoritative voice of Greek patristic orthodoxy: 'the awareness
that God exists is implanted by nature in everybody'.[10] God's existence
is something of which human beings are innately aware. We need to
pause and try to recreate an approach to the world – a way of being in
the world – which finds the divine or the sacred immediately visible in
the world.

Thomas has two further, somewhat more technical, arguments. First,
he offers a form of the ontological argument: when we understand the
meaning of the word 'God', it follows that God exists. Then, since God
is truth, as Scripture says, and we plainly live in a world where there is
truth, there must also be something that we call 'God'.

These are serious arguments, presented skeletally, but which would
not be difficult to spell out and strengthen. Thomas dismisses the ontological argument very rapidly; but there has been much highly sophisticated discussion in recent philosophy.[11] It would be easy to recast the
argument from the existence of truth to the existence of First Truth along
the lines that the common sense correspondence theory of truth trades
on a metaphysical realism which implies theism.

Thomas replies, anyway, that, if the divine presence in the world were
manifest, the proposition 'God exists' would be self-evident, and therefore could not be contradicted. Yet, the proposition can be – has been –
denied: 'The fool said in his heart: There is no God' (Psalm 13 (14): 1;
52 (53): 1).[12]

Here, again, we need to pause and consider how strange it is that
Thomas needs to – anyway in fact does – cite Scripture in evidence that
God's existence has been – not just may be – denied. For us, of course,
atheism is an entirely familiar intellectual position. Thomas, on the other
hand, turns to the revealed word of God to hear of someone denying the
existence of God.

From the outset, then, atheism, for Thomas, is a properly theological
concept. It will be many pages before he introduces the concept of sin,
but what he surely assumes is that atheism is in effect a sin: it is the fool
who says in his heart: 'there is no God'.

Argument is required, then, but it is those who sinfully deny the divine
presence in the world with whom Thomas is in conversation, not
philosophers with open minds who wait to hear arguments that might
compel them to accept the truth of the proposition 'There is a God'.

In effect, Thomas invites the sinful denier of God's existence, or
(rather) the future pastors whom he is instructing in case they ever meet
such a sinner, to turn to look at the world in which we live. Again and
again, Thomas takes his stand on the reality of the world – thus, for him,

on the world's intelligibility and goodness. It can only be on the basis of what owes its existence to God that God's existence can be brought to light for us, by the mediation of logical argument. It is as if Thomas wants to isolate the fool's sinful subjectivity by turning our attention to the realities of the visible world. But a good deal of metaphysics is in place: specifically, the traditional doctrine of the convertibility of the transcendental concepts: unity, truth, goodness, beauty and being.[13]

God in himself is utterly and totally intelligible, Thomas assumes, giving as the reason for this that God's nature is identical with his existing, a truth that he at once promises to demonstrate in Question 3. Thus, in what on the standard view are often supposed to be pre-theological and religion-free ways of demonstrating God's existence, Thomas already anticipates the doctrine of divine simplicity, his most fundamental theological principle, some would say.

This is another, usually overlooked, indication that the question whether God exists, though preceding the question of God's nature in the text, is not pre-theological conceptually, as is often assumed.

That God's existence is something that does need to be argued for, Thomas holds, is based on the fact that we do not know what God's nature is – as the doctrine of divine simplicity will say. In other words, the God who is present in the world as source and goal of all things is so much more mysterious than those who see signs of divinity everywhere believe that argument is required. The point of insisting that argument for God's existence is required is, then, not to convince hypothetical open-minded atheists, or even to persuade 'fools', so much as to deepen and enhance the mystery of the hidden God. From the start, the 'theistic proofs' are the first lesson in Thomas's negative theology. Far from being an exercise in rationalistic apologetics, the purpose of arguing for God's existence is to protect God's transcendence.

Moreover, as Thomas notes, taking it that we need no philosophical theory to justify saying so, the only way that we come to know more about anything is by working from things that we do know – things which he at once glosses as 'effects'.

In other words, from the outset, article 1 of question 2 is pervaded by theological assumptions. The Bible itself tells us of the possibility of denying God's existence; it's a sin. The doctrine of divine simplicity spells out why we cannot know what God is. This ignorance of God's nature requires us to reason to God's existence from the world. God is much stranger than those who see his presence everywhere realize. That an argument is needed for the existence of God is Thomas's first move in resisting idolatry. But it then turns out that 'those things of which we do have knowledge' are already describable, without argument or explanation, as 'effects' (*effectus*).

That is precisely what might seem to be in question. Why should we regard features of the world as 'effects'? Is that not what argument for the existence of God is supposed to achieve – to demonstrate, philosophically, that things are 'caused' in such a way that they may be called 'effects', thus of some 'cause'? The aim of a proof of God's existence by inference from the existence or nature of the world should surely not take it for granted that the world is an 'effect'. From the outset, however, Thomas sees the world in a cause/effects perspective. More properly, perhaps, he is relying, tacitly, on the doctrine that the world is created. The demonstrations that 'God exists' which he will offer are articulations of the already accepted presupposition that the world has a creator – not arguments that start from features of a world that are not yet identified as 'effects'. In a religious climate in which people see the hand of God everywhere in their lives, Thomas wants to introduce a degree of distance, at least to shift from seeing everything sacramentally or animistically, to contemplating the world in the light of a radically apophatic understanding of the divine nature. God's presence is just not so obvious as people assume, Thomas is saying.

The allusion to the doctrine of divine simplicity already shows that Thomas is taking it for granted that the creator – the 'cause' of these 'effects' – is radically unknowable.

Thomas deals with the three claims that God's existence is self-evident as follows. First, however much we may be aware that what our human nature desires is a happiness to be found only in God, this awareness does not count as knowing that God exists. A certain awareness of God is implanted in us, Thomas agrees, in the sense that we naturally desire beatitude (an often repeated axiom, one of the basic principles of his theology); but, as he will show much later (ST 1–2.2), we are easily mistaken or deceived about where our beatitude is truly to be found. Human beings desire to be with God, we may say, but which God, whose God?

As regards the ontological argument: those who hear us speaking of 'God' do not always understand us to mean 'that than which nothing greater can be thought'. Indeed, Thomas contends, there have been people who believed God to be something physical. The first question he will consider, after the arguments establishing the existence of something everyone calls 'God', is whether this God is a body (cf ST 1.3.1).

Then, while no argument is needed to show that there is truth in general, Thomas thinks, the obviousness of this does not reveal that there is First Truth. As Thomas will spell out much later, *prima veritas* is that which gives rise to faith: God himself (ST 2–2.1.1). By that stage, in the *Summa Theologiae*, we can have no doubt that Thomas is discussing the God who is author of the Law of Moses and of the New Covenant in Christ (cf. ST 1–2.98–108).

Once again, then, if we overlook what Thomas will spell out only much later, what he writes here (ST 1.2.1) might easily seem pre-theological. Thus, in article 1 of question 2 Thomas considers whether the existence of God needs to be demonstrated. In article 2 he considers whether God's existence can be demonstrated. This time the thesis he will oppose is to the effect that there is no place for reasoning to the truth that God exists – it is solely a matter of faith. Here again, but for the opposite reason, argument would be redundant.

Again citing John Damascene, it seems that logical argument is excluded: there can be no syllogism without a middle term; but we cannot know of God what he is but only what he is not, which means that no argument can even begin.

Taking the third objection, it surely has to be said that, if we could demonstrate God's existence, it would have to be from his effects; and his effects are obviously incommensurable with him: God is infinite, his effects are finite; which excludes any move from the finite to the infinite (*finiti ad infinitum non est proportio*).

These are again arguments it would not be difficult to expand. The thesis that God's existence is solely a matter of faith adumbrates the kind of fideism with which we are very familiar in the philosophy of religion today. Secondly, we might say that the nature of God is so radically mysterious that we can say nothing of God at all. Thirdly, equally familiarly, the qualitative difference between finite and infinite seems so unbridgeable as to rule out any argument by analogy from the world to God.

In their way, as theologians familiar with the work of Karl Barth would perhaps think, these objections to the position that Thomas wants to adopt amount very much to 'Barthian' objections to 'natural theology'.

Thomas is steering his way between the claim that argument for God's existence is unnecessary because God's existence is so manifest in the natural world, and the claim that argument is impossible because God's existence is solely a matter of supernatural revelation. He wants to deny both that God's presence is transparently obvious to 'natural reason' and that God's presence is totally hidden except to 'supernatural faith'. Characteristically Thomas is searching for a middle way.

Thomas thinks that this middle way is mandated by Scripture – Romans 1:20: 'the hidden things of God can be clearly understood from the things that He has made'. That is to say, it has been divinely revealed that the existence of God can be demonstrated by reasoning from the existence and nature of the world. It is a matter of faith that God's existence can be discovered by reason. As a believer, Thomas is permitted, and perhaps even required, to use reason to argue from the nature of the world to the existence of God. In other words, Christian revelation itself allows us to entertain the possibility of making God's existence evident 'from things that have been made' (*per ea quae facta sunt*).

The Scriptural Authority

Citing Romans 1:20 is contentious. In fact, like Exodus 3:14 (as we shall see in chapter 5) and 2 Peter 1:4 (see chapter 9), this is a biblical text that plays a key role in Thomas's theology but only because it has accrued to itself from the beginning a wealth of significance that goes far beyond the bare meaning which a modern exegete might detect and concede.

Joseph A. Fitzmyer, in the *New Jerome Biblical Commentary* (1989), explains that the passage comes in a lengthy account of how, through the Gospel, the uprightness of God is revealed as justifying the person of faith (Romans 1:16–4:25).[14] In detail, the Gospel is the powerful source of salvation for all (1:16–17); negatively, without the Gospel God's wrath is manifested towards all human beings (1:18–3:20). Echoing a common Jewish belief at the time about the culpability of pagans in not acknowledging and reverencing God as they should have, Paul – 'in this quasi-philosophical discussion' – maintains that there is 'an inceptive, speculative sort of information about God that . . . the pagans could not help but have'. He does not mean philosophers only; nor some 'primitive positive revelation'. By 'contemplating the created world and reflecting on it', they should have perceived, 'through its multicoloured facade . . . the great "Unseen" behind it'. Romans 1:20, Fitzmyer goes on, was cited at Vatican I in support of the thesis that God can be known with certainty by the natural light of human reason from created things, which does not mean, however, that Paul and the Council were saying 'exactly the same thing'. On the contrary, Vatican I was dealing with the 'capability' of the human mind to know God, prescinding from *de facto* knowledge, whereas Paul states as a fact that God is known from created things. He speaks of 'impiety and wickedness' when pagans fail to acknowledge the creator properly; Vatican I passes no such judgement. On the other hand, the question of whether human beings are capable of knowing God without grace is beyond Paul's perspective.

Fitzmyer's discussion, as we should expect, both takes the text seriously and considers the wider theological use to which it has been put. That is to say, for a biblical commentator working in the Catholic tradition, the meaning that has been found in, or projected on, a given passage, over centuries of interpretation, cannot be ignored. As Hans

Georg Gadamer would put it, the history of the effect a text has had is inseparable from its meaning.

Many different interpretations of Romans 1:20 are available. As John Ziesler notes, in his commentary on the passage, it has been much debated whether Paul implies that something of God can be known apart from divine revelation.[15] 'What can be known about God is plain to human beings, because God has shown it to them', as the previous verse says: meaning, Ziesler thinks, that the creation implies the creator and that, for Paul, God has created the world such that all human beings are able to draw this inference. 'If this is natural theology, then Paul is a natural theologian.' For Ziesler (who is not Roman Catholic), Paul simply takes the existence of God as given, and assumes that God's nature can be discerned in the created world – having in mind such texts as Wisdom 13:1–9: 'For from the greatness and beauty of created things comes a corresponding perception of their Creator' (etc.).

That interpretation is repeated by Pope John Paul II in the encyclical *Fides et Ratio* (§22) where it is taken for granted that Romans 1:20 is 'a kind of philosophical argument in popular language', developing what is already in the Wisdom literature. Indeed, somewhat provocatively, this Pauline text is said to affirm our 'metaphysical capacity as human beings' – *potestas hominis metaphysica* – which (it at once turns out) our sinful condition prevents us from fulfilling in the way that God's plan intended: 'this ready access to God the Creator [has been] diminished' (but only 'diminished', not obliterated).

John C. O'Neill, to take another example, doubts that Romans 1:18–32 was written by Paul at all – 'The language in which the argument is expressed is unlike Paul's usual language in both vocabulary and style'.[16] Nevertheless, whoever wrote the passage, O'Neill has no problem about finding 'natural theology' in verse 20, calling it a 'valid' if 'concise summary' of a 'proof' for the existence of God that was already five hundred years old, being found in the Greek philosopher Anaxagoras (500–428 BCE), and, nearer Paul's day, in Hellenistic Jewish apologetics.

Whatever the differences among these readings of Romans 1:20, they all bring to mind what Barth wrote in his famous commentary, in a passage translated by Edwyn Hoskyns as follows:

> Plato in his wisdom recognised long ago that behind the visible there lies the invisible universe which is the Origin of all concrete things. And moreover, the solid good sense of the men of the world had long ago perceived that the fear of the Lord is the beginning of wisdom. The clear, honest eyes of the poet in the book of Job and of the Preacher Solomon had long ago rediscovered, mirrored in the world of appearance, the archetypal, unobservable, undiscoverable Majesty of God.[17]

Thomas would have understood that passage, even if the seas of language run much higher than his ever do. Inveighing against the corruptions of religious arrogance, much more eloquently than Thomas ever does, Barth nevertheless allows that there remains 'a relic of clarity of sight, a last, warning recollection of the secret of God . . . A reflection of this secret lies even in the deified forces of the world, even in the deified universe itself . . . from time to time this bare relic of the Unknown reasserts itself in the presentiment of awe'.

More recently, Douglas A. Campbell, with evident Barthian sympathies, questions this interpretation.[18] He argues that the sequence Romans 1:18–3:20, far from setting out Paul's ideas, on natural theology or anything else, is, on the contrary, an exposition of precisely the theological position that he is out to 'undermine' and 'savage'. The commitment to natural theology in Romans 1 – which Campbell happily acknowledges – is just one more element of Paul's putative opponents' doctrine of salvation by works that Paul is out to discredit. Far from our being able to cite Paul as an authority for doing natural theology, that is to say, he becomes an authority, on the contrary, for outlawing any such enterprise.

Campbell does not conceal his satisfaction about the implications for natural theology of his exegesis. In his first footnote, he reminds us that Thomas Aquinas took Romans 1:20 as endorsing the doctrine of general revelation and natural theology, and, more specifically, as 'the warrant for his Five Ways'. Moreover, when Thomas explicates the verse in his Romans commentary, he 'supplies philosophical proofs' (a bad move to make, Campbell of course would think).

While noting 'an intriguing argument' made by Eugene Rogers, seeking to reduce the difference between Barth and Aquinas, Campbell prefers Barth's famous description of how natural theology, after the rediscovery of Aristotle, got the upper hand over Catholic theology, something that finally became apparent at the First Vatican Council, 'which canonises the supreme achievement, *Spitzenleistung*, of Thomas Aquinas'.[19]

Either way, the exegesis of Romans 1:20 turns on alternative, indeed incompatible, theological preconceptions: either the text ceases once and for all to provide biblical legitimacy for natural theology (as with Campbell) or (with Fitzmyer, Ziesler and O'Neill) it voices Paul's endorsement of a commonplace that echoes well beyond New Testament revelation.

An Intriguing Argument

The 'intriguing argument' advanced by Eugene Rogers, reducing the distance between Thomas Aquinas and Karl Barth by insisting on the importance of reading Question 2 of the *Summa Theologiae* in the light of Question 1, should not be so easily dismissed.

Rogers is out to show that, on the basis of their reading of Romans 1:20 and its context in their respective commentaries (Barth's *Shorter Commentary* dating from 1956, rather than the famous commentary), Thomas and Barth end up by maintaining essentially the same position about the possibility of natural knowledge of God. Apart from the interest of this thesis for theologians, and in particular for interpreters of Thomas and of Barth, the implications for philosophers of religion and their understanding of the Five Ways are obviously important. In short, the claim is that the natural theology found in Question 2 of the *Summa* is much the same as the natural theology in the commentary on Romans.

As regards Barth, Rogers argues that, in the *Shorter Commentary*, 'an explicit openness to natural theology appears, which, however narrow and hedged round with conditions, only leaves space for the sort of natural theology that Thomas offers'.

However that may be, it is the bearing of Thomas's reading of Paul on the Five Ways that should make philosophers of religion reconsider the standard account. No doubt, if Thomists who believe the Five Ways can and even should be extracted from their theological context and judged from the point of view of natural reason as purely philosophical chains of inference, the Barthian objections stand – and also, quite independently of Barth, the objections within Thomism itself. On the other hand, if the second question of the *Summa* is read in the light of the first, which does not seem a very daring move to make, it turns out (Rogers contends) that Thomas is saying nothing substantially different from what we find in his Romans commentary.[20]

Thomas's main activity was expounding Scripture, if we may recall another banal truth, and the *Summa Theologiae* expounds Christian doctrine for students who may be presumed to be already steeped in Scripture. There is no need to regard the *Summa* as a substitute for Scripture.

Equally, we may surely suppose that the citation of Romans 1:20 in article 2 of Question 2, far from being a contextless slogan, is simply a reminder of the much fuller treatment Thomas assumes his students to have had in the customary biblical course. In effect, we should regard biblical references in the *Summa* as an invitation to turn to the biblical commentaries where the same topics are discussed.

Furthermore, if nature as it actually is is always already shot through with grace, and human reason is never entirely detachable from affectivity and sensibility, which are surely not very contentious Thomist thoughts, the kind of natural theology that Barth feared may not be rightly ascribed to Thomas. Natural knowledge of God's existence independently of the life of grace, Rogers insists, is not something that Thomas ever imagined. The function of the cosmological arguments in the *Summa Theologiae*, he concludes, is to 'fulfil the charge of sacred doctrine to leave no part of the world God-forsaken'. Yet, as Rogers says, the one place in the *Summa* in which Thomas is commonly regarded as having abandoned Scripture for philosophy is the exposition of the Five Ways.

The Anguish of Philosophy

So much has happened in Christian theology since the thirteenth century, that there are questions which could never have occurred to Thomas and to which we cannot even guess at or extrapolate how he might have responded. On some issues, on the other hand, we can sometimes pick up clues. He did not have to say anything about Barthian suspicions of natural theology in general, or about the quarrels among modern Thomists over the interpretation of his work. On the other hand, there are occasional hints that he would not have endorsed one version of natural theology *juxta mentem D. Thomae*, as T.C. O'Brien pointed out.[21] Starting from the position that Aristotle and 'many other *philosophi*' have advanced conclusive arguments to the effect that there is only one God, Thomas adds that there are many truths about God which they could not have investigated: truths for example about divine providence and omnipotence and that God alone is to be worshipped (cf. ST 2–2.1.8).

The *philosophi* dependent on natural reason are, for Thomas, pre-Christian 'wisdom-lovers' such as he takes the philosophers of antiquity to be. He does not mean what we mean by 'philosophers': as lovers of wisdom, the philosophers of ancient Greece and Rome are implicitly theologians (Aristotle explicitly so). Philosophers who practise their thinking in independence of or indifference to religious questions never figured even in Thomas's imagination. When he says that certain truths about God can be – have been – discovered by 'natural reasoning' he never imagines that these thinkers lacked or suspended all religious interest in the world. 'Because Aristotle saw that there is no other human knowing in this life except through the speculative sciences, he held that human beings cannot reach a complete, but only a relative fulfilment. Thus it is clear what great anguish the noble genius of philosophers has experienced over the course of time' (*Contra Gentiles* 3.48). Aristotle's metaphysical labours, Thomas thinks, culminated in a certain *angustia* – not, of course, Kierkegaardian *Angst*, more like an Aristotelian *aporia* – but still not the usual perception of Aristotle.

'That there is one God can be proved by reason, but that God has an immediate providence over all things . . . is a matter of faith' (*Compendium Theologiae* 2.246), Thomas says elsewhere. Again: 'The philosophers have made no mention of the virtue of penitence for the reason that pardon for sin and atonement have reference to God's providence over human actions . . . the philosophers have given no consideration to virtues directive of human acts as these bear a relationship to God's providence, but only in their relationship to a human good' (*4 Sentences* 14.1.1.3).

In short, as O'Brien says, 'To portray St Thomas as the proponent of a philosophical discipline about God, complete in all but Trinitarian details, is a caricature'. Pre-Christian philosophy is always already religious; natural reason is always already engaged in metaphysical, ethical and indeed scientific investigations, which finally imply the dependence of the world on the unique 'principle' which is both beginning and end of all that exists (*principium et finis, arche kai telos*). But that the beginning and end of all things is God as revealed to Moses and in Jesus Christ is not something that natural reason could discover, by any chain of inference.

For Thomas, natural theology could not be the kind of theodicy which supposedly justifies the ways of God before the bar of human reason. To say that human beings have a beginning and end in a unique first and final cause is one thing – itself a discovery open to natural reasoning only within an already religiously apprehended world. It is, for Thomas, quite another matter to regard this 'cause' as the loving and forgiving God in whose providential care the world exists. Providence, pardon for sin, atonement, and so on, lie outside the perspective of pre-Christian wisdom-lovers: unsurprisingly, there is no mention of repentance in Aristotle's *Ethics*. Even the theologically orientated metaphysics of antiquity (as Thomas supposed it to be), the best reasoned knowledge of the existence of the *arche kai telos*, could only leave one in a certain 'anguish'. Such natural knowledge of God would come to term, so to speak, only as one learned the language of sin, conversion and repentance. Either way, knowledge of God, attainable by natural reason, pre-Christian or within his own exposition of Christian doctrine, has an existential dimension, as we might say: culminating in the frustration which is *angustia*, or involving the virtue of penitence. For Thomas, who never needs to spell this out, natural theology is always in amalgam with the wisdom-lover's personal ethical and religious history.

Believing Under Conditions

Another clue to Thomas's understanding of natural theology lies in the third objection that he brings against himself in connection with the Augustinian distinction between believing God (*credere Deo*: believing what God says), believing in God (*credere Deum*: believing that God exists), and what has rather awkwardly to be translated as believing unto God (*credere in Deum*: the faith by which one is personally committed to God) (ST 2–2.2.2).

The objection is that even unbelievers (*infideles*) are said to believe in God (*credere Deum*); does this count as faith? Well, no, Thomas replies: 'believing that God exists is not something that non-believers do under the description of an act of faith; they do not believe that God exists under the conditions which faith determines; and so they do not truly believe that God exists, because, as Aristotle says, with regard to simples, defective knowledge is not knowing at all' (ST 2–2.2.2).

Victor Preller brought this remark to the fore, rightly noting that the reason that Thomas gives for his claim is 'rather complex'.[22] We need not go into Aristotle's ontology: the interesting point for us, in this unique, almost throwaway remark, is that Thomas clearly thinks that the proposition 'God exists', held as true by a non-Christian, on the basis of theistic proofs, does not mean the same as the proposition 'God exists' held by a believer. Pagans, or methodologically atheist philosophers, may believe on rational grounds that 'God exists'; but this would not be believing truly that 'God exists', since they do not hold this belief *sub his conditionibus quae fides determinat*.

Notice that Thomas is not saying that the philosophical conclusion that God exists is not the same as existential faith in God's existence (*credere in Deum*): he does not even consider that. His point is, rather, that even the proposition 'God exists' means something radically different when held on the basis of philosophy and 'under the conditions that faith determines'.

Neither of these texts demonstrates conclusively that Thomas had no idea of the wholly pre-theological natural theology that was to develop within neo-Thomism. Frustratingly, he does not spell out what the faith-conditions are for the claim that 'God exists' to be truly about God. Presumably he means that, under grace, the mind of the believer would be conformed to God and the will motivated by God. That would be believing as *credere in Deum*, spelled out in the next line in terms of 'the will's moving the mind and other powers of the soul towards the end'. But the contention one would like Thomas to have spelled out is the shocking remark that *infideles* believe in the existence of God but 'not truly' – shocking, at least, if one was tempted to think that the Five Ways are

theistic proofs that reach the conclusion that God exists in some way
that is foundational for Christian faith.

The Five Ways

Finally, it is worth spelling out just how various are the interpretations
this section of the *Summa Theologiae* has spawned.

Timothy McDermott, for example, in the standard English edition,
says that 'the five ways should be thought of as five ways of disclosing
ultimate causality within non-ultimate causality'.[23] He holds that the
word 'God' means what it ordinarily means (ST 1.13.8), namely 'that
which exercises a universal providence over things ... transcending all
things, at the beginning of all things, separate from all things' – 'what
everyone calls God'.

That is to say, on McDermott's reading, the word is not understood
as meaning a generic deity, in some pre-Christian, methodologically
atheist sense. Thomas is not trying to provide philosophical foundations
for the conviction that God exists. Instead, he is trying to put into words
how such a conviction arises, and to reveal its validity.

Being pre-modern, Thomas never imagines us as inserted into a
not-yet-intelligible world. On the contrary, he sees us from the outset,
as McDermott puts it, in a logical space, an intelligible world. We do
not impose logic upon putatively raw experience; the intelligibility in
things themselves is disclosed as we rational animals engage with them.
We live and move and have our being, so to speak, in the world as the
logical space in which things disclose their intelligibility. According to
McDermott, the 'logical community of concepts in our minds' is
grounded in a 'real community of nature in things'. 'To exist, as St
Thomas sees it, is to have significance, to have point, to play out a role'.
Thomas's 'theistic proofs' do not begin from a world which 'just is' and
from which we have to deduce its 'cause'. On the contrary, the idea of
'just being' would have been unintelligible to him. His idea of being –
'the seminal idea of his philosophical view of the world' – is not about
'an arbitrary thereness of things for sense-experience', as it might be for
us, but 'a logical and significant thereness in a community of the universe revealed to man by knowledge and love'.

In other words, if Thomas's Five Ways are exercises in natural
theology, this natural theology always already includes a certain pre-
theoretical and practical ontology, spontaneous and primordial –
in effect, a communion in being.

Furthermore, the image or model of this concept of being,
McDermott suggests, is that of an intentional action: 'being is playing

out a role, realizing a significant conception'. In other words, 'since action is in turn conceived as the expression and execution of some agent's desire (giving point to the action), the being of things is conceived as fulfilling a role desired by someone, as the expression of someone's love'. What this means, in short, is that the very idea of 'all things' with which Thomas inaugurates the Five Ways, already includes tacit belief in the world as a communion of being, in effect as the expression of an agent with mind and will.

Once again, whatever may be the case in neo-Thomist natural theology, Thomas's 'theistic proofs' should be read as explicitations of an *a priori* communion in being – a sense of being in the world that rests on no foundationalist philosophical theorizing but is simply taken for granted.

Eric Mascall, the best known Anglican Thomist, would probably not have dissented from McDermott's view but would certainly have emphasized that 'the real function of the famous Five Ways . . . was not to provide five independent arguments for the existence of God from finite beings, but to manifest by five different expositions the character of finite beings as radically dependent on a transcendent, self-existent infinite Being'. He sees the basis of the cosmological arguments for theism as consisting in an intuition or 'contuition' of God and finite being together – not unlike McDermott's presupposed communion of being.[24]

As Mascall noted, what appears to many readers as a purely rational proof of the existence of God is embedded in a writing which clearly assumes from the start that God exists and is what the Christian revelation assumes him to be: 'It seems that God does not exist . . . On the contrary, God tells us himself, *ex persona Dei*: "I am who am", Exodus 3.14' (ST 1.2.3).

God has proclaimed his own existence. The truth of the proposition 'God exists' has been divinely revealed – and now we may look for ways to demonstrate or manifest it, ways in which to probe or test it.

So far from being, as often seems, an arid and lifeless philosophical abstraction, the God who is subsistent being itself is a description, Mascall says, 'fertile of all the fullness of Catholic devotion'.

The 'real value' of the Five Ways is that they 'prompt us to look at things with such attention and understanding that we grasp them in their true ontological nature as dependent upon God, and so grasp God's existence as their creator'. For Mascall, far from offering rational justification for believing in God, the Five Ways are an invitation to place everything in the presence of God, prayerfully and worshipfully. Few of us take the time to sit down and look but 'one of the essential prerequisites . . . for an acceptance of Christian theism is a contemplative and reverent attitude to finite beings'. To understand the arguments for

Christian theism in this way 'a certain moral integrity is needed'. Going through the logic of the theistic proofs, Mascall seems to mean, cannot be separated from practising virtue: prayer, reverence, awe and wonder. Then, 'when we look back, in the light of revelation, upon God as reason has shown him to us', Mascall concludes, 'we are able to see that *ipsum esse subsistens* is . . . the sacred abyss', referring us to a 'convinced theist of the Thomist persuasion' (Maritain in fact).

Edward Sillem listed ten recent interpretations of the Five Ways, each different from the other, some 'conflicting', most (he thought) unknown in Britain. He dislikes the use of Thomas to counter modern philosophy, Cartesian epistemology, and so on. He distrusts 'too exclusive an emphasis on apologetics'. This leads to an 'all too ready assumption that the Five Ways, on their own and apart from the context in which they exist, are all that is needed . . . engendering an attitude of mind which will fail to think of the Five Ways as Aquinas himself thought of them'. He insists that the question about God's existence is part of the study of the divine essence (ST 1.2 prologue). Instead of being a preliminary issue to be settled before we get on to the question of God – 'is there any God anyway?' – Thomas is concerned with the divine essence itself and not simply with God as the cause of created things – which would be the topic in natural theology. He does not have to prove that God exists before he gets on to the divine essence. On the contrary, he assumes that, in considering what God has revealed about himself, his essence, we begin by considering, very briefly, the ways in which his existence has been established.

According to Sillem, the arguments are quite unoriginal, *and that is Thomas's point*. He is writing neither for nor against philosophers in the modern sense, but for colleagues and students who feared the arguments inherited from the newly discovered pagan thinkers. Faced with theologians who believed that we know of God's existence without having to think, either because it is self-evident or because it is purely a matter of faith, Thomas wanted to open up a better understanding of reasoning and equally of the mystery of God.[25]

The five arguments in the *Summa Theologiae* are all unoriginal, handed down from ancient philosophy, as McDermott and Sillem both note. Leo Elders is only one of the many scholars who provide the details of the genealogy of the arguments. Since these details are not always easily accessible, we may summarize them as follows.

The first of the Five Ways – 'anything in process of change is being changed by something else' – is to be found in Plato (e.g. *Phaedrus* 245c–e), reformulated by Aristotle (cf. *Physics* VIII X 266a 10 to 267b25; *Metaphysics* XII, VI–VIII 1071b1 to 1074b15). The key idea is that of a primary mover on the fringe of the spheres. Like Chossat, Elders sees Thomas's arguments as inseparable from ancient cosmology. Briefly, there must be something perfect beyond what is imperfect; bodies are manifestly imperfect and movable, so there is something perfect and self-moving.

The second way – 'if there were no first cause there would be no causes at all' – comes from Plato's *Timaeus* but more immediately from Scripture: Acts 17:28 and Isaiah 26:12.

The third way – 'there must be something owing its existence to nothing other than itself' – is foreshadowed in Plato and Aristotle but best formulated by Philo of Alexandria, then found in Proclus, Augustine and Ibn Sina: in effect, God is *ipsum esse subsistens*.

The fourth way – 'there are degrees of being, goodness, etc.' – is basically Platonic, though found also in Aristotle, in Christian authors like Augustine, Denys and Anselm, and again in Ibn Sina: our intellectual and affective activities imply a perfect being, absolute truth, ultimate fulfilment of our desire, and so on.

The fifth way – 'everything in nature is directed to its end by something intelligent' – is widespread in the ancient world and wherever religion flourishes: Xenophon, Plato, John Damascene – the most successful proof of all according to what Thomas says in his commentary on the Fourth Gospel.[26]

Moreover, according to Elders (perhaps a little fancifully), these five arguments are arranged as an ascent, taking the reader more and more deeply into the mystery: God is not an item in this physical world, but the cause of everything, self-subsistent, the goodness we desire, and the one with a mind by which all things are directed to their destiny.[27]

McDermott, Mascall, Sillem and Elders are only four of innumerable variant estimates of the status and function of Thomas's arguments for God's existence: representing metaphysics, asceticism, historical contextualism and genealogy.

Mascall cites Maritain. This returns us to the kind of interpretation that is quite characteristic of French Thomists. In his *Approches de Dieu* (1953), Jacques Maritain contends that the 'philosophic proofs of the existence of God', specifically the Five Ways, are 'an unfolding, on the level of rational knowledge, of the natural prephilosophic knowledge implied in the primitive intuition of the act of being'. This 'natural intuition of being' is not all that esoteric and arcane, on Maritain's account. On the contrary: 'Once a man has been awakened to the reality of existence and of his own existence, when he has really perceived that formidable, sometimes elating, sometimes sickening or maddening fact I exist, he is henceforth possessed by the intuition of being and the implications it bears with it'. This 'primordial intuition' is a sense of my own existence and of the existence of things, simultaneously – yet first and foremost of things:

> When it takes place, I suddenly realize that a given entity – man, mountain or tree – exists and exercises this sovereign activity to be in its own way, in an independence of me which is total, totally self-assertive and totally implacable. And at the same time I realize that I also exist, but as thrown back into my loneliness and frailty by this other existence by which things assert themselves and in which I have positively no part, to which I am exactly as naught.

In this 'sudden flash of intuition' one realizes that 'this solid and inexorable existence, perceived in anything whatsoever, implies . . . some absolute, irrefragable existence, completely free from nothingness and death'. There is nothing odd about this 'sense of being'. For the medievals it was 'an atmosphere too habitual to be regarded as a surprising gift'. For them – for Thomas – proofs of God could take the form of skilful unfolding of logical necessities – 'without losing the inner energy of that intuition'. Indeed: 'This logical machinery was surreptitiously enlivened by the deep-seated intuition of being'. Before proposing the proofs to anyone, Maritain contends, it would be necessary to be assured that he or she is 'alive to the primordial intuition of existence, and conscious of the natural knowledge of God involved in this intuition'.[28]

One may, of course, return with relief to more conventional discussions in the analytic tradition.[29]

Chapter 5

STORIES OF BEING

The most intractable conflict of interpretations centres on Thomas Aquinas's description of God as 'self-subsistent being' (*ipsum esse subsistens*) and the related doctrine of divine simpleness.

These two doctrines, as Anthony Kenny notes, are regarded by Leonine Thomists as Thomas's 'most profound and original contributions'. He goes on to say, however, that 'even the most sympathetic treatment of these doctrines', such as he himself tries to offer, 'cannot wholly succeed in acquitting them of the charge of sophistry and illusion'.[1]

On the other hand, Jacques Maritain, the French Thomist philosopher, declares that, in saying 'subsistent being itself', or advancing the doctrine of divine simpleness, namely that 'in God there is no real distinction between essence and existence', one 'designates, without seeing it, the sacred abyss which makes the angels tremble with love and with awe'. It is like a formula in chemistry, he even says, which would set off an immense explosion.[2]

In a recent encyclical, *Fides et Ratio*, Pope John Paul II insists on the importance, in what he clearly regards as the poor state of Catholic theology, of 'the philosophy of being': 'a dynamic philosophy which views reality in its ontological, causal and communicative structures'; a philosophy which is 'strong and enduring because it is based upon the very act of being itself, which allows a full and comprehensive openness to reality as a whole, surpassing every limit in order to reach the One who brings all things to fulfilment' (§97). In a footnote we are directed to the address which the Pope delivered at the Angelicum in Rome in 1979, commemorating the revival of Thomist studies encouraged by Pope Leo XIII. Here again, the Pope commends 'the philosophy of St

Thomas' as 'a philosophy of being': that is to say, 'a philosophy of the "act of existing", *actus essendi*, whose transcendental value paves the most direct way to rise to the knowledge of subsisting Being and pure Act, namely to God'. We may even call this philosophy, the Pope concludes, 'the philosophy of the proclamation of being, a chant in praise of what exists'.[3]

Ticking Over, Metaphysically

The seas of language run high, in such remarks. The hardest thing, for English-speaking readers, even those who are friendly towards Thomas, is to cope with talk of Being. The word simply does not have the semantic charge, the metaphysical aura, that *esse* has in Leonine Thomism, or *l'être* in French philosophy in general, let alone *das Sein* in Heidegger's German.

There is nothing new about this. A.E. Taylor, for example, to name one of the prominent figures in pre-analytic philosophy, speaks of 'reality', never of 'being'. As he explained in a later edition, he wanted his book to be understood 'in a definitely theistic, indeed in a definitely Christian sense', which might not be the reader's natural impression. When he wrote of 'the Absolute', he meant 'that simple, absolutely transcendent, source of all things which the great Christian scholastics call God'. Indeed, when he spoke of created beings as 'appearances' of the Absolute, he meant by this 'precisely what St Thomas, for example, meant by the doctrine that they have being by "participation"'.[4]

Outside professional philosophy, G.K. Chesterton notes, perhaps ruefully, that the word 'being' reminds us of fantastic professors in fiction, who wave their hands and say, 'Thus do we mount to the ineffable heights of pure and radiant Being', and the like. The word has 'a wild and woolly sort of sound; as if only very vague people used it; or as if it might mean all sorts of different things'.[5]

Evidently aware of philosophical debates about our knowledge of anything outside our own heads, Chesterton satirizes philosophers who ask of a child looking at grass, what does he actually know; indeed, does he know anything? Some of them would claim that grass is 'a mere green impression on the mind'; thus that the child 'can be sure of nothing except the mind'. Against such scepticism, Chesterton rightly says, Thomas would insist that – 'long before he knows that grass is green' – the child 'knows that something is something'. In Thomas's terminology, that is to say, 'the child is aware of *ens*'. Then, 'very profoundly, but very practically', Thomas insists that, with this knowing that something is something, there immediately enters the idea of contradiction. Whatever the child sees, when he sees it, he knows it is not true that he does not see it. Thus, in a general way, the difference between Yes and No, between truth and falsehood, appears. What also becomes clear, Chesterton goes on to say, is that while the ordinary thing at any moment is something, it is not everything that it could be. In other words, in everyday pre-philosophical discourse, we recognize the existence of a 'fullness of being'.

This is about as far as Chesterton goes. Among non-academic readers his book has had more influence than any other written in English, in portraying Thomas. He has a good understanding of the polemical dimension of Thomas's work. Quite deliberately, he expounds Thomas's views over against the 'heretics' with whom he 'fought': specifically over against Manicheanism. He does not conceal his own conviction that the Reformation – 'the sixteenth-century schism' – was 'really a belated revolt of the thirteenth-century pessimists', 'a backwash of the old Augustinian Puritanism against the Aristotelian liberality'. He insists on seeing Thomas as 'the only optimist theologian'; and indeed on seeing Catholic Christianity as 'the only optimist theology'. In the end, Chesterton allows himself to say that 'the praise of Being' (by Thomas) is 'the praise of God as the Creator of the world' – nothing more wild and woolly than that. Indeed, that last phrase is quite like the papal encyclical's doxological conception of ontology.

Anthony Kenny, among the most distinguished analytic philosophers of his generation, is also a careful exponent of Thomas Aquinas. He devotes 28 of the 80 pages in his widely read introduction to a chapter headed 'Being'. He does not question that Thomas was 'a great metaphysician'. He holds, however, that the main concepts of his metaphysics, far from 'constituting . . . a coherent system of philosophy', often involve 'ambiguity and confusion'. Many of his key concepts, like substance and accident, matter and form, property, quality, category, and intention, are concepts that we use every day, with their remote origins as technical terms in Aristotle's philosophy. The greater part of Kenny's discussion is devoted, very usefully, to explaining these concepts and sorting out how they differ in various ways and to some extent both from modern English usage and from Aristotle's. For example, as Kenny notes, Thomas was himself a substance, in his terminology, like anyone or anything else about which this or that may be predicated: an odd way of talking now. Again, a substance, for Thomas, is perceptible only in its accidents (colour, size, etc.), which does not mean, however, that the substance itself is some mysterious entity behind the perceptible accidents, as (since Locke) we might be inclined to think. The discussion leads to the problems (insuperable as Kenny thinks them) about substance and accidents in the doctrine of transubstantiation, and about how, by identifying the soul with the form of the body, Thomas could coherently maintain the doctrine of the immortality of the soul.

As regards talk of *esse*, as Kenny notes, Thomas is entirely familiar with the use of the verb 'to be' as a copula, linking subject term to predicate term in a sentence, as in 'Socrates is wise'. He also uses the verb as the grammatical predicate to indicate the existence of what corresponds to the subject term, as in 'God exists' – a way of talking which is in English, Kenny says, 'rare and archaic' (cf. e.g. ST 1.3.42). Indeed, on Kenny's account, when we say that God just *is* – meaning the 'actualization of being' – we are saying nothing.

Thomas sometimes compares 'being' with 'living': 'for living things, to *be* is to *live*'. Fine; but this does not mean that living is a separate activity from breathing, moving, eating, loving, and so forth, an activity supposedly accompanying or underlying these and suchlike activities. Kenny suspects that Thomas thinks of the 'actualisation of being' as something over and above the multifarious activities which constitute this or that entity's 'being'.

Without mentioning him, Kenny no doubt shares the suspicions voiced by J.L. Austin, in a famous footnote: the thought that 'existing' describes something that things do all the time – 'like breathing, only quieter – ticking over, as it were, in a metaphysical sort of way'.[6]

Divine Simplicity

The doctrine of divine simplicity made good sense to the likes of A.E. Taylor. Some who object to the thesis, one suspects, believe that it commits us to a picture of God as a bare, characterless monad, something like the neo-Platonic One. Thomas has no such picture in mind. Indeed, it does not seem, on the face of it, a very problematic claim, as he outlines it.[7]

Having identified something (in the *Summa Theologiae*) as the world's unmoved mover or First Cause, that is generally called 'God' (ST 1.2.3), Thomas at once allows that this deity might be spatially extended and corporeal (1.3.1). (This possibility shows how little Thomas thinks the Five Ways have achieved.)

The problem that he now discusses arises not from philosophy but from Scripture. In the Bible itself God is often described and invoked as a physical being. This is a question Thomas no doubt expected students to raise, in the course of reading Scripture. No doubt presuppositions about his account of God so far, as being of the God indistinguishable from the deity of ancient Greece, get in the way of our appreciating this but in fact it is the Bible, not supposedly substantialist metaphysics, that encourages the thought of God as an entity.

Thomas cites five passages in Scripture which attribute physicality to God (in Job, Genesis, Psalms, and Isaiah), and counters with one in the New Testament (John 4:24: 'God is spirit'). When physical characteristics are ascribed to God in Scripture (as of course they often are) we have to remember that divine realities cannot be communicated except imaginatively, metaphorically, *sub similitudinibus corporalium* (cf. ST 1.1.9). These unavoidable anthropomorphisms need to be submitted to logical analysis.

As John 4:24 makes clear, God is not a physical being. To spell this out, Thomas appeals to the standard philosophical jargon of the day. He wants to establish that God is not a created being of any kind. God is not composed of matter and form, as creatures are that grow and decay (ST 1.3.2). God does not differ from his own nature, as the individuality of a particular human being differs from what it is to be human in general (3.3). God's nature does not differ from his existence, whereas any particular human being might never have existed (3.4). God cannot be brought into the scheme of genus and species, as we can, as if God were the best instance of the class 'deity' (3.5). God is not a thing with properties, a substance with accidents, as beings like us are (3.6).

In short, whether we regard this as logical analysis or metaphysical deduction or as negative theology or regard it as all three, we have to deny all these standard features of material objects of God: God is in no way 'composite'; God is 'altogether simple' (3.7).

Few who believe in God, these days, are likely to be tempted by the idea of God as a body. Denying that God is a being with qualities, as created beings are, leads to a conclusion some readers find bizarre. In particular, since God is not a being with properties, we cannot say that God is, for example, wise or just, as if wisdom, justice, and so on, are qualities that God might or might not have. On the contrary: 'God must be his own godhead, his own life, and whatever else is predicated of him' (ST 1.3.3). No doubt, we may go on picturing God as a being with virtues; but that remains an anthropomorphic conception.

Knowing the Unknowable

The doctrine of divine simpleness seems to make God so utterly different from anything created – so 'totally otherwise' – that any claim to have knowledge of God would be ruled out on the grounds that that which is 'simple' could never be known by 'composites' such as we human beings are. So one might reasonably think.

Thomas sees the problem (ST 1.12). Things are knowable insofar as they are realized. God is wholly realized, with no potentiality yet to be fulfilled – which makes God maximally knowable (1.12.1). On the other hand, what is maximally knowable in itself is not knowable by any particular mind if there is an excess of meaning over that mind – rather as the sun, which is maximally visible, indeed itself source of all light, cannot be seen by a bat because of the excess of light (Thomas's favourite analogy).

All this might suggest that no created mind can ever see God – 'as some have said' (precisely whom Thomas has in mind is not clear). God must be so radically mysterious that no human being could ever know him.

Such a thesis is not acceptable, for Thomas: it is *alienum a fide* and also *praeter rationem*: estranging us from the Christian faith and setting us outside the bounds of reason.

'We shall see him just as he is' (1 John 3:2). Thomas never tires of recalling this promise. That is to say, as he expands it: 'The ultimate beatitude of a human being consists in our highest activity, which is exercising the mind; if the created mind were never able to see the Godhead either we would never attain beatitude or our beatitude would consist in some other than God – which is contrary to faith' (ST 1.12.1).

As usual, Thomas's theology is focused on the end, the *finis* or *telos*, which is the promised face-to-face communion in which the blessed see God as he really is and accordingly themselves 'become like him' (1 John 3:2).

As regards reason: 'there is in us a natural desire to know the cause when we see an effect, that is how wonder arises in us in the first place; so if the minds of the rational creatures that we are were incapable of ever touching the First Cause of things this desire of our nature would remain unfulfilled' (ST 1.12.1) – enough said, Thomas clearly thinks, locating himself in the tradition from Plato onwards: there is a human desire for knowledge which is rooted in *wonder*.[8]

To deny that God can ever be known by creatures such as we are thus goes against the promise made in Scripture and would thwart the desire for wisdom which motivates the philosophical tradition. The divine essence – God in himself – is, indeed, 'beyond description', 'in no way representable by any created likeness' (ST 1.12.2).

In the ordinary economy of knowledge, the human mind in the cognitive act is identical with what is cognized, in a certain way. The world's actually being known is the mind's actually knowing: the formal identity of knower and known. Truly knowing something is, in a way, becoming like it.

For the blessed to see God face to face, what is required is 'the light of divine glory strengthening the mind' – 'In thy light shall we see light' (Psalm 35 (36): 10), one of Thomas's favourite mantra-like quotations.

In further detail: 'The divine essence is existence itself; hence as other intelligible forms, of course not identical with their existence, are united to our minds in a kind of existence in which they actualise our minds, so the divine essence is united to a created mind as something actually being understood, the mind's being made actually understanding by the divine essence itself'.[9]

When God is 'seen as he is', in the bliss of face-to-face communion, what happens is that what is actually known is itself how the mind actually knows: the object is itself the medium. The divine reality occupies the minds of the blessed in such a way as to be the condition as well as the object of knowledge. The face of God, so to speak, is seen in its own light – in the light of the divine glory. When the blessed human mind sees God in himself, 'that very divine essence becomes the form through which the mind knows'. Seeing God face-to-face is so immediate – unmediated – that the human mind may even be said to become 'deiform' (12.5).

Thomas's discussion, here, then, of our knowledge of God, is entirely dominated by the biblical promise of face-to-face vision. He spells this out in terms of complete identity between the human subject and God in a 'deiforming' event. Aristotle's mind/world identity account of knowledge is called in now as enabling us to see how the blessed might indeed become one with the object (God) – without being absorbed or extinguished.

Thomas's interest is often supposed to lie in developing a proto-empiricist theory of knowledge in the wake of Aristotle either for its own sake or in opposition to Augustinian illuminationism or to defeat Cartesianism *avant la lettre*. It then looks as if, perhaps with a certain reluctance and a certain amount of massage, he has to squeeze in the abnormal case of beatific vision. Yet, given his deepening attention to the works of Aristotle in tandem with reading St John and St Paul, it seems much more likely that he wanted the mind/world identity account in place precisely to highlight the extraordinary character of the consummation of the human mind in the ultimate bliss of deiforming knowledge of God.

The utterly grace-given 'beholding and reflecting the glory of the Lord' (cf. 2 Corinthians 3:18) could be located in this Aristotelian account of the economy of human knowledge far more pointedly, even poignantly, than in the Augustinian neo-Platonism Thomas inherited. The radically 'incarnationalist' naturalism of Aristotle perhaps struck Thomas as (providentially) far better designed to identify and protect the specifically

Christian dispensation of grace than the dualistic metaphysics of the Platonist tradition.

Metaphysics of Exodus

In every other Western language but English it has long been barely possible to do philosophy, let alone study Thomas Aquinas, without referring one way or another to the work of Martin Heidegger, and so to his several attempts to retrieve (as he thinks) the occluded difference between beings and being, *Seiendes* and *Sein* – between actual entities of whatever kind and the light in which all entities become visible or intelligible as such. Certainly, since the 1930s, the study of Thomas has been heavily affected by Heidegger's reclaiming of the 'question of being'. In particular, the question is much discussed as to whether Thomas's description of God as *esse subsistens*, 'subsisting being', is an exception to Heidegger's retelling of the entire metaphysical way of thinking from Plato onwards as constituted by 'forgetfulness of being', or 'abandonment by Being'.

One important movement, labelled Existential(ist) Thomism, began in France, initially at least quite independently of Heideggerian considerations.

The key figure, Etienne Gilson, brought out the first version of *Le Thomisme* in 1919; revised and expanded several times, this became by far the most influential exposition of Thomas's thought.[10] From one edition to the next, it is not difficult to trace Gilson's growing emphasis on Thomas's 'metamorphosis' of Aristotle's divine self-thinking Thought into God as 'He who is' – 'a supremely existential God'.

In 1926 Emile Bréhier, in the first volume of his *Histoire de la philosophie*, declared that Christianity had exercised no influence whatsoever on the history of philosophy. For Gilson, at least, this book, aimed at school and university students, was an attempt finally to put an end to Christianity as a serious intellectual option. Two years later, in a set of lectures in Brussels, under the title 'Is there a Christian philosophy?', Bréhier insisted, more technically, that Christianity and philosophy are incompatible, the one being purely 'mysterious, the other purely rational'.

This set Gilson off. Invited to deliver the Gifford Lectures in the University of Aberdeen, Gilson seized the opportunity to show, not only that the very idea of 'Christian philosophy' is perfectly intelligible, but that Christian philosophy is actually to be found, in abundance, in the Middle Ages.[11] As a 'historian who deals with ideas', he sought to show that 'the spirit of mediaeval philosophy' is nothing other than 'the spirit of Christianity penetrating the Greek tradition, working within it, drawing out of it a certain view of the world, a *Weltanschauung*, specifically Christian'.

The first two lectures were devoted to 'Christian philosophy'. Nobody would speak of Christian mathematics, biology or medicine; why of Christian philosophy? Certain Thomists grant that no Christian ever constructed a philosophy, except Thomas Aquinas, and they hold that he did so on a purely rational basis, that is, without appealing to Christian doctrine. Such Thomists, Gilson contends, admit, in effect, 'the paganization of Christianity by Thomism', with which Thomas was then charged by rationalist historians (like Bréhier), on the one hand, and, on the other hand, by Protestant theologians (Luther and Calvin are attacked throughout Gilson's lectures, with gusto). On either view, Thomism is 'nothing but Aristotelianism rationally corrected and judiciously completed'.

Over against all this, Gilson appeals to the *speculative* as well as the practical elements in New Testament Christianity. Indeed, to deny the speculative would be to deny that Jesus himself 'taught the doctrine of the Heavenly Father, preached faith in divine providence, announced eternal life in an everlasting Kingdom'.

Far from being corrupted by Hellenization, the most primitive Christianity sprang out of Judaism and the Bible, but was always already 'full of ideas about God and his divine government which, although not properly philosophical in character, only needed to fall into the right soil to become fruitful of philosophic consequences'.

In brief, 'the fact that there is no philosophy in Scripture does not warrant the conclusion that Scripture could have exerted no influence on the evolution of philosophy'. Rather, why should we refuse to allow that Christianity 'might have been able to change the course of the history of philosophy by opening up to human reason, by the mediation of faith, perspectives as yet undreamt of?'

Gilson writes of the 'laborious gropings' of Plato and Aristotle, as they sought to say something about God. Compared with these efforts 'how straightforward is the method of the Biblical revelation, and how startling its results!'

This brings us to the following famous passage:

In order to know what God is, Moses turns to God. He asks His name, and straightway comes the answer: *Ego sum qui sum, Ait: sic dices filiis Israel; qui est misit me ad vos* (Exod. 3:14). No hint of metaphysics, but God speaks, *causa finita est*, and Exodus lays down the principle from which henceforth the whole of Christian philosophy will be suspended. From this moment it is understood once and for all that the proper name of God is Being and that, according to the word of St Ephrem, taken up again later by St Bonaventure, this name denotes His very essence.

Appealing to Exodus 3:14, Thomas contends that, among all the names of God, the one that is eminently proper is *Qui est* – 'He who is', the name that means 'nothing other than being itself' (cf. ST 1.13.11).

In short: 'There is but one God and this God is Being, that is the corner-stone of all Christian philosophy, and it was not Plato, it was not even Aristotle, it was Moses who put it in position'.

Obviously Gilson did not suppose that God spoke in Latin. Moreover, in a long footnote he insists that he is not maintaining that Exodus 3:14 is 'a revealed metaphysical definition of God'. On the other hand, 'if there is no metaphysic in Exodus there is nevertheless a metaphysic of Exodus' – which he goes on to insist is to be found throughout the patristic tradition. In particular, he cites Ephrem of Nisibis, Gregory of Nazianzen, Gregory of Nyssa, Cyril of Alexandria and finally Hilary of Poitiers.

What Gilson holds, then, is that the Lord God's self-identification as 'I am who am', as reported in Exodus 3:14, lies at the back of the tradition of Christian theology, Greek and Latin, which culminated in the thought of Thomas Aquinas: God as Being. As he says: 'the Christian revelation exerted a decisive influence on the development of metaphysics by introducing the identification of God and Being'.

Gilson cites Adolphe Lods (1867–1948), the French Protestant exegete, then the leading authority, who maintained that the meaning of Exodus 3:14 is simply that God 'is what he is, the being undefinable by man' – an explanation, Lods says, that 'does not lack grandeur, but is apparently too theological, too lacking in spontaneity, to express the original idea of the Madianite [sic] god'.

'This is a question for Hebraists', Gilson says, a trifle cavalierly. His main concern is to insist that, whatever experts in biblical Hebrew say, 'the patristic-mediaeval philosophy is a correct development of this text'.

The One Who Is

This is another hermeneutic crux. If modern scholarship tells us that a word could never have carried the meaning, even embryonically, that later interpretation exploits, we might be inclined to dismiss that whole tradition. For Gilson, on the other hand, the self-identification of God in the Pentateuch, obscure and barely intelligible or translatable, once carried into the Greek of the Septuagint and diffused in the Jewish diaspora, working its way into the Hellenistic Judaism represented by Philo of Alexandria, passing into patristic theology, eventually, with the help of Moses Maimonides, comes to fulfilment in Thomas Aquinas's 'Christian philosophy' – the ancient Greek quest for the cause of being radically transformed by the biblical revelation of the God who says 'I am'.[12]

By the fourth edition of *Le Thomisme* (1942) Gilson was affirming that Thomas's philosophy was the true 'existentialism'. At that point, in France anyway, no one made much distinction between Heidegger's philosophical work and existentialism. In the context of various philosophical projects that stressed the priority of existence over consciousness, of the 'existential' over the intellectual, of action over theory, and so on, it became clearer and clearer to Gilson that Thomas's 'existential metaphysics', as he put it, 'succeeded in forcing its way through that crust of essences which is but the outer coating of reality', thus allowing us to 'see the pure Act of existing as one sees the presence of the cause in any one of its effects'. Metaphysics properly conducted 'does not culminate in a concept, be it that of Thought, of Good, or One, or of Substance. It does not even culminate in an essence, be it that of Being itself. Its last word is not *ens*, but *esse*; not *being* but *is*'.[13]

According to Gilson's grand narrative of the 'fall' of the metaphysical tradition, within Thomism itself, the sixteenth-century Dominican commentator on Thomas, Thomas de Vio, better known as Cajetan, allowed himself to be contaminated by Scotism, and reduced Thomas's metaphysics of the existential act of being to an ontology of substance.[14] Failing to understand the innovative move beyond Aristotle that Thomas made, a move in metaphysics prompted by the Christian doctrine of creation *ex nihilo*, Cajetan and his followers into the 1930s represented Thomas as focused on the forms and essences of beings only, and not on the existence of all things as participation in the pure actuality which is God.

The word *esse* – 'to be' – is a *verb*, Gilson insists: a *doing* word, a word that designates an *act*. Historically speaking, it took the 'self-revelation of the existentiality of God' in Scripture to help philosophers to reach – 'beyond essences' – 'the existential energies which are their very causes'. This entirely unforeseeable revolutionary development, Gilson thinks, occurred to Christian thinkers when 'the Jewish-Christian Revelation had taught them that "to be" was the proper name of the Supreme Being'.

Yet this insight is very hard to maintain: 'Human reason feels at home in a world of things, whose essences and laws it can grasp and define in terms of concepts; but shy and ill at ease in a world of existences, because to exist is an act, not a thing'. We live in a world of facts; what we have to do, however, is to view the world as 'a world of particular existential acts all related to a supreme and absolute Self-Existence' – and that is 'to stretch the power of our essentially conceptual reason almost to the breaking point'.

The 'fundamental truth' that Thomas reached, 'on the strength of straight metaphysical knowledge', comes out when he says, for example: 'all knowing beings implicitly know God in any and every thing that they know'[15] – the kind of thing Thomas says, Gilson notes, wherever he speaks of the natural (albeit confused) desire we have for beatitude (citing ST 1.2.1).

This is what Augustine understood, Gilson says, when the Psalmist taught him to hear all things proclaiming the glory of God and thus their creator, citing for example *Confessions* 7.10:

> I recognized that "because of iniquity you discipline man" and "cause my soul to waste away like a spider's web" (Ps. 38:12 (39.11)), and I said: "Surely truth cannot be nothing, when it is not diffused through space, either finite or infinite?" And you cried from far away: "Now, I am who I am" (Exod 3:14). I heard in the way one hears within the heart, and all doubt left me. I would have found it easier to doubt whether I was myself alive than that there is no truth "understood from the things that are made" (Rom. 1:20)

According to Gilson, 'quite apart from any philosophical demonstration of the existence of God, there is such a thing as a spontaneous natural theology': 'God spontaneously offers himself to most of us, more as a confusedly felt presence than as an answer to any problem, when we find ourselves confronted with the vastness of the ocean, the still purity of mountains, or the mysterious life of a midsummer starry sky'.

These feelings are, of course, not 'proofs' – they are the 'facts' which prompt philosophers to ask questions about the possible existence of God. Where metaphysics ends, religion begins. Thomas takes us to the God of natural theology, beyond the concept of thought, of good, of the one, of substance, or of being – to posit an Act – 'the supreme Act of existing whose very essence, because it is to be, passes human understanding' (he quotes ST 1.3.4) – that takes us to 'the mystery of existence'.

Again and again, Gilson insists that this is the culmination of true metaphysics – of pure philosophy – but of course he has been saying all along that it took God's self-revelation to Moses to get the thought going in the first place that God is the 'to be' which we cannot know. It is not easy to see how this theologically generated doctrine could ever be discovered in purely metaphysical reflection. And this becomes even less easy to understand when we find Gilson insisting that we have to penetrate beyond the philosophical theses which constitute 'Thomistic philosophy' to the underlying 'deep religious life and secret fervour of a soul in search of God'.

There is no interior life or spirituality to be found by digging into Thomas's work, so Gilson thinks. The *Summa Theologiae*, with its abstract limpidness and impersonal transparency '*is*' Thomas's interior life crystallized under our eyes, so to speak. This is the best way to read it. Recalling the hymn '*Pange lingua*', Gilson insists that Thomas's philosophy is as beautiful as his poetry is thoughtful.

Perhaps one should recall that Gilson was writing programme notes for concerts in 1913, defending Debussy, for example. In 1939 he published a book on Dante. In 1959 he gave the Mellon lectures in Washington, *Painting and Reality* – not, as he said at the start, an effort by a philosopher (as he thought of himself) to interpret paintings but an attempt to show how paintings express the philosopher's question: why is there something rather than nothing?

In 1958, visiting Freiburg to receive an honorary doctorate, Gilson heard Heidegger lecture and was moved to tears. Heidegger 'is taking us to the only real metaphysical problems. I believe he could . . . help us not only to deeper insights into his own thought, but even into that of . . . Thomas Aquinas'.[16]

While many regard 'Gilsonian Thomism' as *passé*, a good case has been made for the view that, in the encyclical *Fides et Ratio*, it is Existential Thomism that is being commended by Pope John Paul II.[17]

Heidegger Against the First Cause

According to Heidegger, 'Christian philosophy' is an absurdity, 'a round square and a misunderstanding'. This remark comes early in the lecture course which he gave in 1935, the text of which did not appear until 1953; but the comment circulated orally from the start and there can be no doubt that it was aimed at Catholic philosophers in Germany who were attracted by Gilson's claims.[18]

Heidegger had some exposure to Thomistic philosophy in the three semesters he spent as a seminarian. His doctorate dissertation, completed in 1913, on 'The doctrine of judgement in psychologism', anticipated his endorsement of Frege's anti-psychologism, and the anti-Cartesianism to be found in *Sein und Zeit*. The account of the being which each of us is, with regard to its being, as he would say, was, of course, only the preliminary to working out 'the question of being' (*die Seinsfrage*). Indeed, the very asking of this question turns out to *be* our way of being. What characterizes us as human beings, over against all other entities, is precisely that we are the ones in the world who can raise 'the question about Being'.

It is an astonishing claim. To contextualize it for our purposes here, we might say that it is a variation on the typically Thomist 'definition' of the human creature as the 'rational animal'. In turn, this is a development of Aristotle's account of the human being as the animal possessed of reason (*zoon logon echon*), which Heidegger will eventually translate as 'that living thing whose being is essentially determined by having the potentiality for discourse'. Thus, human beings are not so much animals endowed with a certain rational nature, as if that were their possession; but beings whose nature is constituted by *logos* understood as meaning *language*.

But Heidegger was after much bigger game. He was interested in carrying through a root and branch rejection of psychologistic and anthropocentric philosophical prejudices, yet only so as to clear the way to reopening the question of the difference between beings and Being, forgotten (as he thought) since Plato. Indeed, he goes as far as to say that what has counted as philosophy ever since Plato is the product, precisely, of obliviousness to this question: 'A dogma has been developed which not only declares the question about the meaning of Being to be superfluous, but sanctions its complete neglect'.

In the academic circles in which this seems a compelling understanding of the history of philosophy, there have long been students of Thomas with their sights set on showing that his philosophy of being is an exception. In the predominantly Catholic countries where Thomas Aquinas is – still – most seriously studied, the local philosophers with whom Thomists choose or feel compelled to interact are mostly Heideggerian in their presuppositions.

Obviously, this interaction gives rise to interpretations of Thomas which are incommensurable with, indeed virtually unintelligible to, readers schooled in English-language analytic philosophy.

Bizarrely as this seems to theologians and philosophers in English-speaking circles, Catholic philosophers and theologians in mainland European traditions now take for granted Heidegger's history of Western philosophy as a history of 'forgetfulness of being'.[19]

The story goes as follows, briefly. It is not the fault of any philosopher, or of the philosophical tradition as a whole, that the 'question about the sense of being' has 'fallen into oblivion'. On the contrary: 'forgetfulness of Being' (*Seinsvergessenheit*) issues from 'Being's withdrawal' (*Seinsverlassenheit*); it is not that philosophers have forgotten being (culpably or otherwise) but that Being has abandoned us. Heidegger is so concerned to eradicate all inclinations to anthropocentric philosophies that he insists on the priority of the 'event' (*Ereignis*) of the self-establishing difference between beings and Being. The human way of being, one might say, is the 'effect' of this wholly uncovenanted and gratuitous antecedent differentiation.[20]

Putting it a little less obscurely, perhaps, the claim is that philosophers have assumed that the boundary of their thought is set by the limits of human experience (metaphysics as concerned, conventionally, with things and properties, parts and wholes, particulars and universals, identity and persistence, space and time, etc.). They have not asked 'the question about the *sense* of being', about what it is that makes it possible at all for us to see beings *as* beings, to see beings, then, in the light of Being. Philosophical thinking, now that Heidegger has enabled us to understand this, needs to develop ways of displaying the 'clearing' (*die Lichtung*), in which beings are revealed for what they are. What we have to learn to do, in another bit of the jargon, is to allow the difference between Being and beings to show up.

The 'ontological difference', so the story goes, has been obliterated from the outset of the Western metaphysical tradition. What this means, essentially, is that, in philosophy, we have always at least tended to represent 'Being' as itself a being, and as having a ground, even as itself being the ground – usually, Heidegger thinks, as the supreme being, in other words: God. Medieval theologians, certainly including Thomas Aquinas, are the ones in whose thinking Being and God have been identified. One type of entity (the divine one) is taken as the standard for Being in general. We have what Heidegger calls 'the onto-theo-logical constitution' of the metaphysical way of thinking: when we think about being, the deity is always already included: onto-theo-logy.

The question, then, for Thomists, after Heidegger, is to see what is to be made of Thomas's concept of God in the light of his favourite description of God as 'subsistent being'. Does such talk exemplify metaphysical obliviousness to Being or may it be claimed as an exception – even, along somewhat Gilsonian lines, the exception that proves the validity of the Heideggerian grand narrative?

Heidegger Against Teleology

Heidegger is very insistent that Being is not in any sense an entity, not even a god. On the contrary, no worse error can be imagined than reification of *das Sein*. There is no Being except in the existence of beings; and beings do not show up except in the light of Being.

The identification of Being with the supreme being, Heidegger maintains, means that ontology is always already theology – in effect, we may say, that the world is always already regarded as divinely created.

The work of thinkers after Heidegger should be to free thinking of being from its theological straitjacket. Being is regarded as a property, alongside other properties of a thing – perceptibility, and so on; so that once again *das Sein*, as the transcendental condition of the possibility of human experience of beings in the first place, is hypostatized and thus misconceived as an item among beings.

God as cause of things 'is the right name for the god of philosophy', as Heidegger famously writes: 'Human beings can neither pray nor sacrifice to this god. Before the *causa sui*, human beings can neither fall to their knees in awe nor can they play music and dance before this god'.[21]

God has persistently been understood as a special being among beings. Indeed, long before Christian theology assimilated Hellenistic philosophy, the latter was already thoroughly theological.

Heidegger's claim that Aristotle's *Physics* is das *Grundbuch* of Western philosophy may be exaggerated.[22] Yet, undoubtedly, Aristotle's argument for the existence of a first mover, in the context of his picture of the world as *physis* and *kosmos* – as 'nature' always already exhibiting a 'beautiful order' – looks very like onto-theo-logy.

In effect, as Heidegger suggests and as Reiner Schürmann worked out in detail, Aristotle's 'world', with its in-built origination and finality, was always already understood as 'made', 'fabricated', if you like 'created'.[23] All along, as a result, in Western philosophy, it is taken for granted, however unwittingly, that there is a divine maker of the world – an origin that commands and a destiny that calls. The rule in the metaphysical tradition has always been to look for something fundamental in virtue of which reality becomes intelligible and thus masterable, so this story goes: the rule of *scire per causas*, thus of establishing 'principles' for thinking and action. Heidegger, according to Schürmann, seeks to show that thinking no longer aims at securing some rational foundation upon which the sum total of knowledge may be erected, any more than action means conforming one's life to the foundation so secured.

As Schürmann puts it, Heidegger's return to pre-Socratic thinking opens up a paradigm (allegedly) for us in the West at last to break free of the 'archeo-logical' and 'telo-cratic' way of thinking. On this reading, Heidegger was out to persuade us of the viability of an economy of practice and thinking which would be 'an-archic' and 'a-telic', so to speak. We should then begin at least – at last – to be cured of nostalgic desire for return to the source (*arche*, *principium*); we should be released from the obsession with achieving the ultimate end (*telos*, *finis*).

Thus, for example, when Thomas argues from effect to cause (as for example at ST 1.2.2) he takes it for granted that the world has a source and an end: that the world is 'made'. For Heidegger, in contrast, to maintain that the world cannot be described as the effect of something else, far from being an admission of the impotence of human reason, is rather an acknowledgement of the inapplicability of the language of causality to the mystery of the world's existence: when we look in vain for an explanation, in this case, the failure is not in our being unable to master the world but in our even trying to do so: 'The human will to explain just does not reach the simpleness of the simple onefold of worlding'.[24]

Thomas After Heidegger

Whether, and then perhaps how, Heidegger's subversion of the language of source and goal in connection with the existence and intelligibility of the world rules out any possibility of saving Thomas Aquinas's philosophy of being could be discussed at considerable length. In Germany alone, several distinguished Catholic thinkers have reconsidered Thomas's metaphysics of God as *ipsum esse subsistens* in the light of Heidegger's story, for example, Gustav Siewerth, J.B. Lotz, and Bernhard Welte.[25] If Schürmann's 'an-archistic' reading of Heidegger's antimetaphysical and anti-ontotheological project is correct, it seems plausible to suspend attempts to reconcile Heidegger and Thomas. On the other hand, among Catholic theologians, none has written at greater length or with such appreciation of the light that Heidegger may cast on Thomas as Hans Urs von Balthasar.[26]

Balthasar's theological project is very different from Thomas's, obviously, in many ways: he writes after the Reformation, the Enlightenment, German romanticism and idealism, and in conversation especially with Karl Barth; but there is a sense, he believed, in which his work depends decisively on Thomas's concept of God as 'actualization of Being', *actus essendi*.[27]

Balthasar endorses Heidegger's grand narrative of the abandonment of Western thought by Being, quite explicitly.[28] When Heidegger rejected the exposition of the distinction between essence and existence that he found in contemporary neo-Thomism, however, he did so, according to Balthasar, on the grounds that essence was conceived by these Thomists as something to which existence might or might not be related. These neo-Thomists had, however, misrepresented Thomas. In fact, Balthasar maintains, Thomas is saying much the same as Heidegger: for both, 'the act of Being, which comprehends within it all that is, is illumination (and thus the original locus of truth), is origin, the greatest proximity (*intimum*) in the greatest distance ('more existent than all that exists'), and at the same time it is nothingness (the non-subsisting), the unity beyond all number'.

Behind all this stands, not Aristotle, but Plotinus, Balthasar notes, though historically Thomas was in no position to know this. But then nor could Heidegger see it either, assuming as he did that Plotinus, as a Platonist, was forgetful of Being – a big mistake, however, Balthasar insists. To the contrary: for Plotinus, 'Being remains a superconceptual mystery' – as Balthasar had already sought to demonstrate at some length.[29]

We have much to learn from Heidegger's anti-subjectivism, Balthasar maintains. We should not yield to the temptation to think of ourselves as subjects, on this side of the world, as if the world stood over against us, on the other side of some gap. Rather, prior to seeing ourselves as subjects over against objects, we need to see ourselves as situated in the 'open' which allows the relationship of subject to object to unfold in the first place: Heidegger's 'clearing' (*Lichtung*), it seems.

To say that we are what we are by being in the light, Balthasar says, agreeing again with what Heidegger once said, settles nothing one way or the other about theism or atheism. Rather, by highlighting our being in the world, as Heidegger does, all that happens, for theology, is that we (re)gain a more adequate concept of our place in the light of Being and may therefore at last be in an appropriate position to ask how God comes in. This is not indifference to the theistic question. Indeed, it cuts more deeply than the metaphysical tradition can. It is not a question of transcending the metaphysical tradition, by climbing still higher; rather, the right kind of post-Heideggerian thinking overcomes metaphysics by climbing back down into the nearness of the near: 'the descent, particularly where we have strayed into subjectivity, is more arduous and more dangerous than the ascent'.

As Heidegger says, neatly, playfully, the world is not the result – *die Ergebnis* – as if it were the effect of some cause, the consequence of some antecedent. Rather, the world is simply *die Er-gebnis*: the original, under-ived, inaugural self-giving. The world is not the product of a fabricator-god; the world's existence is its own gift.

Balthasar obviously likes the Heideggerian language. But, as he rightly notes, it is very biblical in resonance and even to some extent in provenance. Heidegger breaks with the (alleged) Platonist motif of grasping and self-promoting *eros* by cultivating a new receptivity towards things which he calls *Gelassenheit*: a 'letting be', a concept, and indeed a practice, which (as Balthasar says) should not surprise those familiar with the intellectual inheritance of Christianity. For Origen, the medievals, Eckhart, Tauler, Ignatius of Loyola, to name but a few, all willing is grounded in 'letting be', freedom lies in *indiferencia*.

More to the point here, as Balthasar goes on to show, Heidegger relies very much on biblical categories: covenant, listening, obedience, fidelity as a precondition of revelation, and so on. Balthasar is quite clear about this. Heidegger simply transfers to the mystery of Being what traditionally has always been said about God: God as hidden precisely in being revealed, God as described, not in the 'sawdust Thomism' with which Balthasar and no doubt Heidegger also were painfully acquainted, but in classical patristic theology (Maximus the Confessor, Denys, John Scotus Eriugena and many others).

The space for theocentric metaphysics opened up to some extent in the thought of Plotinus and Denys, so Balthasar goes on, is identified, uniquely, by Thomas Aquinas. He is the one who acknowledges the difference between, on the one hand, the *actus essendi*, understood as 'non-subsisting abundance which attains a state of rest and self-realization from and within finite essences' and, on the other, '*essentiae* which attain to reality by act, without however reducing or subdividing the infinite act'. Heidegger is right to reject it when 'a pedantic scholasticism turns the mystery into a "real distinction"'; but in Thomas, so Balthasar maintains, 'this structure' – the distinction in the created order between existence and essence – 'remains the sign of the indeterminate non-absoluteness, speaking in Christian terms, of creatureliness' – 'for how can a non-subsisting act of Being generate subsisting Beings from itself alone, and how are the essences to acquire a closed and meaningful form?'

The seas of language are running high again. These are the questions, Balthasar supposes, that prompt Thomas towards describing God as 'subsisting and absolute Being'; but Heidegger, being of the 'post-Christian age', 'revokes' the Christian distinction, and creates the notion of a superconceptual *actus essendi*. In short, he identifies the negations of classical apophatic theology with the nothingness of the act of being which constitutes the world. Though he goes beyond Aristotle, as Thomas does, perceiving the distinction between Being and the beings as a mystery impenetrable to reason, thus allowing him to charge philosophy from Plato until now as motivated by unthinking obliviousness to the absence of Being itself, Heidegger does not construe this 'difference' as Thomas does, in the Christian way, as a sign, indeed *the* sign, of creatureliness. Heidegger falls back, Balthasar thinks, into identifying being and beings: a claim that would need a good deal more explanation than he provides.

Towards the close of his discussion, Balthasar focuses on the positive. For the Christian theology of God's glory which Balthasar is composing, Heidegger's later work is the most fertile available, philosophically. He keeps our eyes on the main issue: the mystery of the distinction between Being and things. If Christian theologians think they can expound the biblical revelation of the living God while bypassing the mystery of this distinction, Balthasar holds, they lose their way: their theology sinks into a positivism abjectly submissive to the jurisdiction of philosophy, or into Teilhardian naturalism.

Balthasar cites a reviewer who describes his theological aesthetics as 'an exceedingly urgent endeavour to penetrate behind Thomas and his Aristotelian-conditioned ontology of the beautiful' in order to see 'the whole of revelation and history in a renewed neo-Platonic-Christian mysticism'.[30] Balthasar believes his project can do justice to the Christian requirement of penitence, conversion, and immediate listening to the word as emphasized by Luther, Kierkegaard, Bultmann and many others, while at the same time remembering the equally biblical Catholic and Orthodox requirement of giving glory in contemplation – holding the two requirements together, as he says he does in his book on contemplative prayer.[31]

Where biblical contemplation sinks into neo-Platonic aesthetic contemplation, the Protestant (Barthian) protest is of course justified – albeit the Protestant nervousness about the unserious aestheticism of Catholicism is exaggerated: Protestant attention needs to be directed to the glory of God, against the temptation to sink into the pseudo-seriousness of existential-subjective grief for one's sins. Yet, in the end, the theology of God's glory must be reformulated directly from biblical revelation itself.

Balthasar's purpose is, no doubt, to retrieve, even to re-create, the pre-Christian vision of Being in all its awesomeness as the cultural environment within which the specifically Christian vision, rooted in God's self-revelation in the biblical tradition, came to expression historically and remains accessible today. In particular, he seeks to bring out the theological *a priori* of the metaphysical vision of goodness, truth and beauty – of Being as such. 'Greek metaphysics was orientated towards the *theion* and the Christian view of reality took possession of this 'natural' aesthetics in order to complete and transcend it on the basis of revelation'.

Unlike Heidegger, with his objections to the onto-theo-logical constitution of the metaphysical tradition, Balthasar is happy to acknowledge philosophy's theological *a priori*.

What is remarkable about Thomas, indeed his 'major creative achievement', is his recognition of the real distinction: a *philosophical* distinction, yet one that, in distinguishing creatures from creator, allows the significance of the divine glory to be located. Indeed, much as with Gilson, Balthasar sees Thomas's theorem of the absence of any distinction between essence and existence in God as a metaphysical achievement – but an achievement, historically at least, only in the light of God's self-revelation as 'I am who I am'.

Thomas's work is a turning point, a *kairos*. He builds on the already theological ontology of the Greeks, seeing Being as dynamically transparent to divinity. He sees human existence as the site for reflecting on Being, in a unique suspension between nature and the supernatural: disposed by nature for God's self-revelation in grace, making no claim to grace but never fulfilled without grace (citing ST 1–2. 5.5), and thus opening up the question of 'natural desire for God'.

Thus, far from being one more case in the history of Being's withdrawal from thought, Thomas is a key figure in the epoch-making transition from an ancient, monistically thinking world which saw philosophy and theology together, to an emerging world which separates philosophy and revealed theology and makes a totality of each. The transcendence of God over the world is secured against deeply tempting pantheism, the adversary against which Thomas's doctrine of God is primarily developed, so as to allow the natural–supernatural theological *a priori* to show up – with the doctrine of the Trinity as the background to Western philosophy. The 'de-essentializing of reality', demanded by Heidegger, is already achieved by Thomas: it is 'an extension within philosophy of the illumination by biblical revelation of the idea of God as creative principle'.

Here, in his own way of course, Balthasar comes very close to Gilson's position about the transformation of Aristotle's metaphysics under the impact of the Christian doctrine of creation.

In short, Heidegger's project to relieve the world of being 'created' depends on a radical misunderstanding of the Christian doctrine of creation *ex nihilo* as always already receiving the world as 'gift'. Where Heidegger sees the world explained in terms of an effect of some cause as demeaningly losing its incomparable mystery, Balthasar's Thomas celebrates the world as a miracle of divine grace.

Balthasar's language becomes quite intoxicated: the 'dark cloud' from India to Greece and Arabia and then from Eckhart to Hegel – 'the perverse demand that [the creature] deny itself in its finite essence' – is lifted. The metaphysics of Thomas is 'the philosophical reflection of the free glory of the living God of the Bible and in this way the interior completion of ancient (and thus human) philosophy' and:

> a celebration of the reality of the real, of that all-embracing mystery of being which surpasses the powers of human thought, a mystery pregnant with the very mystery of God, a mystery in which creatures have access to participation in the reality of God, a mystery which in its nothingness and non-subsistence is shot through with the light of the freedom of the creative principle, of unfathomable love.[32]

Far from being 'sophistry and illusion', Thomas's identification of God as *ipsum esse subsistens* in the light of the doctrine of divine simpleness is a 'breakthrough' in the history of thinking about God.

Idipsum

There is no way of reconciling these incommensurable interpretations of Thomas's doctrine of God as *Ipsum esse subsistens*.

Readers who work in the tradition of Anglo-American analytic philosophy are gripped by the principle enunciated by Frege and Russell, to the effect that 'exist' is not a first-level predicate. Thus 'God exists' does not predicate the property of existing of God; it is equivalent rather to 'Godhood is instantiated': that is, the property of being divine has at least one instance. According to Christopher Williams, Thomas's concept of God as *ipsum esse subsistens* is completely empty.[33]

In the perspective in which Gilson, Balthasar and most Thomists operate, on the other hand, no concept is richer. God is self-identified as 'I am He who is' (Exodus 3:14).

From the outset, the Jews who translated the Pentateuch into Greek rendered Exodus 3:14 (Hebrew *'ehyeh 'asher 'ehyeh*) in terms of the verb 'to be': *ego eimi ho on*.[34] This is no doubt the background for the use of the formula 'I am' as God's self-description in the Passover *Haggadah*. Equally, the writer of Revelation 1:8 puts into God's mouth the same text: 'I am . . . the one who is, who was, and who is to come'. Philo comments on Exodus 3:14: "no name at all can properly be used of Me, to Whom alone existence belongs' (*Vita Mosis* 1.75). It is also the background for the self-descriptions ascribed to Jesus in the Fourth Gospel.[35]

In Greek and Latin patristic writings the Exodus text is understood as God's self-revelation as 'Being itself', 'the subsisting act of all existing'. Augustine for one usually cites Exodus 3:14 including the words 'I AM has sent me to you'. He distinguishes God's *nomen misericordiae* – 'The LORD, the God of Abraham, Isaac, and Jacob' – and God's *nomen substantiae* – 'I AM WHO I AM'. That is to say, Augustine sees no problem in identifying the Lord God who commissions Moses for the role that he is to play in the continuing history of the salvation of the Israelites with the God who is self-revealed as Being itself, *ipsum esse*.[36]

Modern commentators sometimes find this unbelievable, but for Augustine the God who is Being itself, immutable, incorporeal, and so on, is simultaneously the God who called Abraham, sent Moses, and for that matter revealed his name at the burning bush. There is no need to set metaphysics and salvation history over against one another.

Even more significant for Augustine is the identification of God as *Idipsum*, 'the Self-Same'. The expression, which Augustine quotes hundreds of times, comes from Psalm 4. In the *Confessions*, he recounts the extraordinary impact Psalm 4 had on him (see book 9). He returns to this psalm (in book 12), in a quite ecstatic outburst: '*itaque tu, domine, qui non es alias aliud et alias aliter, sed id ipsum et id ipsum et id ipsum, sanctus, sanctus, sanctus, dominus deus omnipotens*' (thou, lord, who art not something other somewhere else or somewhere else otherwise but the same and the same and the same, 'holy holy holy Lord God almighty') (citing Isaiah 6:3 and Revelation 4:8). Here, as the reference a few lines on to God as 'one trinity and triune unity' (*una trinitas et trina unitas*) shows, Augustine is taking the doctrine of God as Trinity for granted. God as *Idipsum*, 'the Self-Same', is Augustine's answer to the question 'Who is God?' – a biblical, indeed doxological and liturgical name which designates also the One whom he addresses in the following words: 'Thou art truly that Self-Same, who never changes, and in thee is the rest which forgets all troubles, since there is no other besides thee' (*Confessions*, book 9). Psalm 4 contains the verse which Thomas often cites: 'The light of thy countenance, O Lord, is signed upon us', which Augustine also likes; but above all, for Augustine, the significant verse is as follows: 'In peace in the selfsame I will sleep, and I will rest: For thou, O Lord, singularly hast settled me in hope'.[37] Obviously, Thomas must often have sung these words, and known Augustine's predilection for addressing God as 'the Self-Same'. Though he seems never to have favoured the expression, it must have resonated whenever he spoke of God as *Ipsum esse*. He must also have known that one of the most interesting stages in the history of the reception of Augustine's naming of God as the Self-Same is to be found in the Cologne school founded by his teacher and friend Albert the Great.[38]

When he spoke of Thomas Aquinas's 'metaphysics of Exodus', Etienne Gilson entered this ancient tradition of interpreting Exodus 3:14. Here we meet the same problem as we saw with the history of the interpretation of Romans 1:20, in an even more acute form. Many readers now, with incomparably better knowledge of the original Hebrew, would regard the Septuagint translation of Exodus 3:14 and the entire subsequent tradition – Jewish, patristic and Thomist – as, exegetically, simply unfounded.

Others, like Paul Ricoeur, think it is impossible to obliterate readings that have shaped 'the intellectual and spiritual identity of the Christian West'.[39] His collaborator, André LaCocque, employs a historical-critical method, taking into account archaeological, philological and historical research, to provide the best available interpretation of Exodus 3:14; but, unusually, he includes historical information about how the text has been read, thus opening his exegesis to developments and enrichments (as he thinks: no doubt some would say corruptions) subsequent to the production of the original text. Indeed, he would question what discovering the original text, unmediated by accumulated readings, could mean anyway. Then, after providing a good summary of the metaphysical readings of Exodus 3:14 from Augustine and Denys to Bonaventure and Thomas, Ricoeur tackles head on the fundamental question as to whether the 'convergence without fusion' of the story of the divine self-naming at the burning bush and the ontological considerations inherited from the Greeks represents 'an intellectual aberration' or, as he is inclined to say, an 'intellectual event': 'Why not suppose that Exodus 3:14 was ready from the very beginning to add a new region of significance to the rich polysemy of the verb "being", explored in other terms by the Greeks and their Muslim, Jewish and Christian heirs?', Ricoeur asks.[40]

Chapter 6

NATURAL LAW: INCOMMENSURABLE READINGS

Thomism is 'one prominent form of natural law theory', according to Jeffrey Stout: like many other theories, such as those of Calvin, Hooker, Locke and Pufendorf, it depends on the idea of a divine lawgiver, which makes it of limited use in pluralistic society. Vernon Bourke, on the other hand, contends that the term 'natural law' should be abandoned altogether in connection with Thomas Aquinas: whatever he meant, it is nothing to do with what modern theories talk about; we should speak of his ethics of right reason.[1]

Standard Accounts

The classical study of the idea of natural law in the development of Western European thought, by A.P. d'Entrèves, remains fairly widely in use as a textbook in university courses in jurisprudence and political philosophy. It is an excellent book. Thomas Aquinas is more cited than any other author. His great *Summae* 'contain the most complete statement of that ideal of a thorough Christianization of life which inspired medieval Catholicism and which found its highest artistic achievement in the Divine Comedy of Dante'.

As an Italian and a Catholic and a great scholar (one-time professor of Italian literature in the University of Oxford), d'Entrèves plainly had no post-Reformation qualms about reason and faith, nature and grace, working in harmony. He rejoices that 'the Protestant Hooker' continued the tradition; the Thomist notion of natural law, paradoxically enough he thinks, lies at the basis of Anglicanism and thus also of 'the English way of life'.[2]

However all that may be, his account of Thomas's view cannot be faulted, as far as it goes. He regards natural law as the basis of morality, in Thomas's conception. He pays no attention to the place of virtue. He does, however, insist strongly on the metaphysical foundation of Aquinas's natural law doctrine, seeing this as supposing the world to be governed by divine providence. Thus, d'Entrèves would have agreed with Stout: Thomas's natural law doctrine is theologically grounded; but not with Bourke's shifting of emphasis from natural law theory to virtue ethics.

The standard account by a philosopher in the analytic tradition, D.J. O'Connor, certainly assumes that Thomas's moral philosophy is dominated by the concept of natural law.[3] What Thomas has to say relates to many practical questions, such as sexual conduct, and, on the other hand, more theoretically, to whether or not judgements of value can be deduced from accounts of empirical fact. From the outset, according to O'Connor, we can set aside Thomas's religious beliefs. His work is of great philosophical interest, comparable with that of Aristotle, Hume and Spinoza. Indeed, in a time when influential moral philosophers have abandoned objective theories of ethics, Thomas's work is of all the more interest. Moreover, it would be superficial to regard his work as mere Christianization of Aristotle; on the contrary, there is profound change of emphasis, and much alteration of detail. The important point is that, while the concept of natural law has a long history, there is no single theory; the common core is that in some sense or other the basic principles of morals and legislation are objective, accessible to reason and based on human nature. The doctrine of natural inclinations is very important – a set of dispositions or tendencies to act and react that we have in virtue of our nature.

The difficulties O'Connor sees include the following. Thomas is so unclear about which of the natural law precepts are primary and which are secondary, and, anyway, allows so much variability at the level of detailed choices, that his position seems little different from any other relativism. Moreover, his notions of nature and of reason seem ambiguous and even vague. Perhaps he sets his standards too high. If we regard knowledge as tentative, experimental, corrigible, and so on, as we surely should, then we cannot but find his ideas about how much we know about human nature much too certain.

The great difficulty with the appeal to natural law in Christian ethics, according to Michael Keeling, is that it becomes 'almost inevitably, the preserve of ecclesiastical authority'.[4]

Keeling characterizes the basic principle of natural law ethics as follows: despite the ways in which human beings keep failing to do so, 'anyone who accepted the discipline of rational thought could both see what the world was meant to be and follow through the moral indications which arose from that fact'. Thomas Aquinas put this principle into the form that has been fundamental in modern as well as medieval 'Catholic understanding of the moral world'. For all the damage done to human nature by sin, it remains possible to see from the creaturely order as it exists the moral end which it was intended to serve. Certainly, 'the divine revelation of Holy Scripture' is required for 'the fullest knowledge of God', 'nevertheless the "natural law", the law given in nature when we perceive the ultimate purposes there, still provided a sufficient moral basis for daily human existence'.

As Keeling rightly says, natural law ethics, as in Thomas Aquinas, does not generate 'widely agreed detailed rules in terms of human moral life'. True, 'many ethical precepts would find acceptance among human beings generally' – yet others, 'such as the control of contraception or possibly of abortion', are 'a matter of controversy, even among Christians'. The 'temptation', to which the teaching authorities in the Roman Catholic Church have persistently yielded, has been to press the theory into far too great detail and, worse, to make the definition of 'natural law' an 'act of authority'. In the encyclical letter *Humanae Vitae* (1968), Pope Paul VI declared authoritatively that the content of the natural law is a matter for the Magisterium to define. With *Veritatis Splendor* (1993), Pope John Paul II has made it impossible for the concept of natural law even to be discussed between Catholics and Protestants.

Keeling seeks to 'define mandates for the whole of humanity', starting from a 'Protestant Christian theological basis'. He is clearly happier with Protestants like Joseph Fletcher than with Karl Barth or Dietrich Bonhoeffer. He contends that natural law, far from being 'the discovery of a plan and even less the discovery of a set of rules for putting a plan into effect' is 'a dance' – 'As the Greek fathers said, life is a *perichoresis*, a dance of the universe led by Christ the Lord of Creation, towards a fulfilment that is not yet seen'.[5]

However that may be, it is significant that a Christian moralist, long experienced in ecumenical and inter-faith dialogue, believes that the very idea of natural law has been appropriated by the Roman Catholic Church, or anyway by the Vatican, in such a way that it is now a useless concept in any conceivable attempt to work out basic principles of a morality which adherents of various religious traditions would endorse.

Non-standard Accounts

There are other philosophical and theological accounts, probably much less familiar. Howard Mounce, for example, questions whether Thomas's conception of natural law is quite what is often assumed: 'Some have taken him to mean that moral principles can be verified as one might verify the law of gravity' – that is, 'by appealing to facts that can be appreciated even by people who otherwise have no sense of good and evil', in much the same way as people who have no sense of the possibility of religion are thought to be able to argue usefully about facts about the world (change, contingency, etc.).

That is not what Thomas meant, Mounce says. For Thomas, 'moral reasoning depends on principles which do not themselves depend on reasoning but are given us by nature'. There is nothing mysterious or metaphysical about this.

Why do we think murder is wrong, Mounce asks: we can easily think of reasons, but it turns out on further reflection that none of the reasons we might cite is any more certain and fundamental than our original conviction that murder is wrong. We might say that murder is wrong because it has bad social effects – but then, when there are no such consequences, we should have to find a different reason. It might be held, on the other hand, that murdering certain persons would have good social effects: that might lead into further debate about the rights and wrongs of assassinating tyrants, and so on. As the 20 July 1944 plot to kill Hitler is enough to show, even assassination in such circumstances confronted the conspirators with a terrible moral dilemma. Partly, no doubt, as officers, they had a problem about breaking their oath of allegiance to the head of state. Also, however, they shrank from an act of homicide which, if successful, was likely to have good political results. This is not surprising. We think there is something wrong with murder, independently of whatever results it might have. The reasoning that might come into the question begins after, not before, some act is regarded as murder. Our reaction to murder is an example of what Thomas means by saying that we have moral principles which are not founded on reasoning but are given us by nature.

For Thomas, moral reasoning is cogent only to the extent that it is framed and informed by principles that are given to us by our nature. We know the difference between right and wrong not because we have discovered it by reasoning but because it is given us as a natural disposition, 'a natural way of reacting to good and evil when they appear', as Mounce says.

If this seems too mysterious we need to consider what the alternative might be. If our belief that some action is right or wrong rests on reasoning, we certainly move far from what Thomas and (before him) Aristotle held. For Thomas it is part of our being created to the image and likeness of God that we have these natural dispositions which provide the principles upon which our moral reasoning can begin to work.

Given that by nature we are drawn to the good and inclined to resist evil, we have a 'natural law' which then requires us to reason, in particular cases. Of course we have to reason; our natural reactions will not do it all. For Thomas, as for common sense, there is something given to us and something that we have to do ourselves.

Moreover, again as Mounce notes, it is mistaken to think that for Thomas natural law enables us to have solutions to every moral problem – he thought, on the contrary, that no such clear-cut solutions were available in most cases.

In short, we always have to work at moral problems. With our practical reason we have 'a natural participation in the eternal law' – 'according to certain general principles' – but 'not as regards the particular determinations of individual cases'.

Obviously, the idea of there being a basis for morality in human nature has plausibility, perhaps a certain unavoidability, in common sense. Without some appeal to the notion that moral behaviour is governed to some extent by an understanding of human nature as (again to some extent) given and shared, what else is there for us but the option between the idea that we human beings create whatever moral values there are or the idea that we simply have to submit to the 'divine command' ethics disclosed by revelation to some Christians? In other words, what else is natural law ethics but an attempt to find middle ground between the doctrine that 'it's right because we judge it so' and 'it's right because God tells me so'? Essentially, whatever the various developments of the idea and their eventual incompatibility, the point of invoking natural law is to maintain a space between what human beings may reason their way into regarding as allowable and what those who speak in the name of God would permit.

At least since the Nuremberg trials, with their charge of 'crimes against humanity', jurisprudential thinking has moved away from legal positivism (Justinian: 'What pleases the prince has the force of law') towards natural law ethics. It comes, of course, in several varieties. In an explicitly Thomist tradition we should note the work of Jacques Maritain.[7]

Among recent theological accounts one of the most interesting we owe to Oliver O'Donovan.[8] Despite 'points of strong sympathy' between his exposition of the moral significance of created order and 'the more realist versions of Natural Law theory', he wants to avoid using the 'classic term' because of the ambiguity that he sees in attributing universality not only to being but to knowledge. He regrets that in the great theological attack on the idea of natural law spearheaded by Karl Barth there was confusion between epistemological and ontological issues, such that some aspects of the doctrine of creation (like 'ordinances') fell under suspicion, leaving a very thin basis for moral deliberation – nothing but the divine command. This was not helped by his subordinating the doctrine of creation ontologically to Christology, leading to 'disturbing results in a series of frankly Apollinarian Christological conceptions'.[9] Barth lays so much emphasis on the unity of divine and human natures in the person of the Word incarnate that he effectively denies the presence of a human mind or soul. Human nature as a whole, and particularly human rationality and moral development, are so marginalized as not to be included in what is redeemed. Over against that view, we need to see that creation and redemption has each its ontological and epistemological dimension: the created order and natural knowledge; the new creation and revelation in Christ. Thus, the epistemological programme required for natural ethics, in the sense of an ethics known to everyone, is very high – even impossibly so – but O'Donovan refuses to conclude there is no ontological ground for an ethics of nature, meaning by this an objective order to which the moral life can respond. If we were to take that line, we should have to say that any certainty we may have about the order which God has created depends solely upon God's own disclosure of himself and of his works. For O'Donovan, it is only in the sphere of divine revelation that we can see the natural order as it really is and so overcome the epistemological barrier to an ethic that conforms to natural law. But nature thus understood involves all human beings and cultures, not excluding a certain 'natural knowledge' which is also part of our created endowment – a position very close, as he says, to what Thomas maintained.

The appeal to the natural law tradition in some form is motivated, obviously, by horror at the abuse of law by so many states. If justice is determined by what the state decrees, as the abandonment of traditional belief in something normative beyond positive law seems to involve, it is not surprising that we should want to return to the principle that the law is always finally subject to what 'natural justice' requires.

Environmental issues, as well as state despotism, invite renewed reflection on the natural law tradition. One of the finest recent retrievals of natural law ethics, and particularly of Thomas Aquinas's version, is provided by Michael S. Northcott, in the context of working out a theological ethics adequate to respect for our physical environment. Thomas's version develops from the natural law ethics to be found in the Hebrew prophets and Paul. It offers 'the strongest conceptual base within the Christian tradition for an ecological ethic'. It remains particularly strong in English culture (Shakespeare, Hooker, Hopkins, C.S. Lewis). On the other hand, it is diminished in the 'humanocentric' conception of natural law in modern papal ethics – which (Northcott contends) fails to maintain the 'deep understanding of the moral significance of created order' in the 'pre-modern natural law tradition'.[10]

Russell Hittinger, among the most persuasive of Catholic exponents of the natural law tradition, deplores the way that natural law, in much modern Roman Catholic discussion, is regarded as functioning independently of the eternal law in the mind of God: 'what began for the Christian theologians as a doctrine explaining how the human mind participates in a higher order of law is turning into its opposite'.[11] For over a century, he says, papal encyclicals have overlooked the theological background as they declared a great number of activities contrary to nature and reason, such as (his list) duelling, Communism, divorce, contraception, Freemasonry, in vitro fertilization and contract theories of the origin of political sovereignty. This, as he says, is not to mention 'the bevy of rights and entitlements that have been declared to be owed to persons under the rubric of justice *ex ipsa natura rei*, by the very nature of the thing'. The problem is not the judgements about the rightness or otherwise of this or that activity, he insists, but the impression that these encyclicals so often create that 'on any vexed issue the minds of the faithful and the gentiles [i.e. non-Christians] can be adequately directed to appeal to elementary principles of natural law'. The fact is that, 'trimming arguments' to fit what everyone is supposed to know irrespective of what they believe about God, and buttressing this with appeals to papal authority, 'would eventually yield diminishing and disappointing results, not only for the gentiles but also for the faithful – especially the moral theologians'. While theologians once upheld the dependence of the moral order on divine providence, Hittinger maintains, there is now a generation of Catholic moralists who have come to think that the rudiments of the moral order ought to be discussed without any reference to divine government, or, for that matter, to created nature'. Careful to note that this is not a result of the reforms of the Second Vatican Council, Hittinger cites Servais Pinckaers in support of his claim that natural law theory had been disembedded from moral theology, and moral theology from the rest of theology, long before that, in the standard exposition in seminary textbooks and suchlike.[12] Thomas's theology was greatly respected but in practice his account of natural law was extracted from its theological context and deprived of its vital connections with beatitude and virtue as well as with the Law of Moses and the New Law. In short, the precepts of the natural law were represented as what every human being is supposed to know by nature, while at the same time being the pronouncements of church authority ('Cartesian minds somehow under church discipline').

Thomas on Natural Law

When we turn to Thomas, in particular to the *Summa Theologiae* and the most widely read text, the first surprise, as with the arguments for the existence of the first cause, is that there is only a single question about natural law (ST 1–2. 94), in the middle of 19 (90–108), in which three deal with human law, eight with the Mosaic law, and three with the New Law of the Gospel. This one question has received an inordinate amount of attention and, abstracted from its context, as it usually is, may be rather misleadingly expounded. Treating the treatise on law, let alone the single question on natural law, in isolation from the rest of the *secunda pars* is plainly to get things out of proportion.

One of the most interesting recent discussions is the 'narrative understanding of Thomistic natural law' offered by Pamela M. Hall.[13] Her first point is that reading the questions on law in the *Summa Theologiae* on their own, without attending to how interwoven they are with the rest, only results in distortion. Her project goes well beyond trying to get Thomas right – which is all that need concern us here.

As Hall notes, discussing several very different commentators, Thomas's natural law is customarily identified with a set of commands and prohibitions, with a set of rules. Some interpret natural law on analogy with human law. For Thomas, however, natural law is linked, time and time again, in the relevant questions in the *Summa Theologiae*, with eternal law: the law by which God governs the entire cosmos. That means, as Hall says, that we need to go back to Thomas's discussion of the nature of divine providence (ST 1–2. 90).

Goodness is found in creatures not only in their 'substance' but also insofar as they are ordered to their 'ultimate end, which is divine goodness'. Rational creatures 'direct themselves to an end . . . through free will, because they can take counsel and they can choose'. Since God is the first cause of freedom on the part of creatures as secondary causes, 'human providence is contained under the providence of God as a particular cause under a universal cause'.

At this point Thomas does not describe how human providence actually works in relation to divine providence. The *secunda pars* is his massive account of how human beings, with minds and wills, direct themselves in decisions of ethical significance and, in doing so, are drawn towards (or away from) God. As Thomas says in the prologue, he will consider human beings on analogy with God, since they are like God, precisely in regard to mind and will.

Thomas starts with an inquiry into the human end, for which no natural good or set of goods can ever suffice (ST 1–2. 1–5), Nothing but God, as known and loved in the beatific vision, can fully satisfy the human desire for truth and the good. Thomas then considers will (6–17), the criteria for good and bad action (18–21) and the emotions (22–48). Following Aristotle, he wants to resolve the issue of the *telos* of human life; then he brings in the concept of voluntariness, incorporating remarks about the passions. He proceeds to consider the virtues, both natural and theological (49–70). Characterizing the only completely and radically fulfilling *telos* for human beings as participation in God's beatitude – already moves a long way from Aristotle; but the lengthy discussion of sin and its kinds, degrees and effects (71–89) departs absolutely from anything that the *Nicomachean Ethics* could have envisaged or included. It is immediately after this that Thomas opens his consideration of law (90–114). That is to say: what Thomas has to say about law, including natural law, follows upon what he says about sin. His consideration of law is part of his consideration of the 'exterior principle' moving us to good, namely, God, who 'instructs us through law and helps us through grace' (ST 1–2. 90 prologue).

Setting law against grace and vice versa would, of course, have seemed unintelligible to Thomas. Law is regarded as a form of instruction, education, intellectual formation; grace is clearly something much more practical and holistic. In principle, Thomas should be able to say a good deal about law, natural and human, without bringing in the Christian economy of salvation, and indeed many read him as doing precisely that; but, as Hall among others insists, the fact is that he does not do so here. On the contrary, human and natural law, as well as divine law, are located firmly in the context of divine providence.

Law (*lex*) is something rational (*aliquid rationis*) directed to the common good by those who are responsible for the community, and adequately promulgated. Thomas distinguishes four kinds of law: eternal law, natural law, human law, and divine law. Natural, human, and divine law, working together, are how eternal law is realized and manifested in and for human beings. This is how divine providence works in the case of human beings, these free and rational creatures who are, as it happens, lamentably prone to sin.

'Granted that the world is ruled by divine providence', as Thomas assumes we believe, 'the whole community of the universe (*tota communitas universi*) is governed by God's mind (*ratione divina*)'. For Thomas, at least on the face of it, there is no place for talking about natural law outside the context of this belief in the sovereignty of God.

More than this, he appeals implicitly to the doctrine of divine simplicity: in our case, rulers have an end outside themselves, to which their legislation is subordinate; but 'the end or *telos* of divine government is God himself, and his law is nothing other than himself'. The *telos* of the universe is to be found in the subsistent goodness of God himself (1.103.2).

For Thomas, it seems, even the Mosaic Law and the Law of the Gospel, let alone natural and human law, are located in the context of eternal law: namely, God himself. Once again, everything in Christian doctrine is related back to God (ST 1.1.7). As the space devoted to them indicate, the Mosaic Law and the New Law are the phenomena at the forefront of theological attention. But neither may be discussed, Thomas thinks, except in the light of the eternal law which is nothing other than God himself, nothing other than the divine light in which the blessed see God.

Granted that 'everything in the world is subject to divine providence and so is regulated and measured by eternal law', it follows that 'everything participates in some way (*aliqualiter*) in eternal law, namely by its impact on them giving them tendencies (*inclinationes*) to their own proper acts and ends'. The kind of creature that we human beings are 'is subject to divine providence in (so to speak) a more excellent way, inasmuch as it even becomes a sharer in providence, providing for itself and for others' (*in quantum et ipsa fit providentiae particeps, sibi ipsi et aliis providens*). Thomas redescribes this: 'there is in us a participating in the eternal reason, by our having a natural inclination to our due activity and end'. And this 'participation in eternal law that is to be found in rational creatures' is what Thomas calls 'natural law'.

Moreover, this is what the Psalmist means, in one of Thomas's favourite mantra-like texts: 'The light of thy countenance, Lord, is signed upon us' (*Signatum est super nos lumen vultus tui*) – 'as if the light of natural reason by which we discern what is good and what evil is nothing other than an impression of the divine light in us'.

Thus it is clear, Thomas concludes, that 'natural law is nothing other than the sharing in the eternal law in the case of rational creatures'.

In short, Thomas's concept of natural law is thoroughly theological, and his appeal is to Scripture (Romans 2:14; Psalm 4:6), not to philosophical authorities or considerations.

One thesis Thomas discusses is to the effect that natural law for human beings is superfluous: the eternal law surely suffices for the government of the human race. He rejects this line of thought: it would work very well if natural law were something quite separate from eternal law but that is just what he refuses to accept: natural law is 'participation in eternal law, in some sense' (*quaedam participatio ejus*). Of course this is not the point that he is making; but it is plain that he would not endorse the idea of a natural law ethics which is autonomous and independent of theological considerations. There may well be room for a theology-free ethics, drawing even on Thomas's distinction between nature and grace; but it seems not to be envisaged here.

Time and again, the eternal law is identified with God himself. Everything created by God is subject to the eternal law but it makes no sense to say that anything divine is either subject to the eternal law or otherwise: 'all that is attributed to the divine essence or nature does not fall under the eternal law, in reality they are the eternal law' (1–2.93.4). God and the eternal law are identical. 'The Son of God', meaning the second person of the divine Trinity, 'is not subject to the eternal law but rather is himself the eternal law' (93.4). The *ratio* of divine providence is the eternal law (93.5).

Turning more specifically to ourselves, Thomas maintains that we all have 'some notion of the eternal law' and secondly we all have within us some bent (*inclinatio*) towards what is consonant with the eternal law (93.6).

It might seem that no one recognizes the eternal law but God himself (93.2). On the contrary, citing Augustine's claim that 'a notion of the eternal law is imprinted on us', Thomas concedes that no one except God and the blessed who see God face to face can recognize the eternal law as it is in itself (its being identical with God himself), yet there are degrees of dawning of its light. For that matter, again following Augustine, 'any knowledge of truth is, so to speak, a ray and share in the eternal law which is the unchangeable truth'; but, more specifically, since everyone has knowledge of truth, *aliqualiter*, we all know the common principles of the natural law, more or less.

Citing Aristotle – 'we are adapted by nature to receive virtues' – Thomas insists that we have a natural instinct for virtue (*inclinatio naturalis ad virtutem*), which may indeed be 'spoilt by a vicious habit', just as our natural knowledge of good is 'darkened by the passions and habits of sin' (93.6).

It may be noted, however, that, for Thomas at least, 'sin never takes away the entire good of [human] nature' (93.6). There always remains a certain *inclinatio ad agendum ea quae sunt legis aeternae*.

The same point is repeated, this time explicitly referring to the natural law: as regards the commonest principles of the natural law, recognized by everyone, the natural law 'can never be deleted from the human heart' (94.6). We may be prevented from doing the right thing in this or that particular instance, for example by lust or some other passion. As regards the less commonly recognized principles (not that Thomas spells out what these are at all adequately), he allows that they may indeed be 'deleted from the human heart', 'either by evil counsel or by perverse customs and corrupt habits'. Robbery is not counted as sin among some people; sins against nature are not always recognized as such. (It looks as if these are secondary principles of the natural law.)

It is perfectly possible that legislators have passed wrongful enactments against secondary precepts of the natural law. Here, clearly, for Thomas, legislation may, at least in some instances, run against the requirements of natural justice. Unfortunately, he does not provide examples, either real or imagined, such as we should need to take the discussion any further.

Though Thomas sometimes speaks of 'precepts' it is more usual for him to refer to 'inclinations': something between psychology and ontology, somewhere on the range between instincts and existential orientations. When he considers the 'content', or the 'extent', of 'the order of the precepts of the natural law' he equates it with the 'order of the natural inclinations' – the instincts and ontological orientations of the human creature (94.2). These turn out to be, first, 'the tendency towards the good of the nature which we share with all other beings' – to preserve our lives; secondly, at the level of the life we share with other animals – 'nature has taught all animals to mate, to bring up their young, and suchlike'; and thirdly, as rational animals, we have a natural inclination to know the truth about God and to live in community, which means that 'it is a matter of the natural law that we have an inclination, for instance, to avoid ignorance, not to offend those with whom one ought to live amicably, and other such related matters'.

We might be tempted to identify divine law with eternal law. In Thomas's usage, however, divine law means the Old Law and the New Law: the whole body of Mosaic legislation, not merely the Decalogue, but including the moral, liturgical, legal and political requirements and prescriptions (ST 1–2. 98–105), and the New Law (106–114, shading into the Gospel).[14] At least in terms of space, he has much more to say about Torah and Gospel than about Natural Law. In fact, as has been clear at least since Chenu pointed it out to students of Aquinas, the growing importance of the Old Testament for Thomas's theology cannot be over-estimated.[15] Partly, no doubt, since the Cathars rejected the Old Testament, mainstream theologians were prompted to study it more assiduously. Mainly, of course, since the Bible was read as a whole, and the Christian dispensation was constantly interpreted as the fulfilment of the Covenant, the Law of Moses, the Prophets and the Wisdom books, Thomas was only an heir to a long tradition of typological exegesis.[16]

As regards the Mosaic Law, Thomas has little to say in his Commentary on the *Sentences* (1256); the massive treatment in the *Summa*

Theologiae is new, and due no doubt to his study of the *Summa* of the Franciscan Alexander of Hales, posthumously completed about 1260 by two of his students.[17]

In sum, in the *Summa Theologiae*, Thomas presents the natural law in the context of Torah and the New Law of the Holy Spirit, in the wider context of an account of the virtues (theological and cardinal) as the moral agent's journey to face-to-face vision with God, all framed by the presupposition that the natural law is a participation in the eternal law which is identical with God himself.

Ethical Naturalism

So it seems, on the face of it. Nevertheless, the thesis that Thomas's doctrine of natural law is completely separable from Christian theology remains an option, capably expounded and defended by Anthony J. Lisska.[18]

Lisska provides an excellent overview of recent interest in Aristotelian ethics, starting with Anscombe's 'Modern Moral Philosophy' and MacIntyre's *After Virtue*. He links natural law ethics with contemporary jurisprudence and philosophy of law. He expounds the reconstruction of natural law ethics by John Finnis, Germain Grisez and Joseph Boyle, continuing with Henry Veatch's objections to their 'revisionist Thomism' (objections he clearly endorses).[19] He has a substantial discussion of human rights and natural law, including the work of Maritain. Throughout, however, taking a hint from a paper by Columba Ryan, Lisska contends that natural law is not something either in the human heart or in the mind of God but a philosophical concept offering an answer to the question of what makes laws possible at all: 'It is the ontological foundation in human nature which explains the possibility of a moral theory and of lawmaking in the first place'. Roughly speaking, Ryan asked the Kantian question: what is necessary theoretically in order to make lawmaking possible? And Thomas, as Lisska reads him, comes back with an Aristotelian response: the possibility of lawmaking is grounded in a theory of human nature.[20]

Far from being based on Christian theology, so Lisska maintains, Thomas's natural law ethics is a version of ethical naturalism, based on a revision of Aristotle's metaphysical account of human nature. Citing Ryan again, suggesting that 'human nature, upon which the whole fabric of the natural law is based, may change and develop', Lisska likes the implied emphasis on the contingent nature of moral decision making: as moral agents, we may have to confront radically new situations in which 'conclusions earlier drawn [from the general principles of natural law] may, in the changed circumstances, have no further application, or only a modified application'.

This seems a considerable distance from the ecclesiastical appropriation of the doctrine feared by Michael Keeling, for example. On the other hand, significantly, the concept of divine providence is not listed in Lisska's index. He constantly glosses the eternal law as a quasi-Platonic set of archetypes, analogous to the Forms, which are found as the divine ideas in God's mind. He seems not to attach much importance to the texts where Thomas identifies eternal law with God, not just with archetypes. For Lisska, Thomas argues for a 'humanist' account of moral theory, which is based upon reason alone.

Back to Theology

According to John Bowlin, in another excellent book, we must not ignore the theological background. Far from being an attempt to provide a morality common to all human beings, a perfectly worthy venture, Thomas was out to provide an exegetical principle for discerning those elements of Torah still incumbent upon Christians.[21]

When we read Thomas it must be in awareness of his otherness, Bowlin contends. For example, he argues that doubts about our most basic moral obligations should not motivate our philosophical inquiry into the character of the moral life. We do not need to be told, by philosophers or anyone else, what our most basic obligations are. It would be insulting to be told how they are justified. We should regard with suspicion anyone whose scepticism about the rightness or wrongness of certain courses of action needed to be supported by moral theories. Perhaps we might not be able to say much about the basis of the obligations that we recognize, but that would not prevent us from thinking that there are some things we should do, others we should never do. Basic obligations aside, of course we rapidly disagree in the specifics, nor should that surprise us. Thomas, at any rate, is not offering to remove basic doubt about good and evil in human action, or to guide conduct in the particular. He is trying to educate Christians who by definition have an untroubled belief in moral realism, and who are to be pastors, hearing confessions, providing spiritual advice, and so on. What he offers is an account of why it is difficult to know what is right and wrong in particular circumstances because of what we are like and what the hindrances and helps are: the moral life, as he says (ST 1–2. 6). If we assume that doubts about obligation motivate our interest in moral philosophy and in natural law ethics, we are surely only looking for security, Bowlin thinks. When the basic inclinations which Thomas describes are turned into the specific prescriptions and prohibitions of our common human nature, then our access to the content of moral obligation in the concrete may seem to be freed from dispute – but are Thomas's considerations intended to dispel basic doubts about what we are to do? According to Bowlin, Thomas is not out to secure us against moral scepticism (an entirely modern project), nor on the other hand does he think his natural law considerations provide an adequate basis for moral guidance. On the contrary, the rest of the *secunda pars*, or rather the *secunda pars* as a whole, shows why a moral agent relying only on natural law – on what we all regard as basically required (no doubt about that, Bowlin thinks) – finds it so difficult to make moral decisions, or to appreciate what decision making involves, or to understand what it is to be good in the first place.

Bowlin reminds us of how the *secunda pars* unrolls. God made us for beatitude, that is to say, for the perfect activity of our highest or deepest powers, with the assistance of 'law', analogously understood, inscribed as 'inclinations' in our nature as rational creatures, partly translatable into legislation by the political community, revealed as Torah and Gospel, in the historical economy of salvation, with the deforming virtues of faith, hope, and charity, and the cardinal virtues – all badly disrupted in our sin-prone condition.

As Thomas remarked, in his last recorded notes on natural law:

> Now although God in creating man gave him this law of nature, the devil oversowed another law in man, namely the law of concupiscence . . . Since then the law of nature was destroyed by concupiscence, man needed to be brought back to works of virtue, and to be drawn away from vice: for which purpose he needed the written law.[22]

That sounds somewhat less than ethical naturalism grounded on human reason. But the conflicting interpretations continue to flourish, at an unprecedentedly high level of philosophical rigour and sophistication.

It is tempting to agree with Servais Pinckaers, however, that abstracting Thomas's questions on natural law from those on the Old Law and the New Law, and from the questions on beatitude and virtue, produces nothing but confusion, and that, whatever happened after his day, he never saw natural law as functioning independently of the eternal law which is nothing other than the creator. But it would be premature to opt for one interpretation rather than one of the many others, in what is currently perhaps the most contested topic in Thomas's work.

One might even be tempted to go back to the finest study of Thomas's theology of law, untranslated into English, by the Protestant scholar, Ulrich Kühn. He places himself in a line of distinguished Protestant studies of aspects of Thomas's theology: H. Lyttkens on analogy (1953), Per-Erik Persson on the relationship between faith and reason (1957), Thomas Bonhoeffer on the doctrine of God (1961), and H. Vorster comparing Thomas and Luther on the concept of freedom (1965).[23] He notes that, although the literature created the impression that neo-Thomism was the only way of reading Thomas, indeed as if not just Cajetan but Thomas himself took a stand against Luther, Thomas nevertheless 'belongs among the fathers of Protestant theology', and 'deserves to be listened to as a pre Reformation theologian, not as a voice in the chorus of post-Tridentine theology'.

Kühn welcomes the work of Catholic scholars, naming S. Pfürtner, Otto Hermann Pesch, E.H. Schillebeeckx, B. Decker and G. Söhngen, as showing that, from within Thomist scholarship itself, Thomas was being freed from the anti-Reformation apologetics which he thinks distorted received neo-Thomist interpretations.

His own study begins with a remark by Heinrich Maria Christmann, in 1958, regretting that Thomas had been pictured for so long more as a philosopher than a theologian – agreeing, then, explicitly with Chenu's insistence, in 1950, that he is more a theologian than a philosopher. He takes us back to Gilson's Aberdeen Gifford Lectures, and insists that Thomas's theology has to be read as the fructification of contemplative study: the teaching of a saint, theologian, mystic. This 'new picture of Thomas' is largely an achievement of French theology, culminating in the sidelining of neo-Thomism prior to Vatican II – indeed this 'new Thomas-understanding' was an element in the 'revolution' of Vatican II, so Kühn thinks.

Kühn traces the history of the idea of natural law through Thomas's work. In the Commentary on the *Sentences* and on Matthew, he shows, law is treated in the light of the virtue of Christ. In the *Summa Contra Gentiles* and in the *Compendium Theologiae* law is treated in the light of God as creator. In the *Summa Theologiae*, by contrast, law is discussed neither in Christology nor in *de Deo creatore*, but in the context of the theology of the moral agent as *imago Dei* returning to God; law is the exterior principle that moves the human being to do well, ultimately to attain beatitude in the communion of saints. Law is oriented to beatitude. Natural law is a kind of reflection of the eternal law – requiring to be taken up into the Mosaic Law, oriented then towards the promise of salvation; and then to be taken into the New Law, in which the believer is instructed by the teaching of Christ interiorized by the Spirit received in the sacraments, the inward grace that allows us to keep the Law and thus attain the righteousness. The essence of what Thomas means is that the New Law is an interior law of God giving himself freely in love to human beings who respond to God's will in complete 'autonomy' – Thomas needs both the metaphysical and the Old Testament.

Whatever Luther feared, Thomas's theology was not entirely subjugated by pagan philosophy. Kühn explains the difference between Thomas and Luther as follows.[24] For Luther sinners become friends of God not only by receiving the divine gift of charity but by the light of the Cross. That we are righteous is something that transcends us: 'righteousness is extrinsic to us' (*justitia extra nos posita*). Thomas, obviously, does not deny the transcendence of Christ is righteousness; but he certainly denies that our being justified is nothing other than Christ's righteousness. There is a sense in which we are ourselves actually justified: righteousness is intrinsic to us, so to speak. For Luther, however, 'all our righteousness is to be sought *extra nos*'. In practice, so Kühn argues, the absence of this '*extra nos*' in Thomas's theology means that his appeal to the image of God is not in the end controlled as it should be by explicit trust in the mercy of God revealed in Christ's Passion. This does not mean that Christ has no place in Thomas's understanding of the relationship between the righteous and God. On the contrary, Kuhn contends, the friendship between the righteous and God rests in nothing other than the grace given through Christ's Passion. Thomas's personal faith is certainly centred on Christ crucified; but his theology, Kühn holds, is not a *theologia crucis*, Cross-centred, as Luther's is.[25]

In short, when Thomas reaches the question of natural law, it is long after he has put in place his theology of beatitude and virtue; he takes natural law to be self-evidently participation in divine providence and always already requiring deeper instruction by the Law of Moses and by 'the Law of the Gospel', as he calls it, 'the grace of the Holy Spirit given inwardly' (1–2.106.1–2). But, for Kühn, Thomas's discussion is not explicitly Christological enough.

Chapter 7

THEOLOGICAL ETHICS

One of the challenges thrown out by Karl Barth was to question the very idea of doing Christian ethics separately from dogmatic theology.[1] In the *Summa Theologiae*, Thomas Aquinas considered the human being's 'movement into God' between the consideration of God (including the coming forth of creatures from God) and the consideration of Christ, 'who as man is the way for us to move into God' (ST 1.2 prologue). This deliberate insertion of moral theology between doctrine of God and Christology has not proved altogether successful.

Thomas and Barth

James M. Gustafson draws attention to 'important affinities and differences' between his own 'Barthian' theological ethics and that of the Catholic tradition following Thomas Aquinas.[2]

Both Thomas and Barth composed ethics in the light of their understanding of God and God's relationship to the world. For Thomas the theological character of ethics is rooted in his fundamental belief that everything proceeds from and returns to God: God as the world's *principium et finis*. For Karl Barth the focus is not on creation but on salvation history: God as commanding and human beings as hearing and obeying. Moral norms are objective for Thomas, because they are grounded in the moral ordering of creaturely nature, and especially of human nature: a view Barth rejects. For Barth, God is related to the world primarily through human beings. For Thomas, by contrast, human beings are related to God, in an important way, through the ordering of nature.

As Gustafson emphasizes, Thomas's understanding of the ordering of nature is theologically grounded: as coming from and returning to God all things are ordered to their ends as God has created them.

This, according to Gustafson, is the chief difference between Thomas and Barth. For both, our responsibility as moral agents is to conform our action to God's will, but they differ over how that will may be discovered. For Barth, what God wills is revealed in the Bible, and on any given occasion our obedience will always be in accordance with God's grace as historically demonstrated in Jesus Christ; whereas for Thomas, for whom the created order is (of course) an effect of God's freely given self-diffusing goodness, human attention to the world is more 'revealing' than anything in Scripture by itself. For Barth, 'the words and acts of God given in particular occasions ground the objective ethics theologically, whereas for Thomas it is the mind of God in which the natural moral law and the revealed law in the Bible participate that grounds objective ethics theologically'. In brief: 'The mediation of the ultimate ground of ethics for Thomas is through continuities and relationships that persist, through laws, and not through the immediacy of a direct command'.

Virtue Ethics

Anyone who studied moral philosophy in the 1950s and 1960s would remember being confronted with a choice: utilitarianism or deontology, John Stuart Mill or Kant, the right course of action decided by calculating the benefit to others or by considering one's duty.[3]

Since then, however, English-language philosophy has witnessed a remarkable renewal of 'virtue ethics': with the focus neither on the happy outcome nor on the purity of the intention of one's moral action but on the kind of person one's action exhibits and requires one to be. The debate was inaugurated by G.E.M. Anscombe's provocative essay.[4]

Dismissing utilitarianism (consequentialism as she renamed it) as barely worthy of attention, Anscombe focused on exposing Kantian duty-for-duty's-sake as continuing, surreptitiously, to feed off the kind of divine command ethics we noted in Barth. It was senseless for philosophers, who bracketed out or had abandoned belief in divine law, to go on arguing about duty, obligation, the categorical imperative, and so on. True, she says, Protestants at the time of the Reformation did not deny the existence of divine law, but they believed that this law was given by God, not to be obeyed, but to demonstrate sinful humankind's incapacity to obey it, even by grace. They believed that Christ was 'only to be trusted in as a mediator, not obeyed as legislator': a doctrine (she notes) condemned at the Council of Trent.[5]

Anscombe proposed, in effect, that the best course for philosophers in a post-Christian culture who sought a completely secular ethics was to reconsider Plato and Aristotle. We should then find, reading them, that 'philosophically there is a huge gap, at present unfillable as far as we are concerned' – a gap which needs to be filled, she contends, by 'an account of human nature, human action, the type of characteristic a virtue is, and above all of human "flourishing"'.

Hitherto, Aristotle's determinative notion of *eudaimonia* (literally: 'having a good guardian spirit'), conventionally translated as 'happiness', was coloured, inevitably, by the modern concept of happiness as a subjectively pleasant life. Indeed, in the 1950s, there were philosophers who expounded Aristotle's ethics as a kind of utilitarian hedonism. Anscombe's conception, like Aristotle's own, of what it is for a human being to 'flourish', focuses on what constitutes the good life: on the life which attains and manifests the good. What is required, then, in the study of ethics, is an account of what human beings must be like, if they have the capacities to achieve this goal.

Ironically, some philosophers, in the van of virtue ethics, notably Bernard Williams and Martha Craven Nussbaum, think that, in rejecting Kantian duty-for-duty's-sake ethics, they are rejecting Christian ethics as such. This is not surprising: even in Roman Catholic moral theology, where Thomism was vaunted as the only authoritative perspective, concern with law, will, rules, obedience, and so on, completely overshadowed interest in happiness, character, reason, virtue, and so on. Obviously, most of the discussion revolves round ancient philosophy; but there is now a significant body of literature involving Thomas.[6]

The renewal of interest in Thomas's analysis of virtue began with Peter Geach's Stanton lectures at Cambridge in the early 1970s. His exposition follows the *secunda pars* of the *Summa Theologiae* quite closely. He opens with what was then, and for most philosophers still is, an extremely provocative question: 'What are men for?' – contending vigorously that there is no good reason for rejecting a neo-Aristotelian doctrine of natural teleology as obsolete. On the contrary, he argues, a moral code that ignores the built-in teleologies of human nature cannot but lead to moral disaster. He then deals in turn with the virtues of faith, hope, charity, prudence, justice, temperance and courage: very much a recapitulation of Thomas's work. Geach writes, explicitly, as a philosopher, though bringing in theological considerations.

At the only significant point where Geach dissents from Thomas he denounces the argument for the unity of the virtues as 'both odious and preposterous'.[7] For Thomas, if you lack any one of the cardinal virtues then you will lack them all; or at any rate the others will be defective. If a man lacks courage is he likely to be just or chaste? If a woman lacks Thomas's virtue of *prudentia*, is she likely to exercise the virtues of justice, temperance and fortitude sensibly? And if she does not practise these virtues sensibly, does she really have them at all?

Plausible as this view may seem, it holds, Geach contends, only if people formed their judgements with rigorous consistency – but 'thank God that they do not'. Indeed, for that matter, not all wrong judgement is bad: 'inconsistency in the right place may save a man from worse errors than if he were not there inconsistent'. For example: 'How much more affliction tyrants would cause if their minions were sea-green incorruptibles, flawlessly efficient and indefatigably industrious!'.

The Secunda Pars

Peter Geach's return to Thomas is little cited; perhaps he expressed himself too abrasively. A much more successful impetus to reconsidering Thomas comes from within the medievalists' guild. 'The great *Summa*', Mark Jordan remarks, 'was written, in some sense, for the sake of writing the *secunda pars*'.[8] By this he means that the point of the whole project lies in Thomas's desire to rethink the treatises on virtues and especially vices in circulation in his day in the light of the account of action, intention and the good that he found in Aristotle's *Ethics*.

The contents page of the *Summa* reveals that beatitude, will, virtue, and so on, and in due course law, grace, and so on, are discussed at great length in the *secunda pars*, thus located between the doctrine of God (including creation) in the *prima pars* and the doctrine of Christ and the sacraments (concluding with the unwritten eschatology) in the *tertia*.

This was an innovation. It might seem better, as it does to many modern theologians, to place Christian ethics and spirituality after Christology. Here, however, instead of treating moral theology as a kind of sequel, Thomas nests 'the movement of the reasoning creature into the divine mystery' between the doctrine of God and the doctrine of Christ (ST 1. 2).

Thomas had not previously composed anything quite like the *secunda pars*. Leonard Boyle has argued, very plausibly, that the *Summa Theologiae* was created for the guidance of ordinary Dominican friars, those who were not to spend their lives in academic pursuits but would be engaged in preaching and hearing confessions:

> By prefacing the *secunda* or 'moral' part with a *prima pars* on God, Trinity and Creation, and then rounding it off with a *tertia pars* on the Son of

God, Incarnation and the Sacraments, Thomas put practical theology, the
study of Christian man, his virtues and vices, in a full theological context.[9]

Unwilling to leave these future pastors with nothing more than the many
confessional handbooks of the day, Thomas wanted to ensure that they
should have their 'practical theology' firmly inserted between what he
often elsewhere speaks of as the two mysteries of faith: the triune
Godhead and the mystery of the Incarnation. Furthermore, Thomas
wanted to blow open the received expositions of vices and virtues (often
in terms of the Ten Commandments). Instead of concentrating on a
catalogue of sins to be assessed for gravity in terms of disobedience to
divine law, he offers a character sketch of the moral agent as such,
drawing especially on Aristotle's *Ethics*. In effect, he sought to develop
an ethics based, not on obedience to this or that divine command, but
in terms of the formation of the kind of person who appropriates and
develops the gifts required for a moral life in view of the promised enjoyment of divine beatitude. His interest is not in the rules we have to follow
but in the kind of people we become, as we practise this or that virtue
or vice – of course in accordance with this or that expression of the divine
law but principally in accomplishing the good in which alone is our ultimate happiness. Thomas tried to deconstruct the sin-dominated moral
theology in the pastors' handbooks of his day, by dispersing the standard list of vices and virtues throughout a systematic consideration of
the human being as moral agent, with goals, capacities, emotions, dispositions, and so on, which have to be integrated, with the help of law
and grace, for them to attain the beatitude which is their ultimate end
(cf. ST 1–2.1).

Thomas's moral theology, thus, is founded not on God's law (biblically revealed or built into creaturely nature) but focused on God's
promise of perfect beatitude (revealed by Christ but best understood as
the divinely given fulfilment of an Aristotelian conception of human
flourishing). Of course, law comes into it; natural law, for Thomas, is
a kind of inscription in rational creatures of eternal law, which is the
divine plan for bringing such creatures to enjoy the beatitude which
they naturally desire but which is granted only by divine grace (cf. ST
1–2.91.2).

More needs to be said, to fill out the picture. But it is not surprising
that Thomas's Christian ethics, the *secunda pars*, opens with a study of
'uncreated beatitude': the 'happiness' which is the ultimate goal of
human life is nothing other than sharing the bliss which is God's own
life. Thomas offers a moral theology, a Christian ethics, centred on one's
becoming the kind of person who would be fulfilled only in the promised
bliss of face-to-face vision of God. It includes obedience to divine law,

as a matter of course, but placed in the context of responding to the gift of divine beatitude.

As it turned out, Thomas was not very successful. To judge by the disproportionate number of surviving copies, the *secunda secundae* seems to have circulated widely on its own. Thus, not only was the *secunda pars* disengaged from the *Summa Theologiae* as a whole, defeating Thomas's purpose of studying moral theology in the middle of the exposition of Christian doctrine, but copies of the *secunda secundae* seem to have been read independently of the *prima secundae*. That is to say, the detailed phenomenology of the specific virtues and vices was studied independently of the preliminary consideration of beatitude, moral agency, and virtue.

From the outset and for centuries afterwards, Thomas's attempt to educate the clergy by replacing the handy lists of sins with a picture of the kind of people God desires, locating this in the middle of courses on the Trinity and the Incarnation, failed to make headway. The clergy preferred to take the *secunda secundae* on its own, reducing it more or less to what Thomas wanted to replace. Even then, it was apparently soon regarded as much too long. By 1290, at the behest of the Master of the Order, even Dominican friars were provided with a slimmed-down version of the *secunda secundae*.

Nature

To assess the role of Aristotle's philosophy in Thomas's exposition of Christian doctrine is never easy. It is a much contested but quite plausible thesis that Thomas's commentary on Aristotle's *Ethics* is an attempt at a self-standing moral philosophy – not of course one that Thomas expected to satisfy him, as a Christian, but an experiment to test how far a pre-Christian account goes.[10]

It is a different move to try (as some have done) to extricate from Thomas's theology a purely philosophical ethics. Denis Bradley, in his recent excellent book, insists that, though Thomas depends on Aristotle's *Ethics* to a great extent, his frequently expressed Christian belief that the final end of human beings is the bliss of seeing God face to face as the New Testament promises is so radically different from anything we might propose as what Aristotle envisaged for *eudaimonia*, that no independent moral philosophy can be extracted from Thomas's theological ethics.[11]

Bradley deals at some length with the dispute between Gilson and van Steenberghen on whether there can be a Christian philosophy and what such a thing might be. In the end, what decides the issue, Bradley thinks, is how we take Thomas's conception of the relationship between a natural happiness and the beatific vision of God. Thomas holds that human beings have a natural desire for the vision of God which they are naturally incapable of fulfilling on their own, without grace. It is a desire fulfilled for them, so to speak, by divine intervention. Any attempt to isolate a purely philosophical ethics from Thomas's work has to negotiate the conclusion that the moral life is to be led in view of a goal which is unachievable.

On one fairly common view, all the same, Thomas's ethical system is regarded as pretty indistinguishable from Aristotle's, with a few changes in virtues and vices: meekness as a Christian virtue, rather than Aristotle's admiration for the 'great-souled' man, and suchlike.

On the standard account, after all, Thomas is best known for demonstrating the existence of God as First Cause of all things: natural theology. He is equally well known for holding that morality is founded on natural law. We might be tempted to think, then, that the clue to uncovering the internal coherence of Thomas's *Summa Theologiae* (if there is such a thing) might lie in the effects of the concept of 'nature'.

This would not be totally implausible. The proposal would go as follows. Thomas mounts his arguments for the existence of God by considering features of the natural world. He considers the divine nature before turning to the doctrine of God as Trinity. He investigates human nature at great length (ST 1.75–102; 1–2. 1–2.70), again before considering what one might regard as the characteristically biblical interest in sin (1–2. 71–89). He believes in the reasoning creature's natural desire for knowledge of the cause of all things. He reaches what he has to say about grace, conversion, justification of the unrighteous, and so on, only after considering the notion of law, at some length, including that of natural law. And so on.

If there is a single notion that runs all the way through, underpinning one consideration after another, it is surely the notion of 'nature'. If Thomas's doctrine of God has any internal link with his ethics, natural theology and natural law might seem to be the connection. That would fit well with the standard understanding of Thomas as primarily a philosopher.

Prudence

Thomas pays a great deal of attention to the virtue of practical wisdom: *prudentia*, Aristotle's *phronesis*. The word *prudens*, as Thomas knew, is a contraction of the word *providens*. Explaining the biblical doctrine of divine providence, he even identifies *prudentia* and *providentia* (ST

1.22.1). It might be suggested, then, that the virtue of prudence and the divine attribute of providence might be a link between Thomas's theological ethics and doctrine of God.

His account of providence starts from the world's being created 'good': it is not only in the existence of things that goodness is found but also in their being ordered to an end, namely their final end, which is the divine goodness (ST 1.22.1). By now, in the *Summa*, we have established that it is by his mind (*per suum intellectum*) that God is the cause of things; we have also seen that the plan for things moving towards their end must pre-exist in the divine mind. This plan is what we mean by providence.

Now the proper function of prudence, Thomas goes on to say, citing Aristotle, is to arrange things to an end: one is said to be prudent if one adapts one's actions to the goal of one's life.

God is the ultimate end, there is no providence or prudence as regards himself; but the plan of ordaining things to their end – that is divine providence. In this sense we can attribute *prudentia* or *providentia* to God.

The word 'prudence', of course, at least in the English language, has the wrong connotations: sometimes a virtue, often more like a vice, it means a habit of being circumspect and discreet, careful above all to avoid undesired consequences of a decision. For Thomas, *prudentia* is a virtue of the utmost necessity for human life. His account goes as follows:

> To live well means acting well. In order to perform an act well, it is not merely what people do that matters, but also how they do it, namely that they act from right choice and not merely from impulse or passion. Since, however, choice is about means to an end, rightness of choice necessarily involves two factors, namely a due end and something suitably ordained to that due end . . . For people to be rightly adapted to what fits their due end, however, they need a disposition in their reason; because counsel and choice, which are about things ordained to an end, are acts of reason. Consequently, an intellectual virtue is needed in their reason to complement it and make it well adjusted to these things. This virtue is prudence. And this, in consequence, is necessary for a good life.
>
> (ST 1–2.57.5)

Herbert McCabe helpfully suggests that Thomas's concept of *prudentia* is what Jane Austen means by 'good sense'. He writes as follows:

> Elizabeth Bennett is shown as having and growing in good sense, in contrast both to the silliness of her younger sisters, who think of nothing beyond present pleasures and, on the other hand, to the pedantry of her elder sister Mary, who thinks that book learning is enough. She also stands

in contrast to her witty and perceptive but almost purely voyeuristic father, who uses his intelligence to survey a life in which he refuses to become involved. Finally, there is a contrast with her friend Charlotte, who succumbs to worldly wisdom and marries the dreadful Mr Collins for 'prudential' reasons. All these people are presented as morally inferior (and thus ultimately unhappy) because they lack good sense.[12]

Perhaps no single word will do; we need stories, as McCabe suggests, in which people either do or do not show 'good judgement'. Translators of Aristotle try 'practical wisdom'; yet here too the phrase has to be filled out, as for example by Nussbaum.[13] Against Plato's attempt (understandable at the time) to discover and articulate a completely non-context-relative concept of the good, which would be the focus of a unitary quasi-science of ethics, so she seeks to show, Aristotle highlights the skill of grasping the salient features of a complex situation, relying on long experience of resourceful and responsive decision making – practical insight, more like sense-perception than deductive scientific knowledge.

There is nothing abstruse or esoteric about Thomas's notion of *prudentia*, then; he is only describing a perfectly familiar feature of many people's character.

As usual, the Aristotelian insight is paralleled elsewhere: for example, in the monastic tradition of biblical exegesis and the ascetic life. Picking up texts such as Hebrews 4:12 ('For the word of God is quick, and powerful, and sharper than any two-edged sword, piercing even to the dividing asunder of soul and spirit, and of the joints and marrow, and is a discerner of the thoughts and intents of the heart'), the early Christians stressed the importance of the skill of discernment. Incorporating insights from the Stoics, such as Cicero and Seneca, the notion of *discretio* (discrimination) comes through monastic authors such as John Cassian, the author of the Benedictine Rule, Gregory the Great, and others, to the friars and then on to the agenda of the university theology faculties in the thirteenth century, decisively helped of course by the pre-Reformation interest in the Wisdom Books of the Bible. No doubt Thomas's emphasis on the centrality of practical wisdom in the moral life was never completely forgotten. Nevertheless, in the 1930s, led by Thomists associated with Le Saulchoir, there was a renewal of interest, proposing Thomas's focus on practical wisdom as the alternative to the then dominant approaches in Roman Catholic moral theology, mostly law-centred.

This emphasis on the virtue of prudence, thus on personal qualities of discretion, practical wisdom and good sense, was not all good news to those more set on retaining the traditional (post-Tridentine) moral theology, with its stress on the objectivity and absoluteness of moral principles. On the contrary, this prudence-based ethics seemed to some much too likely to succumb to subjectivism. Instead of taking the expert interpretation of a rule as basic in moral dilemmas, the Thomist position was in the end finally to appeal to the judgement of a wise person.

Thomists like M.-D. Chenu and J. Tonneau among many others, lamented the failure in the 1950s to understand the originality of Thomas's moral considerations. Chenu tells us how shocked he was by the rigid and systematic way in which exponents of the *secunda pars* detailed the Aristotelian language of the presentation while paying little or no attention to the biblical and patristic spirituality of the text. Tonneau regretted having to acknowledge how many Thomists were able to read and expound the text without having a glimmer of its originality and significance.[14]

Among excellent studies in English of Thomas's doctrine of prudence we should note Mahoney in *Seeking the Spirit*, connecting prudence with wisdom and discernment and the gifts of the Holy Spirit. More recently still, we have the outstandingly good book by Daniel Westberg.[15] Partly, this is a comparison of Thomas's interpretation of Aristotle's account of practical reason, *phronesis*, with lines of interpretation in recent Aristotelian scholarship (D.J. Allan, R.-A. Gauthier, Anthony Kenny, David Charles, M.C. Nussbaum). Mainly, however, the thesis is that the moral-spiritual life, as well as reflection on it, depends on the practice of the virtue of prudence and not on knowledge of natural law, especially not modern, perhaps Suárezian, notions of natural law, according to which Aquinas's moral theology would be based on the premise that natural law alone suffices to generate a complete code of human conduct, provided that one expends sufficient intellectual energy on deriving specific conclusions from general principles. No such natural law ethics is to be found in Aquinas.

That practical wisdom is so central in Thomas's understanding of the moral life reflects his repeated emphasis on the wisdom as well as on the will of God. He sees a certain analogy between divine providence and the habitual practice of the prudent human being: an analogy, however, that seems not to do much work. It does not look like the key concept that establishes the unity of the three parts of the *Summa Theologiae*.

The Image of God

The prologue to the *secunda pars* makes it abundantly clear that the starting point is actually the human creature as image of God, insofar as we are authors of our moral lives. Having considered the 'exemplar', Thomas says, namely 'God and what has come forth by his power according to his will', we now proceed to consider the 'copy', 'insofar as we too are sources of our own works, as having freedom of choice and power over our own deeds' (ST 1–2. prologue).

Perhaps this is where to look for the key to the inner coherence of Thomas's theology. He begins by quoting John of Damascus, as always the voice of Greek patristic theology, to the effect that our being made in the image of God means our having minds, free will and autonomy.

The point in the *secunda pars*, we might then say, is to present the human creature as moral agent, not in terms of human nature, but explicitly in the light of the relationship between the human being as *imago Dei* and God as exemplar, and all with an emphasis on freedom, divine and created, and against the background of the patristic tradition.

As regards the 'image of God' theme, Thomas takes Genesis 1:26 as his authority: 'Let us make man to our own image and likeness'; but that does not stop him from offering three fairly plausible objections to the thesis (ST 1.93.1).

Isaiah 40:18 questions the thesis: 'To whom have you likened God? or what image will you make for him?' That is to say, how is talk of God's being 'imaged' in a human being to be distinguished from idolatry? Isaiah is thinking of man-made bodily images, Thomas says; what we are talking about here, however, is the spiritual image to himself that God makes in a human being.

Secondly, we have a text from Colossians 1:15: 'Who is the image of the invisible God, the First-Born of every creature'. Surely Christ alone is the image of God? Indeed, Thomas explains, Christ is 'the perfect image of God, reflecting perfectly that of which he is the image' – which is why he is said to be the image, absolutely, and never *ad imaginem*. The human being, on the other hand, is indeed said to be the image but this is qualified as *ad imaginem* by reason of being an imperfect image. Indeed, the image of God in a human being exists 'as in an alien nature'.

Thirdly, according to Hilary of Poitiers, 'an image is of the same kind as that which it represents'; but there is no kind common to both God and the human creature. In reply to this objection Thomas agrees that a creature is one with God or like God only according to a certain analogy or proportion.

The little word '*ad*' is decisive in the explanation. There is indeed a likeness to God in a human being, not however a perfect but an imperfect likeness; hence the movement, the approach, indicated by '*ad*', the Latin preposition meaning 'towards'. A small bit of grammar carries a good deal of theology.

Every creature, including the animals, bears a certain likeness to God, by being and living; but, properly speaking, intellectual creatures alone are made to God's image (1.93.2).[16]

But there are two more arguments to consider. Again citing Paul (Romans 8:29), what about predestination? And anyway, hasn't the human race lost the image of God by sin?

The latter question, Thomas explains, invites us to distinguish the image of God understood as consisting in the conformity of grace and of glory. The image of God is to be found in human beings in three ways. In the first place, every human being possesses a natural aptitude for understanding and loving God; we are created capable of worshipping our creator; and this aptitude consists in the very nature of the mind, which is common to us all. At this level, so to speak, the image of God is always in a human being, whether or not that person is a sinner. Thomas always resists the doctrine that human beings lost their reason at the 'fall'. For rational animals to be deprived of their minds by sin would be for them to cease to be human at all.[17]

In a second sense, our being in the image of God consists in the conformity of grace, inasmuch as we actually or habitually know and love God, though of course always imperfectly. The image of God in this sense is to be found 'only in the just'. Even now, that is to say, those who have received the divine gifts of faith, hope and charity are, to some degree, with a certain consistency, men and women of faith, characteristically hoping for the promised face-to-face vision of God, and manifestly charitable.

To say that a human being has the *habitus* of faith or of charity does not, of course, mean, as some think, that they have faith or charity as their interior possession, as if God's giving them these gifts had ceased when they received them. All that Thomas means is that, when you know certain people, you see they are usually charitable. Charity has become, for them, almost 'second nature'. The alternative, which Thomas resists, is the idea that having the faith, or being charitable, is always a one-off moment-to-moment event in a quite unpredictable series of episodes. Some people, Thomas thinks, just are charitable: you are not always surprised by how they behave. Many others, as he knows, perform acts of charity from time to time, but only under pressure, unexpectedly or even unwillingly.

Thirdly, our being in the image of God means our knowing and loving God perfectly, something to be found 'only in the blessed' (i.e. in heaven), when the divine image in us would consist in the likeness of glory: 'The light of thy countenance, O lord, is signed upon us' (Psalm 4:7(6)), one of Thomas's favourite quotations.

Thomas next tackles the thesis that the image of God in the human creature is the image of the divine nature, not of the Trinity of persons.

It is unlikely that Thomas has anything like the monotheistic and unitarian God in mind here, of which some theologians would suspect him. He is absolutely clear that the image of God in the human being is Trinitarian – not of God with the Trinity bracketed out, nor of the Son of God, but simply of God as Trinity.

It might seem as if the image of God is not only in the mind but also in the body (93.6). Here, citing Ephesians 4:23,24 and Colossians 3:10, Thomas contends that we are given to understand that the renewal which consists in putting on a new nature is to do with the mind (*metanoia*). So, repeating that in every creature including animals there is a likeness to God by way of a trace, he argues that this is true of human beings as well but the distinctive thing is that, by finding a procession of the word in our minds and a procession of love in our wills there exists an image of the uncreated Trinity – the uncreated Trinity is distinguished by the procession of the Word from the Speaker, and of Love from both of these (cf. 1.28.30).

The point is reinforced in the following article (93.7): 'first and chiefly, the image of the Trinity is to be found in the acts of the soul, that is, inasmuch as from the knowledge which we possess, by actual thought we form an internal word; and thence break forth into love'.

'After all', Thomas writes (93.5), 'in God one nature exists in three persons', so 'being in God's image in the sense of imitating the divine nature does not exclude being in God's image in the sense of representing the three persons; indeed one follows on the other'. Nobody is saying that the image of God in us perfectly represents God; on the contrary, there is the greatest difference between this trinity that is in us and the divine Trinity; but when God the Trinity made us in his own image we are talking about the image of the whole Trinity (*imago totius Trinitatis*). It needs to be underlined that this is a dynamic conception: the human creature images the processions of Word and Spirit within the triune Godhead in his or her acts of understanding and loving.

As Merriell shows, being the image of God as representation of the three Persons refers in the first place to the analogy that holds between the processions of word and love in the mind and the processions of the Persons in God, but includes also an element of configuration, or conformation.[18] For God acts on the mind as the object specifying its acts of understanding and love, perfecting the analogy, the proportionality, between the mind and the Trinity by conforming the acts of the mind to the inner activity of the divine Trinity. By including this element of conformation Thomas is saying that the mind has to be turned, directly or indirectly, towards God, if we are to discern the image of the Trinity in the human being – 'the uncreated Trinity is distinguished in terms of the procession of a word from the speaker and of love from both . . . Now

since the rational creature exhibits a word procession as regards the intelligence and a love procession as regards the will, it can be said to be an
image of the uncreated Trinity by a sort of portraiture in kind (*per
quandam repraesentationem speciei*) (93.6) – and:

> if we are to see an image of the divine Trinity in the soul, it must be looked
> for principally at the point where the soul approaches most closely, in so
> far as this is possible at all, to a portrayal of the divine Persons in kind.
> Now the divine processions are distinguished from each other in terms of
> the procession of a word from its utterer and of a love connecting them
> both. But as Augustine says, there can be no word in our souls without
> actual thinking. And so an image of the Trinity is to be looked for in the
> mind first and foremost in terms of its activity, in so far as out of the aware-
> ness we have we form an internal word by thinking, and from this burst
> out into actual love' (93.7).

This 'bursting out into love' (*in amorem prorumpere*) is used only
once elsewhere (ST 1.43. 5). It is not an expression in Augustine's *De
Trinitate*, the text Thomas is relying on. Anyway, the mission of the Son
takes place according to 'a conditioning or informing of the intellect such
that by means of it the intellect bursts forth into the passion of love'.
Augustine usually speaks of love as the force that connects and yokes
together, but here Thomas seems more struck by the explosive character
of love.

Is it just a coincidence that the phrase is to be found only in these two
places (ST 1.43. 5 and 93.7)? Certainly, Thomas never adverts explicitly
to any analogy between our being dynamically the image of the Trinity
and the indwelling of the Trinity in the graced human being.

Finally, since we refer the divine image in the human creature, ultimately, to the verbal concept born of the knowledge of God and to the
love derived from this, Thomas can conclude that the image of God is
found in the soul according as the soul turns to God, or possesses a
nature that enables it to turn to God (93.8).

In sum, if we yield to the temptation of picturing humankind as a
static and unmoving mirror image of God, and combine that with the
assumption that Thomas's God is the static divinity of 'classical theism',
we may see a link between the doctrine of God and theological ethics.
If, on the other hand, we read Thomas's discussion of the image of God
properly, we surely find the link precisely in the Trinitarianism. It is precisely as we perform acts of knowing and loving, particularly acts of
knowing and loving God, that we are imaging God as Trinity. The triune
God is not a static entity; the image of God is not static either. Thomas
has a very dynamic concept of the nature of the triune Godhead – very
much as a triad of mutually related activities; so it is no surprise that the

image of this God occurs in the 'event' of a human being's actually knowing and loving.

The unity of Thomas's doctrine of God, Christology and theological ethics might, then, be found in the Trinitarianism of his mature theology as a whole: the moral agent as image of God, with the exemplar in God and the perfection of the image in Christ. But Merriell, after a thorough examination, is surely right in objecting that the references to the image of God, frequent for sure, are scattered through the second and third parts of the *Summa* really on no apparent system. The theme of the human being actually knowing and loving God as the dynamic imaging of the triune Godhead is mentioned only once after question 93 and that is in a quotation from Albert the Great's definition of sacramental character (ST 3. 63. 3). So much for an attractive theme! It is difficult to maintain that the theme is even implicitly present throughout the *secunda pars*, guiding Thomas's account of how the moral agent reaches fulfilment in communion with God.

At most, in contrast to readers who take it for granted that Thomas's God is a static entity and the human creature its mirror image, we have enough textual evidence to argue that the moral life as actually understanding and loving is the practical and dynamic 'imaging' of the God whose act of being is always also actually understanding and loving.

Beatitude

The 'consummation of the whole theological enterprise', Thomas says, is 'our reflection on the Saviour himself and on what he has done for human beings' (ST 3. prologue).

Christology, far from being a postscript to a theological system supposedly worked out independently of it, is conceived rather as the 'consummation'. To our modern way of thinking a project needs a foundation and we are inclined to regard the entire edifice from the foundations upwards. For Thomas, on the other hand, with his teleological focus on everything, the sense of a project is bestowed by the intended achievement. Far from being a kind of appendix to his exposition of Christian doctrine, Christ and the sacraments are the climax.

This is what Thomas says, in the prologue to the *tertia pars*: 'Because the Saviour our Lord Jesus Christ, "saving his people from their sins" as the angel bore witness (Matthew 1:21), demonstrated to us in himself the way of truth by which it is possible, by resurrection, to attain the beatitude of immortal life', 'now that we have considered the ultimate end of human life and virtue and vice' (in the *secunda pars*), 'the consummation of the whole theological project' is 'consideration of the Saviour himself and the benefits he has bestowed upon humankind' (ST 3 prologue).

Spelling this out: first Thomas will consider the Saviour himself; then 'his sacraments, by which we attain salvation'; and thirdly, 'the end of immortal life to which we come through him by resurrection'.

The final questions of the *Summa*, which of course Thomas did not live to write, were thus to have dealt with eschatology, in effect with the new creation in Christ, eternal life as the beatific vision, no doubt, but the beatific vision as radically and definitively Christ-won resurrection. What it is possible for human beings to attain, by resurrection (*resurgendo*) is the 'bliss of everlasting life'.

Suppose, then, that Thomas's whole theological project, including the moral theology, has its focus on *beatitudo* – might this provide the key to the connection between the doctrine of God, theological ethics, and Christology?

Consider some of the opening remarks of the *secunda pars*:

> If we think of gaining or possessing or of being conjoined in any way with that on which our hearts are set, then our ultimate end means something in us (*ex parte animae*) for that is how we become blessed; but in the sense that what is desired as ultimate end is that in which beatitude consists, that which makes one blessed, then we have to say that beatitude is something in us yet dependent on something transcending us (ST 1–2.2.7).

There is certainly a perfection of the soul (*quoddam animae bonum inhaerens*); but that in which beatitude consists is something *extra animam* – not any created good (ST 1–2.2.8). It has to be, can only be, the universal fount of good, the unrestricted object of bliss for all the blessed, the boundless and complete subsisting good (cf ST 1–2.2.8). In brief: 'Human blessedness resides in God alone'.

No doubt we can detect Plato's dialectic of the good, communicated through Denys and Augustine – *beata vita hominis Deus est*; but the Psalmist is just as present – *beatus populus cujus Dominus Deus ejus* (Ps. 143(144).15). Thomas, after all, taught in the intervals between chanting the praise of God in choral recitation of the psalter.

The *secunda pars*, it may surely be plausibly maintained, is entirely controlled by these opening considerations. We should not rush into the philosophical questions: acting for a purpose, action theory, and so on, all of which is of course there. The introduction to all that, its *a priori* condition, is Thomas's characterization of God as 'object' of the bliss of all the blessed – '*objectum*', of course, in the mediaeval sense of 'that which confronts us, provokes and evokes response from us'.

The 'object', in pre-modern discourse, is that which attracts the attention of the human being – evoking or provoking, focusing or occluding, this or that act of reasoning or choosing – not, as we tend to think now, something inert and shapeless that requires us to project or impose significance upon it.

So beatitude is the uncreated good – God – who alone can fill the heart completely by his infinite goodness (ST 1–2.3.1). And beatitude is also, simultaneously, something created in the heart, since it is nothing other than our receiving God – our joy with God.

The exposition of virtue ethics is, thus, focused on the divine beatitude which is shared by the blessed but already able to be anticipated in the moral life here and now. Ethics, for Thomas, is not so much founded on reason or law as motivated by anticipated happiness.

But then, as Thomas would expect us to remember, his doctrine of God culminated in the thesis that 'God is beatitude' (ST 1.26). This is a claim Thomas goes on to repeat – for example, early in his virtue ethics: 'In God there is bliss by nature: his being is his doing, enjoyed by none other than himself' (*In Deo est beatitudo per essentiam: quia ipsum esse ejus est operatio ejus, qua non fruitur alio, sed seipso*) (ST 1–2.3.2) – a scandalous statement to many ears today, of course – it seems selfish and egocentric of God to be perfectly happy without us.

Again, early in the *tertia pars*, one of the 'reasons' for the Incarnation is that what is bestowed on us by Christ's humanity is the full participation in divinity which is humankind's true beatitude and the completion of human life (ST 3.1.2). It is by Christ's humanity that we are drawn into the destiny of beatitude: the blessed knowledge of God for which we remain open as made in God's image (ST 3.9.2). And in many similar remarks Thomas acknowledges that the beatitude in which human beings may share by God's grace is the beatitude laid open in the Incarnation.

Short History of Beatitude

The concept of beatitude was placed on the moral theological agenda in 1956, by Roger Guindon.[19] He claims that, since the Reformation and especially since Kant, one of the major objections to Catholic and certainly Thomist moral theology has been the emphasis on the primacy of beatitude. Whether translated as 'flourishing', 'well-being', or (most commonly) 'happiness', this ancient Greek notion of *eudaimonia* seems quite inappropriate as the focus of Christian ethics. Kant, for example, was deeply opposed to what he dismissively called 'happiness theory' (*Glückseligkeitslehre*): the focus on happiness, rather than on duty, could only lead to 'egoism', placing the determining principle of action in the satisfaction of the individual's desire. The last thing worthy of Christians was to want to be happy.

But the doctrine of happiness has a long and chequered history. To consider only what he says about the Middle Ages, Guindon shows that the idea of beatitude was overshadowed by that of law, in the twelfth and early thirteenth centuries in Latin theology. This did not mean that the theme faded entirely from view. On the contrary, he documents it in Anselm of Canterbury (c.1033–1109), through to Hugh of Saint Victor (d. 1142) and above all in Peter Lombard. These provide the background for Thomas Aquinas.

Again and again we return to the doctrine of creation. The creation of the world is explained by the immense bounty of the God who wills to share his goodness. We can participate in God's beatitude by knowledge and love, anticipating here and now what will only be fulfilled eschatologically. Indeed, it is in view of their participation in divine bliss that reasoning creatures were created in the first place. As Lombard says: 'The good will's aim is beatitude, eternal life, God himself'.

All this was in place when theologians in Paris discovered Aristotle. Albert and then Thomas took the lead in completing (as they perhaps thought) – radically transforming, we might now think – Aristotle's account of *eudaimonia*: no longer the happiness of becoming godlike by coming to understand the world but the blessedness of face-to-face vision of God in heaven. Thomas loves to quote 1 John 3:2: 'Beloved, now we are the sons of God and it does not yet appear what we shall be: but we know that, when he shall appear, we shall be like him; for we shall see him as he is'. In considering the mystery of the unity of the divine nature, for example, he asks how God may be known by creatures:

> The ultimate beatitude for human beings consists in our highest (deepest) activity, which is the activity of our minds. If created minds could never see the essence of God, either we would never attain beatitude or beatitude would consist in something other than God – which is contrary to faith – for it is in [God] that is to be found the ultimate perfection of the reasoning creature because that is the source of our being. (ST 1.12.1)

As so often, it is Greek patristic authorities that Thomas cites: Denys and (here) John Chrysostom (c.347–407).

In short: the beatitude which is God (at ST 1.26) is the beatitude which is the ultimate fulfilment of the human heart and mind (ST 1.12.1); it is the beatitude which motivates the moral life (ST 1–2.1–5); it is the beatitude made accessible to human beings by Christ's humanity (ST 3. prologue); it is the beatitude enjoyed by Christ himself (ST 3.10).

In short: Thomas's theological ethics centre on beatitude, understood as eschatological participation in the divine life, attainable only in union with Christ.

Gifts of the Spirit

Finally, in case Thomas might seem to neglect the Holy Spirit, it should be noted that his exposition of virtue in the *Summa Theologiae* culminates in three questions on the gifts of the Spirit (ST 1–2.68–70), and his account of law, eternal, natural, human and Mosaic, culminates in the question on the New Law which is nothing other than the grace of the Holy Spirit given inwardly to the believer (ST 1–2.90–108).

Introducing the questions on the gifts of the Spirit, Edward O'Connor maintains that they offer the most complete and lucid account of Thomas's 'theory of the divinization of man by grace through the action of the Holy Spirit, teaching, guiding and strengthening' – not, then, merely a decorative pious appendix.[20] Rather, these questions make the transition to the grace-filled life which is radically different from the life of virtue expounded so far: the Gifts are the introduction to the divine life already here and now; the union face to face with God which is beatitude (1 Cor. 2:9–10 and 1 John 3:2).

O'Connor directs us back to the so-called 'infused virtues' (ST 1–2.63): virtues because they qualify our minds and hearts to respond and act in ways proportionate to the vision to which we are called; 'infused' because beyond our power to bring about. And these are not just acts of faith, hope or charity, that might occur from time to time, under a special inspiration of the Holy Spirit; but excellences of character, such as we see in men and women of faith, hopeful and charitable people.

Furthermore, the Holy Spirit works in the individual moral agent in such a way that he or she works also: this co-operation is not pictured as necessarily competitive (ST 1–2.68.3). No one can reach the inheritance of the land of the blessed unless moved and led by the Holy Spirit (68.2). And the whole point is that by the gifts of the Spirit we are 'disposed to become more readily mobile to divine inspiration' (68.1).

Thomas describes the beatitudes (ST 1–2.69), initially the lists in Matthew and Luke; but he relates them eventually to the 'beatitude which is to come, in hope of which we are already called blessed' (ST 1–2.69.3).

It is tempting but would be fanciful to suggest that Thomas's account of virtue as such culminates in an appeal to the beatific vision. The main interest in these questions is rather to stress that, for all that has been and will be said about the theological and moral virtues (faith, hope, charity; prudence, temperance, fortitude, justice), 'in no way are human beings so made to flourish in regard to the ultimate end that they no longer need to be moved all the time by a higher (deeper) prompting of the Holy Spirit' (ST 1–2.68.2).

For Thomas, there is no movement of the moral agent towards this promised face-to-face vision of God except by the continual inspiration of the Holy Spirit.

The best way of describing the moral considerations in the *Summa Theologiae* is not as virtue ethics, let alone as divine command ethics, but as an ethics of divine beatitude.

Chapter 8

QUARRELS ABOUT GRACE

The most bitter controversy within twentieth-century Thomism, and in Catholic theology at large, was set off in 1946 with the publication of Henri de Lubac's book *Surnaturel*.[1] Rereading key texts in Thomas's work, he took them at face value, insisting that they mean exactly what they say: human beings have a *natural* capacity for face-to-face vision of God, which however is granted only by a *supernatural* gift: 'In one way, beatific vision or knowledge is beyond the nature of the rational soul in the sense that the soul cannot reach it by its own power; but in another way it is in accordance with its nature, in the sense that by its very nature the soul has a capacity for it, being made in God's image' (ST 3.9.3).[2] As created in God's image, fallen and sinful as they are, human beings retain an innate capacity for ultimately enjoying the bliss of eschatological communion with God. The Christian paradox, as de Lubac calls it, is that the soul is *naturally* open to a face-to-face communion with God which can only be granted *supernaturally*.[3]

To say this horrifies certain theologians. For others, however, like Aelred Squire, the claim is only 'a kind of creative recognition of what is already somehow obscurely known':

> It may seem a somewhat startling leap to make, but to the great spiritual masters of the undivided Church, the revealed doctrine of man as having been made in the image of God universally inspires this feeling of glad recognition. They go on, in fact, to take it seriously for what it claims to be, a long lost memory of their true selves, and from that all the rest they have to say follows. Their doctrine is concerned to arouse in their disciples a sense of the implications of a memory they believe could not have been initially reawakened without a divine intervention.[4]

In short, nature is predisposed for grace, the world is naturally waiting for the gospel – though it is only after the fact that this becomes clear. Far from coming only as an unwelcome and disorientating shock, the Christian dispensation turns out to offer the beginnings of a fulfilment of dimly apprehended longings. As Thomas puts it (*Contra Gentiles* 3.54): 'The divine substance is not beyond the capacity of the created intellect in such a way that it is altogether foreign to it, as sound is from the object of vision, or as immaterial substance is from sense power'. Communion with God is indeed 'beyond the capacity of the created intellect in the sense that it exceeds all its powers' – but that the realization of this possibility transcends all human effort does not mean that God is 'so to speak, something entirely extraneous (*quasi aliquid omnino extraneum*)'.

As so often, Thomas takes a great deal for granted. He thinks within the Christian economy, instinctively and unembarrassedly, unlike many modern theologians who, whatever their personal religious stance, examine it from outside, as impartially and objectively as they can. He presupposes as a common background, already known because inhabited, in daily liturgical and ascetic practice, an entirely Christ-centred view of the world and thus of the relationship between the created and the divine. The 'consummation of the entire theological business', as he says, is reflection on 'the Saviour and what he has done for humankind' (cf. ST 3. prologue).

Ultimately, though he never needs to make this explicit, the absence of anything like the modern sense of divine grace as alien to 'fallen' human nature is due to Thomas's confidence in traditional Chalcedonian Christology: 'Just as [Christ's] all holy and blameless ensouled flesh was not destroyed by being divinized but remained in its own limit and category, so also his human will has not been destroyed by being divinized, but rather was preserved'.[5]

As Thomas puts it, the mystery of the Incarnation 'took place by God's uniting himself in a new way to the created, or, more precisely, by the created's being united to him' (cf. ST 3.1). In the creature who is the man Jesus Christ, so Thomas holds, the entire created order is united to God: Christ is not only head of the Church but also head of all human beings (cf. ST 3.8.1–3). In being united with the divine, we may surely say, the created nature was 'not destroyed but rather was preserved [saved]' – one of Thomas's favourite themes: nature saved, not destroyed, by 'divinization'.

Surnaturel

Many – perhaps the majority – of the Thomist commentators at the time reacted strongly against de Lubac's interpretation. For them, perhaps surprisingly, it was not a happy thought that fallen and sinful human beings nevertheless have a natural desire for the vision of God – fulfillable only by God's grace, for sure, yet responding to something deep in our nature.

It is always a good question to ask of theologians what they fear. In this instance, one fear, on the part of those who believed that the Thomist synthesis was an unsurpassable recapitulation of earlier theologies, was that de Lubac's reconnecting Thomas with his patristic inheritance was driven by an anti-modern archaizing nostalgia. Over-simplifyingly: if we have perfection, why delve into how it was achieved? It is the genetic fallacy to think that knowing how a position was arrived at brings you any nearer to deciding its validity.

More particularly, de Lubac's reading of certain texts was bitterly contested. Nobody denied that Thomas often insists on the immediate vision of God promised in Scripture (1 Cor. 13:12; 1 John 3:2, etc.): 'We shall see God face to face, in the sense that we shall see him without a medium, as is true when we see a man face to face'; 'in this vision we become most like God and partakers in God's beatitude', when we shall 'eat and drink at God's table, seeing him in the way that he sees himself' (cf. *Contra Gentiles* 3.51).

On de Lubac's reading, of this and many similar texts, Thomas thought that there is a natural desire for truth that philosophers recognize, which is fulfillable only, as theologians understand, in the ultimate happiness of face-to-face vision of God (ST 1.12.1).

Many Thomists regarded this as an exorbitant claim. For one thing, they rejected de Lubac's ascribing their interpretation of the texts in question to blind acceptance of a misinterpretation introduced by Cajetan.[6] According to de Lubac, Cajetan assumed that Thomas was an Aristotelian, working with a definition of nature from Aristotle's *Physics*, which effectively turned human nature into a reality essentially closed in on itself, with its own intrinsic powers, desires and goals. Out of fear of the supposed Reformation doctrine of the depravity of human nature, such theologians as Cajetan opened the way for post-Reformation Catholicism to insist so much on the value of nature that they ended with a two-storey model of nature and grace, juxtaposing the two, as it were, treating grace in relation to nature as essentially extrinsic and adventitious.

Some, following Cajetan, argued that this natural desire to see God is the desire of a human being always already inserted in the history of salvation – that is to say, an already supernaturally graced desire, and not a purely natural desire at all. Here de Lubac cites, as well as Cajetan, John of St Thomas.[7] Much more provocatively, as he must have known, he names modern adherents of this view, headed by Réginald

Garrigou-Lagrange, at the time by far the most eminent Dominican theologian in Rome.[8] Next, wickedly, de Lubac mentions George Tyrrell, regarded at the time as an 'apostate Jesuit' and by far the most notorious of the Modernists.[9] Finally, de Lubac mentions A.-D. Sertillanges, by then the grand old man at Le Saulchoir, the theology faculty of the Paris Dominicans.[10]

Secondly, in a different Thomist line, it was argued by such as Suárez and the Carmelites of Salamanca that Thomas's *desiderium naturale* is not an 'innate longing' but merely a rather vague and ineffective velleity.[11]

In contrast, others allow that Thomas means a real natural desire but argue that it is not a desire for the beatific vision but for a purely natural knowledge of God. This view, according to de Lubac, was perhaps inaugurated by Silvestri Ferrariensis (1474–1528), another of the great Dominican commentators, and was certainly held by Sylvester Maurus (1619–87), one of the best representatives of Jesuit theology in his day. Yet, it seems clear enough, these no doubt famous men in their day are mere shadows: if we follow up de Lubac's footnote we find that he is really getting at Pedro Descoqs (1877–1946), whose classes he attended in 1922–3, the leading Suárezian Thomist of the day, and no doubt the chief of the Jesuit theologians whom he wanted to discredit.

In short, one way or another, all the most prominent Thomists had misunderstood Thomas, for all their different and indeed sometimes irreconcilable interpretations.

Most provocatively of all, perhaps, de Lubac denied that Thomas 'chose' 'the Aristotelian system' for its 'moderate ontological realism' as best for reconciling faith and reason in expounding the Christian mysteries. On the contrary, Thomas did not have to 'choose Aristotle', Aristotle was already there – 'an Aristotle more or less Alexandrianized, neoPlatonized, Arabized'. To cap this provocative remark de Lubac cites Ernest Renan, in particular his 1852 book on Averroism.[12] In other words, most of the Thomists in 1946 still had to learn from a book published a century before, by the most notorious of all the 'apostates', that Thomas Aquinas's Aristotle was effectively a Neo-Platonist.

Unsurprisingly, *Surnaturel* roused a good deal of opposition. Important as the issues were, one wonders whether the controversy need have been so acrimonious. In retrospect, as one recalls the names de Lubac mentioned, it looks as if, with what can only be calculated insults, he himself set off the disputes in which the issues were perhaps obscured. Few now doubt that when Thomas taught that human beings have a natural desire for the vision of God he meant what he said.

When de Lubac revised the book, in the two volumes which came out in 1965, *Augustinisme et théologie moderne* and *Le mystère du surnaturel*, he documented his reading of Thomas on natural desire, insisting that it was by no means innovatory, isolated or unprecedented. He cites Pierre Rousselot, already in 1908, in his remarkable book *L'intellectualisme de saint Thomas*, attacking 'those who would reduce the whole desire for the intuitive vision according to St Thomas to a secret transformation effected historically in man by grace'. That is to say: desire for the vision is not already supernatural.[13] He cites others, in the 1920s, asking how Cajetan's exegesis could ever have been put forward or taken seriously for so long. He delights in quoting Garrigou-Lagrange's remark that it was simply unbelievable that the majority of commentators since Cajetan could have got Thomas wrong, and in citing the sarcastic comment by A.M. Motte: 'No need to read the texts, then; Saint Thomas *cannot* have said it!'.

In short, the significance of de Lubac's challenge to the considerable variety of Thomist interpretations prevailing at the time can now best be recaptured by studying the ramifications of the network of scholarship which he disrupted so effectively.

The 'Thomist' Axiom

'Grace does not destroy nature, but perfects it' is the most cited 'Thomist' axiom (e.g. ST 1.1.8.2). Thomas's earliest appeal to the axiom is in his commentary on Boethius's *De Trinitate*, dated to 1257–8 (the text survives in his own hand): 'the gifts of grace are conferred on nature in such a way that they do not destroy it but rather perfect it.'

In fact, however, the axiom is not exclusively or even particularly characteristic of Thomas's theological outlook. On the contrary, the earliest recorded appearance is to be found in Bonaventure's *Commentary* on Peter Lombard's *Sentences*, dated to 1248, and thus a few years earlier than Thomas's, dated to 1252–6. The axiom may not have been a commonplace at the time but clearly Thomas was not the only theologian to appeal to it.

In post-Tridentine theology, admittedly, the axiom came to be used by Catholic apologists, as a slogan against supposed Protestant assumptions about the utter depravity of fallen human nature. In this sense, it became a principle dividing Christians in the West more than any other. 'Grace does not destroy nature', as Thomas says (ST 1.1.8), 'but perfects it, which is why natural reason ministers to faith and the natural inclination of the will ministers to charity'. Traditional Reformed Christians – but also Catholics in the officially suppressed but actually still flourishing 'Jansenist' tradition – regard human reasoning as much too twisted by human sinfulness to be easily related to Christian faith, just as they are inclined to regard the Christian practice of charity as cutting across the natural desires of human will.[14] In their view, human reason is more likely to be humbled than perfected by divinely given faith, just as *eros* is likely to be thwarted by the specifically Christian virtue of *agape*. To such Christians, the harmonious interaction between faith and reason, charity and natural love, and thus between grace and nature, that is postulated and expected in the Thomist tradition, remains deeply problematic.

In *Church Dogmatics*, II/1 Karl Barth undertakes a searching examination of the main theses of natural, and therefore (as G.W. Bromiley and T.F. Torrance say in their editors' preface) Catholic theology. The problem, allegedly, is that, in Catholic theology, there is a distinction between the *possibility* of knowledge of God as considered in natural theology and the *actuality* of knowledge of God as historically revealed in the Christian economy of grace. This, in turn, it is claimed, displays an underlying split between God's being and God's action. It is precisely this split which (Bromiley and Torrance say) Barth's theology is out to eliminate. To do so, he has to do his best to understand why natural theology – 'the theology of the natural man' – should be so persistent. In the end, of course, natural theology issues from the human desire to secure our own position in face of life and death. The Barthian has no right to deprive the 'natural man' (as the Catholic is assumed to be) of his only trust in our natural powers prior to bringing him to true knowledge of God in Jesus Christ.

In due course, however, Barth accepts the axiom, with the qualification that it means that, besides the negative moment of grace in radical condemnation of sin, there is radical transformation of the sinner in the light of divine patience. What Barth has in mind, in his remarkable consideration of the patience of God, is the way that God 'takes up the cause of the creature, the reality distinct from himself, in such a way that he accepts it as a reality and intervenes for it in recognition, not in suspension, of its reality'. God's mercy 'does not act in such a way as to overpower and blot out its object'. God does not 'annihilate' the creature, or control it 'in such a way that grace means the catastrophic destruction of nature'.[15]

Having said all that, Barth finds it possible, going into the small print, to 'admit the truth of that maxim of Thomas Aquinas' – 'grace perfects nature' – insisting, however, that it 'is so often put to dangerous use and in the first instance was no doubt dangerously meant'.

Barthian Anxieties

The trouble with Catholics, so Barthians fear, is that when they appeal to this axiom they gloss over the negative side.

Consider what George Hunsinger says, in his important book about Barth.[16] Instead of saying that 'grace does not destroy but perfects nature' we should say that 'grace perfects nature *precisely by destroying it*' – a contention that would indeed make a Catholic theologian, at least in any Thomist tradition, somewhat uneasy. It sounds much too paradoxical – perfecting by destroying!

It turns out, in a footnote, however, that Hunsinger understands his reformulation as follows: 'Grace perfects human nature as created only as grace destroys human nature as fallen'. That would be a version of the axiom acceptable to theologians in the Reformation tradition, Hunsinger thinks. He takes it for granted that it could not be what a Catholic would mean. On the contrary, the typical Catholic move (he thinks) simply misses how entirely, and not just partially, 'created nature' is deformed by sin. By appealing to some 'natural potentiality' to account for the human being's 'continuity of self-identity' through the 'abyss of this unheard-of transition', namely from death as a sinner to resurrection as a new creation, Catholics reveal that they do not understand 'the actual miracle and mystery of grace'.

This is the deepest split between traditional Catholic doctrine and the doctrine that issues from the Reformation, so Hunsinger thinks. This 'Thomist', and more generally Catholic, thesis, according to which human beings have the capacity to choose between sin and grace, and, moved by divine grace, can then 'co-operate' in their sanctification, is rejected by Barth. It implies that grace and freedom presuppose a capacity to choose which is itself not destroyed by sin but by which the human being remains responsible, so that the passage from a life of sin to a life under grace implies that the same subject persists, who is converted, and the same divine vocation.

'The typical Protestant worry' is that 'Catholic theology takes neither sin seriously enough as sin, nor grace seriously enough as grace'. By regarding salvation as a 'process', 'sin and grace are understood as quantities'. That is to say, sin and grace are regarded, as Hunsinger puts it, 'as matters of degree, as susceptible of increase or decrease, and therefore as *complementary or correlative*' (my italics).

This means that sin and grace, as Barth puts it, 'are compared and pragmatized and tamed and rendered quite innocuous . . . The practical consequence of all this is that the misery of humankind is not regarded as in any way serious or dangerous'.[17] For sin and grace to be regarded as really 'the dangerous matters that they are', so Barth continues, they have to be seen 'as totalities which do not complement but mutually exclude one another'. In other words, as Hunsinger says, 'one cannot be a little bit sinful or a little bit righteous' – any more than one can be 'a little bit pregnant or a little bit dead'. Putting it a little less graphically: 'Sin and righteousness are predicates that either apply to us as whole persons before God, as intensively and extensively as possible, or not at all'.

According to Catholic theology, in other words, human beings are *partly* sinful and *partly* graced. This is because salvation is a *process*, depending on how well the redeemed sinner *co-operates* with divine grace.

What must be blocked, at all costs, Hunsinger contends, is the very idea of 'our cooperation in the work of redemption'. We must listen to the gospel as understood by the Reformation: 'Christ's righteousness and life become ours as a gift that is received not by works but by faith alone'.

On the other hand, Hunsinger allows, there is a place for talk of growth or progress in the Christian life. His hunch, now speaking ecumenically, is that, when it comes to considering how this gulf between Catholics and Protestants is to be overcome, we might return to baptism as both a gift and a vocation – as a once-for-all saving event to be combined with dying and rising with Christ as our daily vocation. Barth, he says, understood the 'again and again' of our dying and rising with Christ but unfortunately was not very explicit about the 'more and more' – a lacuna where the Catholic theologian might be permitted to enter the discussion. On the other hand, 'the future of Roman Catholic theology', not just of ecumenical dialogue, 'will depend', Hunsinger thinks, on eliminating the traditional conception of salvation as an existential or ecclesial 'process', 'in favour of a richer, more complex, and more truly christocentric soteriology'.[18]

In the footnote to this last phrase Hunsinger advises us that this would mean that the idea of 'process' would be controlled by the idea of 'participation'. 'Seeing salvation as a process of divine/human "co-operation", in which human efforts help bring salvation into being, is something which Reformation-oriented Protestants will feel must be completely avoided as contrary to the gospel'. What would be acceptable, on the other hand, would be 'one's "existential appropriation" of the salvation that has already been given and received by faith' – always remembering that 'even the faith by which Christ is received is and remains his gift'.

Hunsinger finds the key difference between Reformed and Roman Catholic doctrine, and specifically between Barth and Thomas Aquinas, in the question whether the justification of the unrighteous is miraculous or not. For Barth, he argues, it has to be a miracle; for Thomas, on the other hand, it is not so (ST 1–2. 113. 10).

Thomas distinguishes three senses in which the justification of the unrighteous might be counted as a miracle. Like the creation of the world, or any other work which can be done by God alone (*a solo Deo*), justification may be called miraculous in the sense of being 'utterly marvellous and strange'. In another sense, as in the case of Paul's conversion, God may move individuals so violently (*vehementer*) that they immediately attain a certain perfection of righteousness, without going through what Thomas regards as 'the usual and common course of justification'.

In the third sense, however, justification is not miraculous, so Thomas argues. It is not like raising the dead, for instance, in which life is beyond the natural capacity of the body. On the contrary, 'the soul is by nature open to grace' (*naturaliter anima est gratiae capax*).

This Hunsinger takes to mean that, for Thomas, 'grace actualizes a possibility inherent in human nature'. In other words, Thomas sees divine grace and human freedom as interdependent. Worse, God's grace is being conditioned by human freedom, which means that grace is not grace at all – 'sovereign, free, and gratuitous'. Divine grace has been made 'conceptually subsequent to and dependent on human freedom' – which means that human nature is 'conceptually prior to and independent of divine grace'.

Well, perhaps. Yet, if we read to the end of Thomas's discussion, characteristically brief as it of course is, we find him citing Augustine: 'the soul is by nature open to grace (*gratiae capax*) since by the very fact that it is made to the image of God, it is open to God by grace (*capax Dei per gratiam*)'. That is to say: it is *by grace* that the soul of the sinner is open to God. Paradoxically, fallen human beings are open to grace *naturaliter* but this is in virtue of their being open to grace *per gratiam*. It seems that Hunsinger assumes that, for Thomas, fallen human nature is capable of achieving God's favour independently of God's initiative. He seems to assume that Thomas has a doctrine of 'pure nature': human beings who are able, independently of divine grace, to bootstrap their way to God. Thomas, on the other hand, quotes Augustine, and surely takes himself to be in the patristic tradition, according to which human nature is open to grace *by grace* – *only* by grace, as we now have to insist, to rule out any idea of 'pure nature'. Thomas takes it for granted that (fallen and sin-prone) human nature is always already under the conditions of God's philanthropic pedagogy – that 'transmutation from the state of unrighteousness to the state of righteousness' (113. 1) – a move which is not in the control of human nature to achieve but for which human nature has a 'capacity'. Justifying grace is acquired not by the sinner's own activity, as it were independently of God's – *sed Deo operante*. But this is to raise the question of *co-operation* – the problem central in all Western theology: the problem of the co-operation between the graceful God and the graced creature.

Of course, this is a hermeneutic crux. As we saw in chapter 3, when Thomas speaks of causation his model (as with Aristotle) is 'agent-causation'. That is to say, causing is always on analogy with a person's own experience of doing simple things and bringing things about. The interplay of divine and human causalities that Thomas regularly invokes is always already the interplay of *agents* who are implicitly modelled on *persons*.

Whether co-operation is necessarily competition is an interesting question. It takes us right to the heart of Thomas's theology. He often quotes Isaiah 26:12: 'Lord, thou hast wrought all our works in us' – which he takes (e.g. at ST 1.105. 5), precisely as *excluding* all competitiveness between divine and human agency.

Indeed, when Thomas speaks of 'co-operation' between creatures and God, he almost always rules out the picture of two rival agents on a level playing field. On the contrary, he sees it as the mark of God's freedom, and ours, that God 'causes' everything in such a way that the creature 'causes' it too.

Thomas is, of course, well aware that it is difficult for some people to understand this, and of how difficult it is to see how natural effects are attributed both to God and to a natural agent (cf. *Summa Contra Gentiles* 3. 70). If the action by which an effect is produced proceeds from a human agent, they are tempted to think, then it surely does not also need to be attributed to God. When a thing can be done adequately by one agent it is superfluous to posit another: either God or the human agent does whatever it is. If God produces the entire natural effect, surely nothing is left for the human agent to do. It is in order to exorcise us from such bewitching thoughts that Thomas returns us to his doctrine of double agency. As he quite flatly asserts, there is nothing to stop us from thinking that the same effect is produced by a lower agent and by God – by both, unmediatedly, of course in different ways.

It is always by divine power that the human agent produces his or her own proper effect: that is the doctrine of creation. It is not superfluous, even if in principle God can by himself produce all natural effects, for them to be produced by us as causes. Nor is this a result of the inadequacy of divine power, as one might be tempted to think, thus giving way to the charms of process theology. On the contrary: it is a result of the immensity of God's goodness (*bonitas*: bounty). It is another implication of the doctrine of creation that God wills to communicate his likeness to things not only so that they might simply exist but that they might *cause* other things. Indeed, this is how creatures generally attain the divine likeness – by *causing* (*Contra Gentiles* 3. 20 and 21).

To repeat: of course the same effect is not attributed to a human agent and to divine agency in such a way that it is partly done by God and partly by the human agent. Rather, what is done is done wholly by both, in completely different ways, but harmoniously, and not necessarily competitively, just as the same effect is brought about entirely by a tool (an axe, for example) and wholly by the agent (in this case the forester).

Greek Roots of the 'Thomist' Axiom

The roots of the famous 'Thomist' axiom lie in Greek patristic theology. What is often supposed (as by Hunsinger) to be an optimistic humanism rooted in Aristotelian naturalism (little more than Pelagianism) is in fact a version of the theology of divine philanthropy, communicated largely through Denys and well established in the West long before Thomas (though that may not make it any more acceptable).

The place to start is a neglected essay by Bernard Quelquejeu.[19] On Thomas's view, as he shows, it could not be the case that what is natural to human beings as created natures was eliminated by sin. That would mean that, as fallen and sinful creatures, human creatures would have lost their very nature. Deprived of their nature, human beings would thus cease to exist or be so lacking in being that they would count as 'evil'. That would bring us much too close to the Manichean denial of the goodness of created being, the doctrine which haunts Thomas's theological imagination as the deepest error to which his age was prone. In connection with freewill, for example, Thomas cites it as a commonplace that 'no natural power is removed by sin' (ST 1.83.2 obj. 3).[20]

Human nature was not constituted by grace, any more than human nature ever existed without grace. The original justice (righteousness) in which Adam was created was an accident of the nature of the species – not as being caused by the basic elements of the species, but as a gift given by God to (human) nature as a whole (1.100.1). Thus, Thomas knows of no instances of pure human nature, neither unfallen nor ungraced. No doubt he would have admitted the logical possibility of pure nature but there is no sign he was interested in any possibility other than nature unfallen and always already graced (Adam) and nature fallen and always already *capax gratiae*.

Thomas explicitly cites Denys (1–2.63.1) – 'that which is in human beings by nature is common to all human beings and not taken away by sin because even in the demons the natural goods persist (*bona naturalia manent*)'.

The distinctively 'Thomist' axiom, then, is a version of a Dionysian thesis. It is sometimes (as at 1. 48. 4) reformulated: 'the readiness of the soul for grace is always diminished [by sins] . . . yet it is never completely removed . . . because it follows from the soul's nature (*semper magis et magis minuitur habilitas animae ad gratiam . . . neque tamen tollitur totaliter ab anima . . . praedicta habilitas quia consequitur naturam ipsius)*'. Here Thomas is writing in an anti-Manichean context. To say that what is good – human nature as created – could be totally destroyed by sin is equivalent, for Thomas, to the fundamental doctrine of the much feared Cathars.

Quelquejeu rephrases the axiom, as follows: 'sin presupposes nature, doesn't remove or destroy it but diminishes its capacity'. That is to say, sin cannot destroy the ontological structure of human nature, or change the created subject's species-specific nature – but it certainly restricts, wounds, and disorders the human creature.

Here, clearly, Thomas is indebted to the Augustinian tradition: Christian salvation is redemption, restoration of a disordered nature, deeply wounded by the Fall. But he is even more indebted to the Dionysian or Greek patristic tradition: salvation as elevation of nature, as divinization, rather than healing.

Deified Creaturehood

The best account in English of Thomas's theology of nature and grace is by Eric Mascall.[21] Mascall begins by reminding us of the orthodox Christian doctrine about the beings of which the world is composed that they are 'dependent realities': neither 'unsubstantial phantoms or hallucinations' nor having 'that independent and self-subsistent reality which is the peculiar property of God himself'. For all this insistence on 'the radical and indestructible difference of kind that distinguishes the Creator from even the most exalted of his creatures', it remains that 'there is a persistent tradition in Christian thought which finds it impossible to do justice to the transformation that a human being undergoes when he is incorporated into Christ except by saying that he is deified'.

Mascall cites 2 Peter 1:4, then turns to H.E.W. Turner's book *The Patristic Doctrine of Redemption* for the authority to say that the terminology of deification passed 'firmly and finally into the Christian tradition' by the time of Origen. He then cites Athanasius and Augustine, and leaps to John of the Cross – thus from the patristic age to the Counter-Reformation – steering between doctrines of grace which would seem to involve the destruction of creatureliness in some kind of absorption into the divine nature and on the other hand doctrines which hold that creaturehood is inherently incapable of deification.

Mascall is worried by late medieval Dominican theologians like Eckhart and Tauler, allowing that it is not clear enough about what they mean, but suspecting they may tend towards stressing deification to the point at which there is suppression of creaturehood – a view to be found both inside and outside Christianity.

On the other hand, again inside and outside Christianity, but its 'most conspicuous manifestation is in certain sections of Reformation Protestantism', there is a view which excludes 'deification' altogether.

Conceding that 'some of the Catholic manualists have stated the doctrine of grace and nature in a very pedestrian and uninspired way', Mascall does not allow that the Catholic view requires a 'two-storey' anthropological dualism (such as Brunner and Niebuhr object to). He denies that the doctrine of nature and supernature in Catholic theology means that the two operate in isolation from each other; on the contrary, 'supernature means the supernaturalization of nature, the elevation of nature by grace to a condition that it could not attain by its own powers'. Then he cites Thomas: 'grace perfects nature without destroying it, but also . . . grace requires nature as its presupposition' (ST 1.1.8; 2.2).

When human beings are said to have by nature a passive capacity for receiving grace this does not mean there has ever existed, in concrete reality, any 'merely natural man'. It means that, historically, God has elevated human beings to an order of existence far beyond what would be expected simply by the fact that we are rational animals – rational meaning far more than 'reason' in the narrow sense, including all those spiritual and cultural powers which distinguish us from the brute beasts (as Mascall notes) – so we might have worked it out and had some knowledge of God as the ground of being (etc) but in fact, historically, we have been elevated by God to a participation in God's own life. 'Grace is thus not merely something added to nature, as an extra storey may be added to a house, but is something that completes and perfects it'.

Then Mascall takes on Barth: grace, when it is given, 'appears as something which contradicts and ignores man's natural constitution altogether' (citing *Church Dogmatics* I/1 and O. Weber). Mascall charges Barth with 'a more violent segregation of grace from nature than anything of which the most plodding Catholic manualists could be guilty'.

However all that may be, Mascall returns from the anti-Protestant polemics to expounding Thomas Aquinas: grace is a participation in the life of God, which is normally brought about by incorporation into the human nature of Christ. The grace which makes one pleasing to God (*gratia gratum faciens*) is a condition in which the graced find themselves. Quite ordinary Christians have an experience which can only be described this way. The Christian doctrine of finite beings as dependent realities means that it is the essence of the finite to be incomplete – to be essentially open, that is, open to the activity of God, who without annulling or withdrawing anything given can always give more – 'The very possibility of deification by grace arises from the fact that creation is a most intimate and incessant donation of the creature to itself by God; it is not a projection of the creature into a lonely and isolated vacuum'. Mascall directs us back to the doctrine of the Incarnation, which is 'an example – and indeed the supreme culmination – of the notion of deified creaturehood'.

An Irresolvable Dispute?

Whether Mascall or anyone else in the Catholic tradition can ever understand Reformation doctrine or Luther specifically is open to dispute. Daphne Hampson, for example, attacking Mascall, speaks of the 'usual uncomprehending and hostile way' in which he writes about Luther's doctrine of grace: 'The emotional heart of Mascall's Catholic position lies in human love for God . . . For Luther it lies in rejoicing in faith, in trusting in God'.[22]

In practice, for Hampson, no Catholic could understand Luther without ceasing to be a Catholic. The 'Aristotelianism' in Catholic thought, she contends, rules out even understanding, let alone accepting, the Lutheran premise. According to Hampson, for Lutheranism, 'apart from God there is no self and this reliance on God has to be reaffirmed in every moment': very like the view we have seen Thomas Aquinas resisting. This means, on the other hand, she says, that, for the Lutheran, 'there could be no constant self which is tempted to think that it could exist in and of itself apart from God' – the selves so tempted all being Catholic, I take it she means. The self, on the Lutheran view, 'can only be the self "in the moment" ', whereas within Catholicism there is, or can be, 'a constant and ongoing sense of self'. In the end, Hampson says, the Lutheran self's grounding in God comes in the doctrine of salvation – 'which is a reinstating of what was intended in creation' – in contrast with those whose sense of self is grounded in 'some doctrine of creation which is relatively independent of salvation'. (No prizes for guessing who they are!)

Catholicism would have to shed the 'heritage from the ancient pagan world' that it carries in order to understand Lutheranism: the two systems of thought are 'strictly non-comparable'.

It is not surprising, then, that, in a more recent Anglican Catholic perspective, Henri de Lubac's retrieval of Thomas Aquinas's account of natural desire for the beatific vision has been described, no doubt provocatively, as a continuation and recommencement of 'the real theological revolution of the twentieth century'.[23] That is to say, de Lubac's theology of grace would be 'the real theological revolution' – not Barth's return to the doctrine of the Trinity. The claim is that the 'overcoming of a grace/nature duality', by Blondel as well as by de Lubac and 'in a very flawed manner' by Karl Rahner, 'finally arrived at a theologically "postmodern" questioning of modern assumptions' – 'whereas Karl Barth remained basically within those assumptions and so within modernity'.

In *Theology and Social Theory*, John Milbank commended de Lubac and the 'integralist revolution' of *la nouvelle théologie*: the view that in real historical humanity there is no such thing as a state of 'pure nature'; rather, every human being has always already been worked upon by divine grace – the consequence of which is that we cannot separate 'natural' and 'supernatural' contributions to this integral unity. Consequently, the social and political cannot be separated from the spiritual. The importance of all this is a recovery of a pre-modern sense of the Christianized person as the fully real person, with a stress on action as a mode of ingress for the concrete supernatural life. As we have seen, Barth's theology harbours a remarkably Cartesian current. Milbank's claim is that Barth never broke free of modernity – he did not get through to the patristic and early medieval view of faith and reason as included within participation in the mind of God: 'to reason truly one must be already illumined by God, while revelation itself is but a higher measure of such illumination, conjoined intrinsically and inseparably with a created event which symbolically discloses that transcendent reality, to which all created events to a lesser degree also point'.[24]

What is lacking in Barth's theology, so Milbank contends, is this older understanding of Christ as restoring to us participation in the mind of God. In seeking to retrieve the sense of the self lost, indeed betrayed, by post-Tridentine Thomist orthodoxy and still misunderstood right into the era of *la nouvelle théologie*, de Lubac 'supernaturalizes the natural': 'our mere desire to see God' is already 'a sign of the actual presence of grace within us' – not of a merely possible gift. One can specify human nature only with reference to its supernatural destiny – which of course does not mean that this destiny is owing to human beings as their due. We are back with the Christian paradox – as one might say of love: we all desire it but it always comes as a gift, love that comes on demand is not love at all.

In their entirely different ways, Daphne Hampson and John Milbank testify to the unresolved and perhaps unresolvable difference over the question of grace between Lutheran and pre-Reformation theologies. The bitter dispute among Catholic theologians half a century ago is subsumed here under a much wider view, framing the most intractable division in the history of Western Christianity.[25]

Chapter 9

DEIFIED CREATUREHOOD

The theme of deified creaturehood, examined by Eric Mascall, warrants some further study.[1] 'God alone deifies', Thomas Aquinas writes, in a rare use of the word (ST 1–2.112.1). If he was economical with the word, he nevertheless had a rich conception of the transforming effect of divine grace on the individual believer which clearly amounts to the traditional patristic doctrine of deification.

Here (ST 1–2.112.1), in the context of whether God alone is the efficient cause of grace, Thomas considers three objections: grace is caused in some sense (1) by Jesus Christ, (2) by the sacraments of the New Covenant, and (3) by angels. 'On the other hand', he declares:

> the Psalm says, The Lord will give grace and glory. No being can act beyond the limits of its specific nature, since the cause must always be of a higher power than its effect. Now the gift of grace surpasses every capacity of created nature, since it is nothing other than a certain participation in the divine nature, which surpasses every other nature. And so it is impossible that a creature should cause grace. For just as it is impossible for anything to set fire but fire, so it has to be God alone to divinize, by sharing communion in the divine nature by means of the participation of a sort of assimilation (*communicando consortium divinae naturae per quamdam similitudinis participationem*).

As to the three problems: yes, the actions of the incarnate Word in his human nature certainly have saving efficacy but only in virtue of the divine nature with which his human nature is conjoined. Yes, we may say that grace is caused by the sacraments but only in virtue of the power of the Holy Spirit working in them. And yes, angels may well enlighten human beings, as Denys says, but only by way of some sort of instruction (a somewhat vague concession), certainly not by justifying the unrighteous.

French Interpretations

Aelred Squire, in a reflection on the cultural situation of the believing and praying Christian in the modern West, contends that the doctrine of sanctification as divinization, so central in the teaching of the Church during the first 12 centuries, has come to be so neglected as to be almost unintelligible.[2]

In particular, insisting that this is not to reproach the able men who taught him as a theological student, Squire notes that they never mentioned the theme in Thomas, let alone tried to explain what it might mean: 'They only represented the school in which they had been trained'. Thus, the version of Thomism which Squire encountered at Blackfriars, Oxford, in the early 1950s, was silent about the divinization theme. Indeed, since the end of the thirteenth century, he contends, Western theology has by and large failed to take this central patristic theme seriously: 'The need to remedy this situation in a satisfactory way is still an urgent one'. He cites Maurice Wiles, 'in a good brief explanation of what the Fathers did mean by the phrase', as maintaining nevertheless that they did not mean the expression 'to be taken with full seriousness'.

According to Squire, here thinking not only of the divinization theme, 'those who have been accustomed to read a great medieval theologian like St Thomas Aquinas in the light of his predecessors, unrefracted through the often curious lenses of later times', would find that he exhibits 'an uncanny sense for the minimal essentials of the claims of the unbroken Christian tradition'. If, on the other hand, we read Thomas in the light of the sixteenth-century commentators, or with late nineteenth- and early twentieth-century expositors in the Leonine Thomist tradition, we are unlikely to see him as an inheritor of patristic theology, holding many of the characteristic theological positions of 'the undivided Church' (viz., before the breach between Rome and Constantinople, conventionally dated to 1054).

For Squire, then, as regards the doctrine of grace, Thomas should be read as a late exponent of the ancient patristic divinization theme. At the beginning of the Christological considerations in the *Summa Theologiae*, for example, quoting what he mistakenly believed to be a sermon of Augustine – 'God has become man so that man might become God': a theme familiar since Athanasius – Thomas argues that what is actually given through Christ's being human is that 'full participation in divinity which is humankind's true beatitude and the destiny of human life' (ST 3.1.2).

Once again, depending on whether one sees more of the past than of the future in this 'transitional author', very different assessments of his thought are inevitable. Presumably the Thomists who invigilated Aelred Squire's study of Thomas neglected the patristic inheritance. On the other hand, Réginald Garrigou-Lagrange (1877–1964), the best known French Thomist, while he held back from using the word 'deification', yet regularly described grace as a participation in the divine nature: 'Sanctifying grace, the seed of glory, introduces us into this higher order of truth and life and is an essentially supernatural life, a participation in the intimate life of God, in the divine nature . . . immensely superior to a perceived miracle and above the natural life of our intellectual and immortal soul'.[3]

The word 'deification' itself is not used, no doubt to avoid obvious misunderstandings of what this theology might involve; but the theme is plainly acknowledged.

By 1960, anyone who studied theology in France, for instance, was aware of the possibility that Thomas Aquinas on grace and sanctification might be best read against the background of the Greek patristic theme of divinization. Indeed, as far as the Thomists of Le Saulchoir were concerned, Yves Congar had welcomed M. Lot-Borodine's epoch-making series of articles on divinization in Greek patristic literature as long ago as 1935.[4]

Moreover, with the appearance of the entry on divinization in the *Dictionnaire de Spiritualité* in 1956, the theme was certainly on the theological map.[5] It is made clear, at the outset of the lengthy entry, that only the key moments in the history of the theme would be considered. The purpose of the entry, we are told, is to lighten the entries yet to appear on divine filiation, on indwelling of God in the soul and especially on the doctrine of grace. Evidently, we are not expected to isolate divinization from these other topics.

The entry is so little known in English-language Thomism that we may usefully summarize parts of it here. According to Humbert-Thomas Conus, who is entrusted with the medievals, Thomas shows much more interest in the theme of the divine indwelling than in divinization. The Franciscans Alexander of Hales and Bonaventure, as well as Albert and Thomas, were all disturbed by the thought that God might be regarded, by pantheistically inclined believers, as actually being in the soul in his own divine nature. The word 'deiform' is often employed by Bonaventure, for instance of deiforming grace making the soul perfect, a bride of Christ, a daughter of the Father, a temple of the Holy Spirit, and the like (*Itinerarium mentis in Deum*, 4): language that Thomas never uses. Or

again, for Bonaventure, it is explicitly to the triune God that we are conformed by grace.[6]

Albert maintains that the supernatural union with God that constitutes the divinization of the Christian must be described in terms of
'created' grace. His fear, that is to say, is that the difference between God
and the soul risked being occluded or denied in certain accounts of divine
indwelling. The notion of created grace, which would eventually be
regarded by critics as placing an intermediary between God and the
justified soul, was intended originally to rule out quasi-pantheism. Far
from granting the human creature possession of a certain quality in
response to which God is obliged to act graciously, the doctrine was an
attempt to exclude the temptation to believe that God actually perme-
ated the sanctified soul in a quasi-physical manner.[7]

Divinization in Modern Theology

The deification theme never completely disappeared from Western
Christian spirituality. It is true, of course, that *De deificatione justorum
per Iesum Christum*, the Latin treatise composed in 1693 in Siam (as it
then was) by the French Jesuit missionary Louis Laneau (1637–96), was
first printed in Hong Kong only in 1887 and not in a French translation
until 1993. Yet it testifies to the continuance of the divinization theology late in the seventeenth century and far beyond Western Europe, in
however subterranean a form, albeit the dossier in the *Dictionnaire* concludes with Laneau.

Once alerted, however, we can trace the divinization theme in even
more unexpected and exotic places – in the north-east lowlands of
Scotland, for example, in the work of William Forbes (1585–1634) and
John Forbes of Corse (1593–1648), 'two theologians of unquestionably
international importance'.[8] All but forgotten as the Reformed Church of
Scotland at last became presbyterian, these men clearly took the patristic doctrine of deification for granted.[9]

More surprisingly still, the deification theme has been discovered in
Luther. Robert W. Jenson lists 'deification' in the index of topics in both
volumes of his *Systematic Theology*, insisting that the patristic concept
of *theosis* is an indispensable element in his inheritance. He emphasizes
that the doctrine is 'the precise opposite of the idealist doctrine that
appears in neo-Protestantism', citing 'no more blatant statement' of this
latter than the encomium of Fichte's conception of the human creature's
community of being with God offered by Emanuel Hirsch in a book published in 1952.[10] According to Jenson, the 'content' of patristic language
about hope for participation in God's own nature is substantially the

same as biblical eschatology. Lutheranism followed Philip Melanchthon, Jenson says, rather than Luther, in understanding justification of the unrighteous in strictly forensic terms. By the participation in Christ which occurs as the believer accepts the word of the gospel, Luther takes it that the believer is 'ontically righteous'. For Luther, justification is 'a mode of deification' – Jenson cites Tuomo Mannermaa, thus completely endorsing the 'new Finnish interpretation', the result of a collaborative rereading of Luther by Orthodox and Lutheran scholars. He rejects 'standard Lutheran exegesis', which is conducted 'mostly by liberal Protestants or philosophical existentialists', deploring their account of Luther as 'theology's great deliverer from ontological thinking'. On the contrary, 'the received scholarly understanding' of Luther 'must now be taken as in large part discredited'.[11]

If there are conflicting interpretations of Thomas, as we are seeing, it looks as if Martin Luther is now open to radically different readings with even more significant implications. The standard interpretation that Lutherans acclaim and Catholics attack, according to Jenson, has little basis in Luther's writings. In effect, if Thomas may be read against the background of patristic theology, looking very different from the received picture, it makes just as good sense to treat Luther in the same way, with much more remarkable results.

Returning to Aelred Squire's sense of the absence of the deification theme in his student days, it may be noted that, by the 1970s, writers in English on Thomas were highlighting his allusions to the divinization theme. R.J. Hennessy, for example, in connection with 'participation in divinity' as the human creature's ultimate destiny and beatitude, notes that this is 'a favourite theme with the Fathers of the Church and can be traced back at least as far as Irenaeus'.[12]

Cornelius Ernst was a good deal more positive: the discussion of God's deifying the justified sinner is a 'thoroughly "Greek" article, in its sources, perspectives and philosophical approach'. In citing 2 Peter 1:4 – '[God] has given us most great and precious promises, that by these you may be made partakers of the divine nature' – Thomas 'seems to be using the language of Greek religious philosophy, no doubt in a Christian eschatological sense'.[13]

2 Peter 1:4

The biblical text 2 Peter 1:4, like Exodus 3:14 and Romans 1:20, has been cited for nearly two thousand years in support of a thesis that no doubt goes much beyond what many modern biblical scholars would allow. Once again, readers will divide over the importance to be given to the uses made of a text in establishing its meaning. For Thomas, as we have seen, Romans 1:20 and Exodus 3:14 as read over many centuries are of fundamental importance in constituting his theology. Incommensurable theologies spring from how the historical trajectory of a text is treated.

The expression in 2 Peter 1:4, Michael Green says, 'certainly looks startling', but this does not inhibit him from allowing that such Jewish authorities as Philo, Stobaeus and Josephus use similar language. He rejects any need to choose here between the Hellenistic and Jewish character of 2 Peter – arguing that 2 Peter 1:4 is equivalent to 'being born from above' (John 3:3; James 1:18; 1 Peter 1:23); being the temple of the Holy Spirit (1 Cor. 6:19), being in Christ (Romans 8:1), or being the dwelling-place of the Trinity (John 14: 17–23).

There is no need, Green thinks, to go with the likes of Ernst Käsemann, for whom 'It would be hard to find in the whole New Testament a sentence which ... more clearly marks the relapse of Christianity into Hellenistic dualism'. Käsemann (a Lutheran theologian, it is perhaps relevant to note) takes it for granted that the author of 2 Peter is recommending 'apotheosis', in the sense of some pagan doctrine of escaping from this corruptible world to gain a divine nature. For Käsemann, indeed, this is one more sign of the 'primitive Catholicism' that creeps ruinously into the later New Testament texts.

Green, on the other hand, an Evangelical Anglican, sees no reason not to place 2 Peter in mid-first century, even prior to Peter's death. In his view, then, the divinization theme is as 'primitive' as the New Testament gets.[14]

On the whole, however, this is a minority view. Malcolm Sidebottom, an Anglican scholar and authority on first-century Christianity, thinks that the type of religion envisaged in 2 Peter is 'entirely different from that of the first age of Christians'. The expression 'partakers of the divine nature', he thinks, 'sounds late'. He agrees that this is the doctrine of deification. He dates 2 Peter to around 130. In effect, he is denying that this is an authentically Christian doctrine. Plainly, if this view is correct, Thomas's doctrine of grace, and the entire patristic doctrine of sanctification as deification, must rest on extremely shaky foundations.[15]

Richard J. Bauckham, on the other hand, in one of the most original and conservative commentaries, dates 2 Peter to 80–90, denying that it is likely to be the latest book in the New Testament.[16] He sees 2 Peter 1:4 as dependent on pre-Christian Hellenistic Judaism, citing 4 Maccabees and the Wisdom of Solomon as well as Philo. He insists that none of these authorities envisages any kind of 'pantheistic absorption into God' – the bugbear of Käsemann and many others, and (as we have seen) precisely the heresy that the medievals, including Thomas, sought to eliminate.

Of course, as Bauckham notes, this 'divinization', for these Jewish writers, is entirely the gift of God's grace, not attainable by any human self-promotion. In the case of 2 Peter 1:4, however, Bauckham contends that what is meant is not human participation in the very life and being of God but rather in the nature of heavenly beings definitively other than God. According to Bauckham, the doctrine of deification is much better supported by the Pauline concept of the Christian's participation in the Holy Spirit (Romans 8:11; 1 Cor. 15: 42–53). This could be what 2 Peter 1:4 means, he thinks; but he doubts if the language requires this.

Bauckham regards Käsemann's 'full-scale theological attack on 2 Peter' as 'excessive denigration', noting that for Käsemann, 'early Catholicism' is 'not so much a historical category as a theological accusation'. For his own part, he seems happy to allow that Christians become partakers of divine nature, preferring to say that this is an eschatological prospect, to be attained at death or at the end of the world, rather than connecting it with concepts such as regeneration, adoption, the gift of the Spirit, and even sacramental experience – as Green does.

It all turns on whether 2 Peter 1:4 and the phrase 'participation in the divine nature' is regarded as a mid-second century contamination of the New Testament by some pagan Greek mystery doctrine of apotheosis, or a perfectly natural Christian transformation of an already accepted Hellenistic Jewish doctrine.[17]

Harnack on Thomas

Harnack looms behind one common reading of Thomas on grace. One need only track the references to deification in the index to Harnack's great work to see how angry the theme makes him.

As regards Thomas, the basic error resides in the underlying concept of God and of grace: 'There was no recognition of personality, neither of the personality of God, nor of man as a person'. What Harnack wants may be rather quaintly expressed:

> If even in earthly relations man cannot be otherwise raised to a higher stage, than by passing into a person who is superior, more mature, and greater, that is, by entering into spiritual fellowship with such an one, and attaching one's self to him by reverence, love, and trust, then the same holds good, but in a way that transcends comparison, of the rising of man from the sphere of sin and guilt into the sphere of God.[18]

According to Harnack, Thomas's model is 'communications of things' (*dingliche Mitteilungen*), whereas what is wanted is person-to-person communion: 'the disclosure to the soul, that the holy God who rules heaven and earth is its Father, with whom it can, and may, live as a child in its father's house – that is grace, nay, that alone is grace, the trustful confidence in God, namely, which rests on the certainty that the separating guilt has been swept away'.

Not even the mystics had a real sense of this; they 'aspired to having intercourse with Christ as with a friend', but it was 'the man Jesus of whom they thought in seeking this'. That is to say, like Augustine and Aquinas, they all, when they thought of God, looked, 'not to the heart of God, but to an inscrutable Being (*ein unergründliches Wesen*), who, as he has created the world out of nothing, so is also the productive source of inexhaustible forces that yield knowledge and transformation of essence'. And when they thought of themselves – these mystics – they did not think of 'the centre of the human ego, the spirit, which is so free and so lofty that it cannot be influenced by benefits that are objective, even though they be the greatest perceptions and the most glorious investiture, and at the same time is so feeble in itself that it can find support only in another person'. Rather, in place of the personal fellowship with God which is grace, they construed grace as 'knowledge and participation in the divine nature'. The more impersonal, objective (*dinglich*) and external this grace becomes, the less surprising it is that it at length becomes 'a magical means, which stirs to activity the latent good agency of man, and sets in motion the standing machine, that it may then do its work'.

Everything turns on the concept of God: instead of the 'holy Lord in relation to guilty man', we get 'the unfathomable power that comes to help man with knowledge and with secret influences of a natural kind'. Thomas has 'the Areopagitic Augustinian conception of God' – God as 'the absolute substance'. Though he rejected the pantheism of the 'Neoplatonic-Erigenistic mode of thought', there are traces of the idea that creation is the actualization of the divine ideas, that is, the passage of the divine ideas into a created form of subsisting. Indeed, with his thesis that God necessarily conceived from eternity the idea of the world, since this idea coincides with his knowledge and also with his being (the doctrine of divine simplicity), it appears that the pancosmistic conception of God is not finally excluded, the 'pantheistic acosmism' is not quite banished (cf. ST 1.44.3).

Conditions of Beatific Vision

The most remarkable discussion in recent scholarship comes from Anna Williams.[19]

Williams claims that Thomas is best understood as a mystical theologian, not in the sense of being interested in mystical experiences, visions, ecstasies and so on, but out to write a theology 'concerned with the conditions of the possibility of union with God'. Mystical experiences might be a product (and may be exemplified by the experience in which Thomas saw something in comparison with which all his writings were 'straw') but this 'mystical theology' is concerned with the union of God and the human being created in God's image. What Thomas is out to do, as Williams puts it, is to describe who God is, and who God has created us to be, and the one in whom this union has taken place most radically.

Thomas is not any kind of Pelagian. Union with God takes place, not in virtue of any merit on our part, nor by practising extraordinary spiritual feats, not because of anything we human beings do, but because of who God is. Thomas's *Summa Theologiae* has often been construed as logic-chopping system-building, philosophy-dominated apologetics, or metaphysical speculation – in contrast with all such views Anna Williams insists that the project is wholly shaped by Thomas's relentless portrayal of God as the God who is intent on union with humanity.[20]

God has destined us for a union with himself that lies beyond our grasp (ST 1.1.1). That destiny, 'man's whole salvation, which is in God, depends upon knowledge of this truth'. That is why we do theology. The teaching which is theology is based on premises known by the light of another science: 'God's own knowledge of himself, shared with the blessed in heaven'. Theological activity is a form of reflection rooted in a kind of active participation in God's self-knowledge – which is nothing other than God's own being: according to the doctrine of divine simplicity there is no difference in God between his nature and his mind and his will. Theology, that is to say, is not so much a human task as a divine self-giving, one of the ways in which we are drawn into God's own life.

Thomas deliberately rejects other theological projects, Williams recalls: projects familiar in his day, that start from the sacraments, the history of salvation, Christ in the Church, and so forth. He is interested in theology as primarily concerned with God – not with history or human experience. Thomas goes 'from God to God' – from God as everlasting bliss in his triune being to God as everlasting bliss shared with the blessed, so to speak.

The impetus to understand God, as Williams puts it, is part of the larger process by which God draws human beings towards himself – the gracing of nature that we may come to glory.

Thomas does not use the term union all that often, Williams notes; but it is surely easy to see that he thinks of beatitude in terms of a certain kind of union. Our fulfilment is not to be found in ourselves, or in any of the good things of this world, it lies outside ourselves (ST 1–2. 3.8). It lies in our attaching ourselves, or being attached, to something that is not us. Yet we are not absorbed, or joined to something in between. Williams insists that, for Thomas, the two beings (God and the creature) are brought into a lasting relation that destroys neither. From one perspective, beatitude is uncreated, and from another it is created. It is the uncreated whom we attain, who comes as sheer gift, unmerited and unowed – and the joy we have as a result is ours – created, then, as we are. Thus, our beatitude is not other than God himself; and as our participation in the divine beatitude it is something that God creates in us.

But now this created beatitude is the life of human activity in which our human powers begin to be fulfilled here and now. Human beings become what they are meant to be only in union with God; and the specifically human activities, the practice of the virtues, are a form of participation in divine beatitude in this life.

Thus, for Thomas, theological activity is a form of sharing in God's being, a form of union with God, an anticipation of the beatific vision. Obviously, this will be fulfilled only in heaven, yet this contemplative union with God is already available, fragmentarily and provisionally: 'in heaven the human mind will be united to God by one continual everlasting activity; but in the present life, in so far as we fall short of the unity and continuity of this activity so do we fall short of perfect beatitude'.

Is this contemplation simply a form of prayer, Williams anticipates our asking. Not really, she thinks, or anyway not only. Beatitude is an operation of the mind by which the mind is united to God in knowing God. Such knowing might indeed result from, or actually be, direct apprehension of God in prayer. But Thomas says nothing to suggest that he means only that. He surely includes, and even focuses on, theological reflection, William argues. For Thomas, after all, our highest activity must be one that engages our highest powers and their highest object, which means contemplative absorption in God.

This highest – deepest – of activities is necessarily intellectual – a conclusion, Williams says, decidedly at odds with modern notions of 'beatitude', 'spirituality' and indeed of what we human beings are. Thomas is certainly not equating beatitude with human satisfaction *per se*, not even intellectual satisfaction. He is not thinking of 'personal fulfilment', unless we mean by this the act by which God brings the graced human creature into face-to-face vision with himself.

What the mind is capable of knowing in and of itself cannot provide the beatitude that is our destiny; Thomas has said that all along. Theological work, prayer, the spiritual life, the practice of the virtues, are theo-centric activities, even eccentric activities – in the sense of ways in which one may be drawn towards God, and drawn beyond oneself.

Thomas differs from many writers, some of whom might be respectable authorities on the spiritual life. It is not reflection on one's experience of God's goodness, or intense awareness of God's presence or absence that motivates unitive love, Williams insists, in Thomas's view; rather, it is meditation on God's nature. The painstakingly technical consideration of the divine nature, simplicity, goodness, transcendence, immanence, and so on, the opening questions *de Deo uno*, may be viewed, or rather should be followed, as a form of meditation, intended to incite the love that leads to union. So far from being rationalistic meta-physics of the first cause, the questions on the divine nature in the *Summa* are in effect an invitation to the student to exercise his or her mind, with whatever depth and clarity may be possible, in repeated denials in God of creaturely qualities, in steadfast recollection that it is possible only to consider what God is not (ST 1.3), in order that in contemplating the uncreated, the mind may be drawn into the life of the uncreated.

Williams focuses on the question in which Thomas considers how the created mind comes into the light: the light of reason, the light of grace, and the light of glory (ST 1.12). The more light there is the more per-fectly the mind sees God. Those who have greater love have more light. But, as Williams insists, contemplation for Thomas is not identified with any particular method or form of prayer, rather it is the activity by which the mind is drawn to God and into the beatific vision. Minds are what we are: we are creatures with minds who can be fulfilled only by knowing the highest object, the richest other, our minds can entertain – God. The gift of grace that is God's self-disclosure, the basis of all theology then, as well of course as of all prayer, means that not only are we not frus-trated in our desire to know what lies infinitely beyond us but we are drawn to a destiny we could never of ourselves have even imagined.

God of the Five Ways

Thomas thinks of the image of God in human beings not as unmoving, a static and immobile mirror image, but as a 'movement' (*motus*), tending towards a certain fulfilment (ST 1.35.2.3, cf 2–2.175.1.2). While it is proper to the mode and dignity of human beings that they be divinized (*ad divina elevetur*) since they are created in the divine image – yet, since the divine good exceeds all human capacity infinitely, the human being needs to be helped *supernaturaliter* to receive this good – which happens by some kind of gift of grace. Thus we may say that, if the soul is divinized (e.g. in mystical ecstasy, *per raptum*) this is not a violation of our nature, but beyond its ability (*non contra naturam sed supra facultatem naturae*).

It is important to recall that possession of God, being possessed by God, which human beings are understood to enjoy in the beatific vision, is not a grasp, or enclosing within their finite minds, of that which is unfathomable. On the contrary, it is an enjoyment in which one is enraptured – captured by, rather than capturing, the One by whom one is enraptured.

In this simple and brilliant reading, Anna Williams invites us to see that Thomas's theology is dominated by God – but that means by the God who seeks to bring human beings into face-to-face communion with himself. Thomas's God, that is to say, is never aloof or separated from creatures, the created order. On the contrary, the divine intention to bring into being creatures destined for union with himself has been there all along. Moreover, carrying her attack on the standard view of Thomas's apologetics even further, Williams argues that, whatever the Five Ways are intended to do, each on its own already suggests not only God's actual connection to the world but also a divine desire to be connected with the world.

The First Mover moves something towards himself; the efficient cause causes something other than himself; the non-contingent being freely gives being to all else that exists; the degrees of being imply the highest being's sharing of goodness and perfection with others; and the divine mind's ordering of the universe towards its divinely ordained destiny presumes the desire to do some such thing.

The God of the Five Ways is the source and end of all (*principium et finis*); but, perhaps since the focus is on inferring the existence of the *principium*, there has been a tendency to overlook the fact that the Five Ways amount to a description of God also as *finis* or *telos*: in effect as the one who is drawing all things to himself. When Thomas considers the divine perfection he includes the perfecting of creatures (ST 1.4); when he considers the divine goodness he immediately thinks of this goodness as shared with creatures (ST 1.6). Thomas says nothing of God which does not simultaneously refer to that which is not God – quite explicitly in these instances.

This becomes more and more clear as we proceed through the *Summa*. When we get to human beings, and what we do, we find that we are considered as images of God. When we get to the questions about grace we find immediately that grace is given that we may be 'deiformed'. And so on.

Mostly, in standard approaches, we think of Thomas in the *Summa Theologiae* as laying down the foundations ('God exists'), proceeding to build up his great system. The simple move that shapes Williams's interpretation is to start, so to speak, from the end. She argues, and no reader could disagree, that the *Summa* situates everything *sub ratione Dei* (cf. ST 1.1.7). Everything is focused on God as *principium et finis*. In the end, everything culminates in our 'seeing God as He is' (1 John 3:2) – in the beatific vision (ST 1.12). The *Summa*, Williams argues, is concerned above all to spell out the conditions for participation by graced human beings in the life of the blessed Trinity.

While never up front about it, Thomas maintains the patristic doctrine of sanctification as deification. Interpreters of Thomas with a background in Harnack are unlikely to agree but, it seems to me, Anna Williams has made a powerful case that Thomas may, and surely should, be read in the light of his commitment to the doctrine of deification.

The triune being of God is bliss, and salvation is the sharing of this bliss. Thomas's theological project no doubt begins by establishing God's existence but his thinking is thoroughly teleological, indeed eschatological: to paraphrase Williams, the *Summa Theologiae* is a study of the transcendental conditions of beatific vision; not foundationalist apologetics but a set of practices for receiving the gift of beatitude.[21]

Chapter 10

CHRIST IN THE
SUMMA THEOLOGIAE

'The Christian faith consists above all in the confession of the Holy Trinity, and it glories especially in the cross of our Lord Jesus Christ'.[1] This remark, dated to about 1265, thus just before he began to write the *Summa Theologiae*, would not seem to many readers to represent Thomas Aquinas's most characteristic thought. On the contrary, the standard interpretation in the English-language literature is that Thomas has little interest either in the cross of Christ or in the doctrine of the Trinity.

The Consummation of Theology

True, Thomas's decision to focus, in the great *Summa*, on God rather than on Christ (cf. ST 1.1.7) means that Christological questions come much later than modern theologians would usually prefer. Even then, he regards the consideration of 'the Saviour of all and the benefits conferred by him on humankind' as the 'consummation of the whole theological enterprise' (ST 3 prologue). A human being, as created in God's likeness, is capable of the blessed knowledge which is the face-to-face vision of God that is our ultimate destiny; but it is only in virtue of Christ's humanity that we are drawn into this bliss (cf. ST 3.9.2).

The decision to structure the *Summa Theologiae* as he did meant rejecting rival schemes. Thomas names three: organizing the exposition of Christian doctrine in terms of the realities and signs (*res et signa*); or in terms of the history of salvation (*opera reparationis*); or in terms of Christ as head and Christians as members (of the Church) (*totus Christus*). He declares that all these matters will be treated in his exposition, right enough, but with reference to God, theocentrically: 'either because they are God himself or because they have a relationship to God as beginning and end (*principium et finis*)' (ST 1.1.7). Other theologians configure things differently, as he knows; but here he sets out to relate everything, including the sacraments, the history of salvation, and even Christ, to God.

On earlier occasions, six at least, Thomas chose to construct his exposition of Christian doctrine on the basis of the articles of faith, dividing them between those that relate to the mystery of the Godhead and those that relate to the mystery of Christ.

The work from which we have quoted, *De articulis fidei*, composed for the archbishop of Palermo in the mid 1260s, turned out to be Thomas's most popular work (277 copies survive), partly no doubt because it is short and deliberately aimed at being memorizable; it was still being widely read in Germany in the fifteenth century. It gives quite a different picture of the shape of Thomas's theology from the standard one (there is no English translation). Indeed, these Creed-structured expositions might be said to provide a much more characteristic account than the *Summa Theologiae*.

Of course, Thomas discusses the articles of faith in the *Summa*. He considered the Creed in the context of the theological virtue of faith. As usual, but only following tradition, he divides the articles of faith into those that relate to 'the mystery of the Godhead, seeing which makes us blessed', and those that relate to 'the mystery of the humanity of Christ by which we have access to the glory of the children of God' (ST 2–2.1.8).

The articles of faith are not cited as providing the framework in the *Summa* for expounding Christian doctrine. On the other hand, it is not implausible to suggest that the originality of the *Summa* was to recast the traditional penitential treatises about virtue and vice in terms of the human being's progress towards beatitude (thus giving us the *secunda pars*), situating this in the middle, precisely, of the consideration of the mystery of the Godhead (the *prima pars*) and the mystery of Christ's humanity (the *tertia pars*). Christian doctrine is handed on, in the *Summa*, with the focus always on the God who is beginning and destiny of rational creatures (cf. ST 1.1.7). The movement towards the promised enjoyment of divine beatitude, which Thomas expounds in the *secunda pars*, is located between the mystery of the Godhead in the *prima pars* and the mystery of Christ's humanity in the *tertia pars*. The structure of the *Summa*, deliberately or otherwise, is a vastly expanded rendition of the Christian faith's polarization between the God who is one and three and the Son of God by whose incarnation, passion and resurrection human beings are brought to fullness of life.

Moreover, Thomas could never have supposed, let alone intended, that the *Summa* would be studied in isolation from his biblical exegesis, as it so frequently has been. While we may be tempted to think the *Summa* is the text of a course of lectures, there is no reason to believe it was ever delivered in class, or regarded by Thomas as anything more than an aid to studying Scripture and disputing doctrinal issues. Nor could he have imagined students of Christian doctrine whose days were not shaped by worship and penitential practices. We have abundant evidence that the friars understood the liturgy as continuous meditation on, and re-creation of, the realities declared in the articles of the Creed: their daily lives immersed them in 'following Christ'.

The model of a 'good theologian' (*bonus theologus*), Thomas notes towards the end of his lecture course on the Fourth Gospel, is Thomas the Apostle, precisely when he acclaimed Christ as 'My Lord and my God', thus proclaiming the humanity and the divinity of Jesus Christ.

The fact remains, obviously, that the *Summa* is not documented every step of the way with New Testament references. Nor is it a '*theologia crucis*', the label Martin Luther gave to the theological principle that knowledge of the Being of God must be derived solely from meditation on the Passion of Christ – though it is not a *theologia gloriae* either, if by that Luther understood a theology which centres on the sovereignty of God independently of Christian revelation.

Thomas's theology is indeed a 'theology of glory'. But that is because the 'consummation of the whole theological enterprise' is 'our Lord Jesus Christ' as 'demonstrating in himself the way of truth by which we are able to reach the beatitude of immortal life by rising': 'the everlasting beatitude which consists in full enjoyment of God' (ST 3 prologue, cf. e.g. ST 3.49.5).

The Christian Religion

How we read the *Summa Theologiae* depends on who the intended readers are supposed to be, as well as on what we may presuppose and supply about the author's faith from the rest of his writings.

The prologue (ST 1) runs as follows:

> Since the teacher of catholic truth (*veritas catholica*) has not only to instruct the advanced but it is his task also to educate the beginners, as Paul says, As infants in Christ I fed you with milk, not solid food (1 Cor 3: 1–2), the purpose we have set before us in this work is to hand on what relates to the Christian religion (*christiana religio*) in a way that is appropriate for the formation of beginners. For we considered that newcomers

to this teaching are greatly hindered by various writings, partly indeed by the multiplication of pointless questions, articles, and arguments, partly also because what is essential for beginners to know is communicated not in a disciplined way but according to what exegesis of books required or what emerged on the occasion of formal disputation, and partly indeed because the frequent repetition of these essential matters has bred boredom and muddle in the listeners' minds. Eager, then, to avoid these and the like, we shall try, with confidence in God's help, to pursue what relates to holy teaching (*sacra doctrina*) as concisely and lucidly as the subject matter allows.

Who these 'beginners' were is one more much disputed question – not of little interest, either, since the answer affects how one reads the text. Perhaps they were the young friars whom Thomas taught at Santa Sabina in Rome in 1265–8, when he started to compose the *Summa*. These would have been run-of-the-mill students who were being trained to preach in the vicinity of the priories in which they had joined the Order. Unlike Thomas himself, they would not have been destined to proceed to the great international universities to study theology.[2]

Such students did not have copies of the book, or access even to a master copy. This might mean, then, on the alternative view, that it was never intended for them. Perhaps the *Summa* was designed, rather, for those who were to instruct them: intended to help the next generation of lecturers to overcome the 'boredom and confusion' afflicting students who found being taken through Scripture in class repetitious and formal disputations over-subtle. The *Summa* reads like the reflective synthesis which might follow years of studying the biblical and patristic texts, and of hearing doctrinal issues disputed in the schools. Perhaps it was meant for lecturers to use as they guided students through the standard practices of exegesis of Scripture and public argument about Christian doctrine.

Judging from his subsequent practice, Thomas never envisaged the *Summa* replacing exegesis or disputation. On the contrary, after starting to write it, he lectured on the Fourth Gospel (1269–72) and on the Epistle to the Romans (1270–2), in both cases authorizing transcripts. The disputations in the main collections may all be earlier than the *Summa*, it is true; but Thomas certainly took part in disputations about the virtues (1268–72) while he was working on related questions in the *secunda pars*.

It looks as if the *Summa* was intended as a supplement to, not a substitute for, the practices of reading Scripture in common, and of formal gatherings to argue out the questions that would arise. On the other hand, Thomas made some scathing remarks in about 1271 about the prevalence of silly questions in theological debates.[3] As he got older, perhaps he became more impatient with an only too recognizable insatiable lust for authoritative solutions to ever subtler problems.

The prologue offers another ambiguous clue. 'Catholic truth' is evidently equated with 'holy teaching'[4] and also with 'what relates to the *christiana religio*', an expression which obviously cannot mean what we mean today by the Christian religion: the religion which is practised by Christians, as distinct from other traditions. (The *Oxford English Dictionary* cites George Berkeley, in 1732: 'The Christian Religion, which pretends to teach men the knowledge and worship of God'.)

Thomas does not use the word univocally. Primarily, *religio* is the first of the virtues annexed to the cardinal virtue of justice (cf. ST 2.2.81). It covers such matters as prayer, worship, sacrifice, offerings and first fruits, tithes, vows and oaths; and the related vices are superstition, idolatry, simony, and so on. He refers often to the Old Testament but assumes that it is 'a dictate of natural reason that human beings should do something to reverence God' – though what, exactly, is not determined by natural reason but is instituted by divine or human law (81. 2). The practices which display the natural virtue of religion (as he considers it to be) come under the cardinal virtue of justice, as rendering what is due: in this case, the debt of worship which creatures owe to God as creator. He places the virtue of religion in the context of honouring one's parents, honouring the sovereign, and suchlike – different kinds of honouring, as he says; yet clearly, he thinks, with a family resemblance. Piety, for Thomas, is ceremony, not private feelings of awe; worship is an expression of the public virtue of justice, not the overflow of religious emotion.

In a related sense, *religio* is 'religious life': the ecclesiastical and social state of persons under monastic vows. ('Religion', in this sense, is found in the fourteenth century, according to the *Oxford Dictionary*.)

What Thomas means in the prologue to the *Summa* is, however, no doubt what he has in mind at the beginning of one of his apologias for the way of life of the friars: 'The purpose of the *christiana religio* manifestly consists especially in this, that it disengages us from earthly things and makes us intent on spiritual things. Hence it is that the author of and consummator of faith, Jesus Christ, coming into this world, has shown those who believe in him, by deed and word, contempt for worldly things'. Thomas is thinking of *christiana religio* as the way of living in the world according to the example of Christ: in the world but not of the world; turning away from worldliness in order to seek the things that are above; in short, 'imitating Christ'.

The purpose of the *Summa*, in short, was to hand on the doctrinal element in 'the things which pertain to *christiana religio*': the imitation of Christ in the network of practices, liturgical and ascetic, but also moral and spiritual, which, unsurprisingly, Thomas simply took for granted in his students.

The Naked Cross

Thomas never mentions himself or his personal beliefs, in the *Summa Theologiae* or anywhere else, but he wrote a good deal about what it is to be a friar, allowing us some insight into the kind of life which he lived. In one of his polemics, he steered away from the Franciscan ideal of abandonment of all property – literally, 'leaving everything' – and picked up the accompanying phrase – 'Lo, we have left everything and followed you' (Matthew 19:27).

'Following Christ' (*sequela Christi*) was a theme familiar since Jerome (c.345–420), translator of the Bible into Latin but in virtue of being founder of a monastery at Bethlehem regarded as an authority on the essence of monastic (religious) life.

In the *Contra doctrinam retrahentium a religione* (1271), another of his apologias for religious life, Thomas allows that voluntary and mendicant poverty is important, but insists on the absolute primacy of charity. Here he highlights Jerome's famous phrase: *nudum Christum nudus sequi*, 'following the naked Christ naked'.

In effect, he is separating himself from the monastic practice of supporting themselves by working the land they owned but also distancing himself from the Franciscan friars' ideal of living by begging. He sees space between the Benedictine way of life in which his early formation took place, and the radical mendicancy of his Franciscan contemporaries. He insists on the primacy of charity in any form of religious life, but connects it explicitly and specifically with the *crucis nuditas*: 'the nakedness of the Cross'.

In the *Summa*, which was being dictated at the same time (1271–2), Thomas takes up these themes – whether Christ should have led a poor life (ST 3.40.3) – but, perhaps surprisingly, he does not cite Jerome's striking phrase – 'following the naked Christ naked'. In fact, the laconic treatment in the *Summa* of what was a burning issue at the time reveals nothing of the passion Thomas actually felt. In chapter 15 of the *Contra doctrinam retrahentium*, however, as Torrell remarks, Thomas 'unveils a personal mysticism of attachment to the poor Christ . . . with a liveliness his usual reserve hardly prepares us for' – which no doubt (as Torrell says) testifies to the struggle he had to undergo with his family to be allowed to be a friar at all, as well as the polemics with the secular masters in Paris about the legitimacy of this novel way of religious life.

This brings us more intimately than anywhere else into Thomas's Christ-centred spirituality.[5]

In any case, even if his personal devotion to the Cross is never on show, Thomas seems to take Jesus as the prototype of the Dominican friar (ST 3a 40, 1): Jesus is said to have chosen an active life of preaching and teaching, passing on to others the fruits of his own contemplation. In other words, he was not simply a monk, engaged in contemplation, but also a preacher, ready to share the Good News with others. This, as well as much else in his writings, suggests how centred on Jesus Christ Thomas's own life, as preacher and teacher, and his conception of the Dominican friars' way of life, actually were.[6]

The Fittingness of God's Becoming Flesh

No one would expect Thomas to work out his Christology in terms of the post-Enlightenment Quest of the Historical Jesus. Like most others, modern Roman Catholic theologians, such as Christian Duquoc, Walter Kasper, and Edward Schillebeeckx, all begin their Christologies, in varying degree, by reconstructing the specific history and unique life and destiny of Jesus of Nazareth. Thomas, however, opens the Christology of the *Summa* with questions about 'the mystery of the Incarnation, in the sense that God has become man for our salvation'. This, in modern jargon, is clearly a Christology 'from above', not 'from below', in the sense of beginning by documenting the setting and history of Jesus and allowing his significance to develop from there.

The first question that Thomas raises is whether it was appropriate (*conveniens*) for God to become incarnate at all (ST 3.1.1). He wants to show, of course, that given that God has in fact become incarnate nothing inappropriate about this follows: '*nullum inconveniens sequitur, Deo incarnato*' (ST 3.1.1). His considerations are all after the event. That God has become incarnate may well seem surprising but since it has happened it is up to the theologian to remove what unease we may feel. It was not to be expected, but on the other hand the Incarnation is not utterly incomprehensible, outrageous and unacceptable – if you think about it. For Thomas, as for medieval theology as a whole, the chief purpose of theological argument was to bring out how fitting the events of God's dealings with the world turn out to be – once what has happened can be taken in and reflected on in a contemplative spirit.

Even within Thomist theology, arguing in favour of the appropriateness of this or that occurrence or item in the history of salvation, has largely been treated as marginal. For Thomas himself, however, this way of arguing is of great importance. In the end, obviously, it depends on

Thomas's conviction that we can reason our way to understanding something of the significance of what God has done and is doing – Thomas's
fundamental conviction that God always acts towards the creatures he
has made in a way that respects their nature. God always acts wisely,
Thomas believes, which is why it is possible for us to work out the appropriateness of this or that happening – after the event, of course.[7]

Thomas lists four reasons for regarding the Incarnation as scandalous:
God should not be united to flesh; God is infinitely distant from us; God
should not become entangled with evil; and God, who transcends the
entire universe, should not be contained in a woman's womb. In short,
it is not difficult to see, these are the objections that would be felt by
those – particularly the Cathars – who regarded matter, flesh and the
body, as radically unsuitable to receive this divine intervention.

These are all objections that Thomas deals with, not by a construal
of the history of Jesus Christ, but by appealing to a particular conception of God:

> It is most fitting to manifest the unseen things of God through things that
> are visible, for this is why the whole world has been created, as Paul says:
> 'The invisible things of God are there for the mind to see in the things that
> he has made' (Romans 1:20); but, as Damascene says, what has happened
> through the mystery of the Incarnation is that 'the goodness, wisdom,
> justice, and power or strength of God are shown'. (ST 3.1.1)

Once again, Thomas turns to John of Damascus, placing himself as
he no doubt supposed in the great tradition of the undivided Church.
He goes on as follows:

> Whatever is appropriate to a thing is that which fits it according to the
> definition of its proper nature; as reasoning is appropriate to human beings
> because this is appropriate to them insofar as they are by nature rational;
> but the very nature of God is goodness (*bonitas*) as Denys says, which
> means that whatever belongs to the meaning of the good is appropriate to
> God.

Again, then, at the key moment, Thomas appeals to what he takes to be
the Greek patristic concept of God as the good. The rest of the argument
is easy to guess:

> Now the very idea of the good implies that it communicates itself to others,
> as Denys says. Therefore it fits with the idea of the supreme good that it
> communicates itself to the creature in the highest way. But, as Augustine
> says, this happens above all when [God] 'so joins created nature to himself
> that one person happens from the Word, soul and flesh. Thus it is mani-
> fest that it was appropriate that God be incarnate'.

Given the fact of the Incarnation, in brief, we can see it as just what we should expect – if (with Denys, Augustine and John Damascene) we already have an understanding of God as freely self-communicating goodness. That is to say, the God whose ways have already been disclosed in the existence of the world and in the history of the people of the Covenant, thus in the wisdom-seeking of ancient Greece and in the Law, the prophets and the Wisdom literature of the people of Israel, turns out to be the God who has united the creature to himself in a new way (ST 3.1.1). But now that this new way has been established it becomes possible, indeed unavoidable and desirable, for the Christian theologian to work out, in retrospect, how the historical event of the Incarnation is prefigured and anticipated, however provisionally and obscurely, in natural religion and in the Old Testament.

The Motive of the Incarnation

As we have come to expect of a theologian whose thought is so entirely dominated by the prospect of face-to-face communion with God, the focus in the *tertia pars* of the *Summa Theologiae* – his Christology – was never going to be on the 'historical Jesus' or even on the Christ whose significance can be reconstructed by New Testament research; it was always going to be on contemplating the purposes of God and on what this reveals about God and about the human condition.

The standard view is that, for Thomas Aquinas, the Incarnation took place solely, or anyway principally, to deal with 'the Fall'. This is regarded as contrary to the views of the followers of John Duns Scotus, who think that it was in God's plan from all eternity for the Word to become human, as a coronation of creation so to speak, irrespective then of the need to rescue sinners from damnation.

As we have just seen, however, it is only after considering the Incarnation as one more communication of divine goodness that Thomas turns to consider the question whether the Incarnation was necessary to save sinful humanity from damnation (ST 3.1.2). He offers a lengthy answer, beginning again by highlighting the Incarnation as 'advancing human beings towards the Good', this time citing Augustine throughout, and culminating with the axiom: 'God became man so that man might become God' – referring to the 'total participation in divinity which is truly the beatitude of man and the goal of human life, granted us by Christ's humanity'. And only after this does Thomas consider whether God would have become incarnate if the human race had not sinned (3.1.3): the locus of the famous difference between Thomists and Scotists about the 'motive' of the Incarnation.

Thomas knew of conflicting views on this question. His allusions are easy enough to follow. His teacher the Dominican friar Albert the Great and the Franciscan friar Alexander of Hales both maintained that, even if humankind had not sinned, the Son of God would have become incarnate. On the other side of the debate, Thomas would have had in mind his two most celebrated Franciscan contemporaries, Bonaventure and Eudes Rigaud, with whom he will align himself. Our only source for knowledge about God's will is Scripture; and everywhere in Scripture the Incarnation is related to sin.

Obviously Thomas was well aware of two schools of thought, though of course not setting future Thomists and future Scotists against one another. Nor was there any disagreement between Dominican and Franciscan theologians over the issue: the Dominican Albert held that the Incarnation would have taken place anyway, whereas Franciscans such as Bonaventure and Eudes Rigaud regarded such speculation as excluded by the New Testament's linking of Incarnation and Redemption. Given that the perspective in which Thomas sees the event of the Incarnation is, initially and predominantly, that of the Dionysian conception of God as the freely and generously self-communicating sovereign Good, there is surely a certain tension in maintaining that but for sin there would have been no Incarnation, and that the reason for holding this view is that 'what comes in virtue of the sole will of God, beyond what is due to the creature, cannot become known to us except as delivered in Sacred Scripture, through which the divine will becomes known to us' (3.1.3). It is perhaps arguable whether the reason for the Incarnation is related to the sin of Adam and Eve 'everywhere in Scripture': the sort of downright assertion that prompts one to re-examine the evidence. Moreover, it may seem somewhat disingenuous to claim that we know nothing of God's will except what we find in Scripture when the free and unconstrained self-communication of the sovereign Good has already been taken as the most obvious way of redescribing the will of God.

For sure, Thomas no doubt saw the picture of God as self-communicating goodness, which he finds in Denys, John Damascene and Augustine, as evidently grounded in Scripture. That might be more difficult to document than his claim that there is no reference in Scripture to the Incarnation except in connection with the Fall. However that may be, the appeal (in ST 3.1.3) to the principle that we know nothing of God's purposes apart from what is revealed in Scripture seems in some tension with the conviction that God's purpose in the Incarnation is to communicate his goodness to the highest degree (3.1.1). The Reformation principle of consulting Scripture alone is beginning to surface, one is tempted to suggest, in the middle of the Augustinian but actually more Dionysian and Damascenian theology of God as the self-giving Good. Thomas has

no inkling of how different (or even supposedly incompatible) the Latin
and Greek patristic traditions should be regarded as being. Here, as elsewhere, he immediately thinks of backing his view with quotations from
Denys and John Damascene – only then invoking Augustine.

Over the question of the 'motive' of the Incarnation, in modern
Scholastic jargon, something of a tension is thus detectable in Thomas's
account: the question is either settled by invoking the austerity of an
incipient *sola scriptura* principle (at 3.1.3) or preempted (at 3.1.1) by the
'Christian Platonism' of the Church Fathers.

The Singular Man

It is no surprise that, having considered the appropriateness of God's
becoming incarnate, Thomas at once moves on to consider, at some
length (qq. 2 to 26), the ontological implications: taking his stand, again
unsurprisingly, on the decision of the Council of Chalcedon: 'two natures
in one person'.[8]

Perhaps it is worth noting then that, right in the middle of this exposition of the logical implications of the union of the divine and human
natures in the divine person of the Word incarnate, Thomas offers an
account of Jesus Christ 'the singular human being' (3.7), in which he
portrays him, tacitly, as the paradigm of the moral agent described at
such length in the *secunda pars*.

Primarily, Thomas is refuting docetist temptations. In his day, the
temptation was to regard Christ as solely divine, in effect as God only
'seeming' to be human (Greek *dokein*: to seem).

Thomas's contemporaries (he thinks), might be inclined to regard it
as superfluous to attribute *gratia habitualis* to the man Jesus: grace is a
certain participation in divinity on the part of the rational creature but
Christ is God not in any participative way but really and truly; Christ
surely needed no other grace than that of union with the divine Word;
Christ's human nature as 'instrument of divinity' (in the phrase from
John Damascene that Thomas likes very much) is used by God and needs
no other grace to perform the appropriate actions. Why should the man
Jesus have – need – to be sanctified, to be transformed by grace?

Against all this Thomas cites Isaiah 61.1: 'The Spirit of the Lord rests
upon him': if one has the Spirit 'resting' upon one, this means that one
is so possessed by divine grace as to be 'habitually' graced.

Thomas does not often refer us explicitly to what he has said earlier
but on this occasion he refers us back to the key question where he contends that 'no other effect but sanctifying grace (*gratia gratum faciens*)
is the explanation of a divine Person's being in a rational creature in the

new way' – 'dwelling there as his temple' (ST 1.43.3). Of course, as Thomas argues here, 'God is in everything, as the cause in the participants in his goodness; but over and above this mode there is a mode specific to rational natures, in which God is said to be as the known in the knower and as the beloved in the lover'. This is why we may say that, 'by knowing and loving the rational creature by its own proper activity (*sua operatione*) touches God himself'.

Here, once again, Thomas appeals to the principle that, in the act of knowing and loving, that which is known and loved is, in a way, actually in the one who knows and loves – in an identity, which is however not an absorption of one by the other. Once again, too, since there is no competition between human activity and divine, it is by one's own activity that one is drawn into God.

In this key article (ST 1.43.3), in the culminating consideration of the doctrine of the Trinity, Thomas is talking primarily about the 'mission' of divine Persons, contending that there is no mission of a divine Person to a human being except through and by 'sanctifying grace' (*gratia gratum faciens*): the grace that makes the recipient pleasing to God. This line seemed then, as it seems to many still, to mean that what is given is not the divine Person himself but only his gifts.

Thomas comes back to the same issue in discussing charity (ST 2–2.23.2): the thesis that grace and charity simply are the Holy Spirit, actively present directly and immediately. There Thomas insists that if the divine love which is charity is in us only as the Holy Spirit, that means that we ourselves are not charitable people, or ever actually acting charitably and lovingly. That is tantamount to saying that we are mere puppets. In the same way, here with regard to the mission of a divine Person, if there is no sanctification of the human being by and through the gift of grace that makes him or her pleasing to God, that means there has been no gift of the divine Person either.

Returning to Christology: those arguments that regard Christ's human nature as being so united to the divinity that his having the *habitus* of *gratia gratum faciens* would be superfluous only turn the man Jesus into a puppet.

Given, then, that, as human, Christ is graced in such a way as to be pleasing to God (ST 3.7.1), that implies he has the virtues (7.2), like any other human being, excluding faith and hope, however, since he enjoys the *fruitio divina* from his conception (7.3–4); but certainly including the gifts of the Holy Spirit (7.5), the gift of fear of the Lord (7.6), the charisms including prophesy (7.7–8), and finally, the plenitude of grace (7.10–13).

This plenitude of grace is what allows the particular individual who is Jesus Christ to be also the 'source of grace', as 'head of the Church' and as head of the human race as a whole (3.8.1–3). The discussion here is pervaded with New Testament references: Ephesians 1:22, Romans 8:29 and 12:4, 1 Timothy 4:10, 1 John 2:2 and so on. The people of Israel are included: 'the patriarchs, by observing the sacraments of the Law, were carried to Christ by the same faith and love by which we also are brought to him' (8.3.3). Finally: 'Christ alone (*ipse solus Christus*) is the one through whom we have access to the grace in which we stand' (8.6.3).

Christology from Below

Once through all the implications of the metaphysics of the union between God and humanity in the Word incarnate, very much on the basis of the decisions of the early Councils of the Church, Thomas turns to consider 'what the Son of God incarnate in the human nature united to himself did or suffered' (3.27 prologue).

This is where something like a Christology 'from below' is introduced. It falls into four main sections. They are each related to the world: Christ's entry into the world (27–39); the unfolding of his life in the world (40–5); his exodus from the world (46–52) and his exaltation after this life (53–9).

The first set, on Christ's entry into the world, deals with questions on his conception, birth, baptism, and so on, including questions about the Mother of God (3.27–39).

Unlike many Roman Catholic theologians, Thomas treated 'Mariology' in the context of Christology. Famously, while conceding that the practice in other traditions of celebrating the Conception of the Blessed Virgin liturgically should be tolerated, Thomas saw no need to hold any doctrine of her 'immaculate conception' (3.27.2). He contends that Mary (like John the Baptist) was sanctified in the womb but he saw no reason to say that she was actually conceived sanctified. (The doctrine, finally defined in 1854, developed first in England; it was propounded by John Duns Scotus in Oxford and Paris, then by Franciscan theologians in general, and was widely accepted in the late eighteenth and early nineteenth centuries; the doctrine is sometimes now held to mean no more and no less than is meant in the Orthodox Church by calling Mary 'all-holy'.)

In the set of questions on Christ's life in the world we have very much a reading of the Synoptic gospels: Christ's mode of life, the temptation narrative, his preaching, his miracles, and the Transfiguration.

Compared with modern historical-critical reconstructions of the life of the man who figures in the Gospels, Thomas's considerations are very elementary. No doubt, on the other hand, these considerations give some insight into the sort of thing he noted as he took students though the Gospels. Largely ignored by professional theologians, Thomists included, these questions were until recently quite familiar to many devout Catholics, extracted and published on their own in French, German, Spanish or Italian translation. Perhaps the post-Vatican II biblical movement has encouraged such people to study the Gospels directly, even to practise a little 'life of Jesus' research, thus rendering Thomas's exposition completely redundant.[9]

The Passion of Christ

That the Christian faith 'glories especially in the cross of Christ' emerges in the questions on the Passion (ST 3.46–52).[10] The first question – 'whether Christ had to suffer in order to redeem the human race' (46.1) – is a meditation on John 3:14 and Luke 24, insisting that God was not compelled to save humankind this way and that Christ chose to die. Of course God could have redeemed us otherwise (46.2) but this way demonstrated how much God loves humankind, provides an example of obedience, and so on (46.3). Asking why Christ's death was by crucifixion, death on a cross, Thomas brings together several patristic motifs: the multiple symbolism of the cross as tree of life, that on which Christ was lifted up, the sign that embraces the whole world; the wood of the cross anticipated by Noah's wooden ark, Moses' rod, and the Ark of the Covenant (46.4). Christ did not endure every type of suffering (46.5); he endured maximum physical pain (46.6) and mental anguish (46.7) but retained the beatific vision (46.8). The time was right, even though Thomas cannot decide whether it was the Passover (46.9); the place – Jerusalem – was appropriate (46.10). In retrospect, being crucified between two thieves was extremely significant – quoting from Isaiah 53:12 as well as Chrysostom, Jerome, Leo, Hilary, Bede, Origen and Augustine, in another tapestry of patristic allusions.

Thomas turns to the question of who was responsible for Christ's death: he laid down his life willingly (47.1–2), out of obedience to the Father's will (47.3), but he died at the hands of men (47.4–6) – with the 'leaders of the Jews' (*principes Judaeorum*) bearing the heaviest guilt, the 'uneducated Jews' (*minores de populo*) being forgiven because of their ignorance, and the pagans including Pontius Pilate being 'much more excusable still, since they had no knowledge of the Law'.

These two questions (46 and 47) cover obvious questions about the Passion of Christ. Question 46 is concerned with what happened, but actually shows much more interest in looking for the significance of the event in cosmic-symbolic terms than in discovering (as we might now want to do) the practical detail of executions by crucifixion. Question 47, concerned with the 'cause' of Christ's death, shows that, when Thomas thinks of causing, he has the responsibility of personal agents in mind.

No doubt these are little more than headings, expecting further discussion. By far the most contentious, from the earliest days of Christian reflection, revolves round the thesis that the man Jesus Christ was caught up in the beatific vision of God throughout his life and even as he died on the Cross (ST 3.46.8; but see 3.9.2 and 3.10.1–4). Thomas cites John of Damascus, as always his principal authority in delicate doctrinal matters: Christ's divinity 'allowed his flesh to act and suffer whatever was appropriate'. In effect, there is no contradiction between Christ's undergoing the *dolor passionis* and enjoying the *gaudium fruitionis*. The cry of dereliction (Matthew 27:46), Thomas will claim, means that God 'abandoned Christ in death inasmuch as he exposed him to the power of his persecutors' – 'he withdrew his protection, but maintained the union' (ST 3.50.2).

That is to say, the cry of dereliction is that of a holy man who, in his suffering, remains certain of the love of his Father. The psalm from which the cry comes needs to be read through to the end, when it will turn out that the psalmist foresees salvation in the midst of his affliction (Psalm 21 (22)).

Here, of course, Thomas is only repeating the traditional doctrine. It no doubt tests modern Christian sensibilities. It is one thing to read Psalm 21 through to the end: thus to put the cry of dereliction in a context which deprives it of the horror of believing Christ to be abandoned by God. It is another matter to interpret the abandonment as meaning no more than that at last the protection against his enemies which he had enjoyed so far was now withdrawn. Perhaps Thomas's is a better explanation at any rate than Robert Bellarmine's: 'Christ's crying out with a loud voice testified to this abandonment in order that all might understand the great price of our Redemption. Up to this hour he had borne all his indignities with such incredible patience and tranquillity of mind that one might have been led to suspect that he had no feelings at all'.[11]

But the test for modern Christians remains. In traditional language, Jesus was simultaneously a *viator* and a *comprehensor*: walking the earth while having the vision that the blessed have of God in heaven. For Thomas, the continuous union with God implied in the beatific vision is only an implication of the hypostatic union: if the divine nature and a human nature are to be united in the Incarnation then there can be no suspension or cessation of the divine nature's being what it is without breaking up the union altogether. Finally, for Thomas, as in the tradition, Jesus is of the same divine nature as the Father – Christ's union with the Father could not be dissolved; it is a logical issue: no Person of the Trinity can exist deprived of relationship in communion with the other two. That, for Thomas, is what – who – the Trinity is.

Here, then, Thomas offers a neat account of the traditional view. Modern theologians want some much more dramatic account of what happens at the death of Christ – a much more comprehensive abandonment of Christ by the Father, and even a disruption of the intra-Trinitarian communion itself. The test that reading Thomas sets invites us to consider what the implications of the Incarnation must be.

The rest of Thomas's discussion offers the same kind of interest: time and again he summarizes the pre-modern view, thus providing a neat starting point for comparison and sometimes challenge.

In question 48 Thomas considers how Christ's death brought salvation, listing the traditional themes of merit, satisfaction, sacrifice and redemption – again offering no more than convenient headings for further discussion. In question 49 Thomas discusses the 'results' of Christ's death: freeing humankind from sin, from the power of the devil, from the debt of punishment; reconciling us to God and opening heaven's gate to us.

Thomas next devotes a question to Christ's death (3.50). The chief interest here is in the then much contested question of the status of Christ's dead body. Again, as with Christ's having the beatific vision, the question explores the implications of the union of the divine and human natures in Christ. When soul and body are separated at his death, as Thomas takes for granted, neither Christ's soul nor his body was separated from the Word of God (3.50.3). What might seem an arcane and obsolete question again sets an interesting test of how the implications of the Incarnation appear to us today.

Thomas devotes a question to the burial and to the sepulchre (3.51), mainly citing patristic themes: the appropriateness of the garden, the tomb/womb symbolism. Finally, considering Christ's descent into hell, Thomas holds that Christ delivered the patriarchs and saints of the Old Testament but did not descend into the hell of the damned (52.6) and could do nothing about infants who died unbaptized (52.7).

Neither of these theses can be anything but a starting point for dissent and development of a very different view. Here, clearly, the only use of consulting Thomas is to see where we need to go now. No doubt it might be instructive to discover why he could not say anything else on these issues. But mainly seeing what he says only confirms our sense of the irreducible gap between what made sense in medieval Christian theology and what needs to be said today.

Of course, both issues are much debated. According to Thomas, Christ's descent into hell freed only those who by their faith and charity were already united to his passion: for them the effect of his passion was deliverance. Thomas insists that Christ's descent into hell freed the 'holy patriarchs' – Abraham, Isaac, Jacob, Moses and so on; for him an important thesis (3.52.5 and 1–2.3.8). His vision of the continuity between the Law and the Gospel, though no doubt quite limited, is nevertheless worth noting. But infants who died unbaptized, Thomas thinks, were not in any way united with Christ in his passion, either by faith or by love. Infants could not come to faith on their own, since they did not yet have the use of reason; nor could they be freed from original sin through the faith of their parents.

This is a trifle less distressing than might appear. In his commentary on the *Sentences* Thomas accepts the then traditional line that there are four hells: the hell of the damned, limbo, purgatory and the inferno of the holy patriarchs. Hell, like so much else in the medieval world, has its own hierarchy. The word 'limbo', used if not coined by the Paris theologian William of Auvergne (died 1230), meaning border or frontier, came eventually to mean a place of natural happiness appropriate for human beings who have neither sinned personally, since they never reached the age of reason, nor were ever granted the grace of Christ, since they died before being baptized.

If this shows how much leeway had to be made up over the centuries as regards the salvation of the unbaptized and of non-Christians in general, Thomas's claim that Christ did not descend into the hell of the damned now seems unduly restricted and timorous to many theologians. To name only one: Hans Urs von Balthasar contends that in his descent into hell Christ endured all that is hellish in its otherness from God and made hell 'a Christological place', where sinners can undergo in a partial way what Christ himself has already endured totally. Anything that Christ does is by definition redemptive, indeed divinizing, which means, according to Balthasar, that we may at least hope for the salvation even of the 'damned'.

This takes us to Christ's Resurrection, his risen body, who witnessed his risen body, the effects on us, his ascension, his being seated at the Father's right hand, and his being judge of the living and the dead (ST 3.53–8).

The question on Christ as judge, and thus the entire Christology, concludes with these words (ST 3.59.6): 'For this reason God has established none other over the whole earth, since the Lord Jesus Christ is one and the same God and man – let this be enough for the present about the mystery of his Incarnation'.

The Christological considerations which begin with the appropriateness of the Incarnation continue with the logical implications of the
hypostatic union (ST 3. 2–19), the New Testament and largely Pauline
themes of obedience to the Father, prayer, priesthood, sonship, predestination, worship and mediation (20–6), the events from conception to
death, burial and descent into hell (27–52), and culminate with a relatively lengthy account of Christ in glory, and finally with Christ as judge
(53–9).

Here Thomas discusses only what bears on Christ's position as judge,
as he notes, deferring consideration of the Last Judgement as such (but
not living to write it). The text is a tapestry of biblical citations. 'In the
court where God judges, through Jesus Christ he will judge the secrets
of mankind' (Romans 2:16). The focus is entirely eschatological: 'God
alone makes souls blessed through participation in him; but Christ is the
one who leads us to beatitude' (ST 3.59.2).

The Sacraments of the Passion

The 'consummation of the whole theological project', as Thomas says,
is consideration of 'the Saviour and what he has done for the human
race' (ST 3 prologue). Christ, for Thomas as for the tradition, is always
also Christ in and with the Church. True enough, no doubt because he
lived before divisions in the Church gave rise to questions about the identity and location of 'the true Church' (the schism between East and West
did not pose such questions), Thomas has no explicit doctrine of the
Church.[12] He could not have envisaged the Church as an optional extra,
or even as 'the creature of the gospel'. For Thomas, Christology does not
conclude with the enthronement of the risen Christ as judge of all the
earth. After considering the mysteries of the Word incarnate, as he says,
we continue with the 'Church's sacraments, which have their efficacy
from the incarnate Word himself' (ST 3.60 prologue). It soon emerges
that the sacraments of the Church, and particularly baptism and the
eucharist, have been instituted for two main purposes: 'to perfect human
beings in what pertains to the worship of God according to the *religio
christianae vitae* and also to counter the failures by sin' (e.g. ST 3.65.1).
Thomas's sense of priority should be noted. It then turns out, entirely in
accordance with tradition, that baptism is 'the sacrament of the death
and Passion of Christ as regenerating the human creature in Christ in
virtue of his Passion', while the eucharist is 'the sacrament of his Passion
as perfecting one in union with the Christ who suffered' (e.g. ST 3.73.3)
– baptism as the sacrament of faith and thus the foundation of the spir-

itual life, the eucharist as the sacrament of charity, being the bond of perfection (Colossians 3:14).

Thomas does not regard the Church or the sacraments as any kind of continuation or prolongation of the presence of the incarnate Word. The *sacramenta fidei* certainly cause grace and effect salvation, doing so however always in virtue of the Passion of Christ. Ultimately, Thomas's Christological considerations bring the reader to the Cross. It would not be a difficult exercise to trace the frequency of phrases appealing in one form or other to *Christus passus*: the Christ who suffered, once for all, as we may add, and 'to save his people from their sins', albeit glossing that immediately as 'showing us in himself the way of truth through which, by rising, we can reach the beatitude of immortal life' (ST 3 prologue).[13]

Chapter 11

GOD IN THE *SUMMA THEOLOGIAE*

One thing is evident straight away. If the Incarnation is an effect of God's self-diffusive goodness, as we saw in the previous chapter, there is something wrong about the received accounts of Thomas Aquinas's God.

Standard Accounts

Jürgen Moltmann, for example, in his widely read book on the doctrine of the Trinity, tells us that Thomas was the first to split the doctrine of God so as to consider the unity of God before the Trinity. Historically, this is far from certain. The point, anyway, is that 'ever since Thomas Aquinas . . . the doctrine of the Godhead's single substance has taken precedence in the West, logically and epistemologically, over the doctrine of the Trinity'. Lurking in this approach, Moltmann sees 'the danger of depriving the doctrine of the Trinity itself of its function'.[1] Discussing the unity of the divine nature first was more than a methodological decision, mistaken or otherwise. Effectively, it means that Thomas believed that the revelation of the Trinity is really only supplementary. He subscribed to 'the doctrine of the substance of the Godhead, of which all three hypostases or Persons partake' – thus virtually denying the Trinitarian differences and endorsing a modalistic, ultimately unitarian theology.

Behind this story, and many others like it, stands Karl Barth:

The fact that the life of God was identified with the notion of pure being, the fact that the idea of God was not determined by the doctrine of the

Trinity, but that the latter was shaped by a general conception of God (that of ancient Stoicism and Neo-Platonism), was now avenged at the most sensitive spot. Starting from the generalised notion of God, the idea of the divine simplicity was necessarily exalted to the all-controlling principle, the idol, which devouring everything concrete, stands behind all these formulas.[2]

Even more colourfully, according to Colin Gunton, in his fine set of Bampton Lectures, 'Being', for Thomas, is 'still essentially Parmenidean rather than Trinitarian in content . . . While the concept of being does not necessarily have Parmenidean connotations, there is no doubt that in Thomas it does'. Thomas's 'unitarily conceived deity' is 'the Parmenidean God of Christendom'; his theology is grounded in 'the essentially Parmenidean synthesis of Neo-Platonism'.[3]

Wolfhart Pannenberg tells a different story. He allows that Thomas considered the doctrine of the Trinity (in the *Summa Theologiae*); but insists that he did so inside an argument that presents God as First Cause of the world. In practice, Thomas 'derives' the doctrine of God as Trinity – almost – from the concept of God as one. The theistic proofs deliver the concept of the one everyone calls 'God': the first mover (ST 1.2.3), which Pannenberg takes to be a purely philosophical idea. Thomas then deduces not just the negative attributes of this first being (simplicity, perfection, etc.), but also its 'spirituality' as knowing (ST 1.14) and willing (ST 1.19). By a chain of logical deductions from the concept of the First Cause of the world he reaches the doctrine of God as internally triune: a being with mind and will. True, Thomas says that knowledge of God as Trinity of persons is available only by divine revelation (ST 1.32.1). But actually he has already effectively derived the doctrine from the metaphysical concept of the unity of substance. This, Pannenberg clearly thinks, is a wonderful achievement; but a doctrine of God as immanently triune that is derived by metaphysical deduction from the concept of First Cause, rather than solely by reflection on God's self-revelation in Scripture as Father, Son and Holy Spirit, is not Christian. For Pannenberg, Thomas's God, far from being 'unitarily conceived', is internally triune – but none the better for that.[4]

Influential Catholic Accounts

Most accounts of Thomas's allegedly non-Trinitarian God cite the 1960 essay in which Karl Rahner criticized the separation of the courses *de*

Deo uno from those *de Deo trino* in Roman Catholic colleges in those days, claiming that the split was not traditional but invented by Thomas Aquinas – 'for reasons which have not yet been clearly explained'. It is a misconception that goes back 'possibly' to 'the Augustinian and western conception of the Trinity'.[5] The effect is that 'it looks as though everything important about God which touches ourselves has already been said in the treatise *de Deo Uno*'. The result, anyway, is that the average Catholic accepts 'monotheism' (Rahner's scare quotes), a non-Incarnational and non-Trinitarian 'cult of the supremely one, undifferentiated and nameless God'.[6]

A decade earlier, in a much less frequently cited text, Hans Urs von Balthasar, the other Catholic theological giant of the twentieth century, also claimed that Thomas has a defective doctrine of God. Bizarrely enough, he charges Karl Barth as well as Thomas with favouring the doctrines of the unity of God, creation, conservation and providence, and especially ethics and eschatology, at the expense of the doctrines of the Trinity, Christology and the Church. The three doctrines that did not interest Thomas – *de Deo trino* (excellent logical analysis but no shaping influence on the project of the *Summa Theologiae*), *de Christo* (carefully done but with no influence on all that precedes in the *Summa*), and *de ecclesia* (simply absent) – are, however, precisely what Christian theology is about, Balthasar contends. Barth is just as one-sided, he thinks. In Thomas's case, anyway, his predominantly philosophical methodology prevents him from doing Christian theology properly. Above all, for him, theology does not deal head on with *singularia*: the very particular historical events, which he treats as mere examples. In the end, Balthasar here prefers Barth, precisely because his theology is practised as *scientia de singularibus*.[7]

Whose God?

As Henri de Lavalette pointed out at the time, in a brief but totally neglected comment on Rahner's essay, what is in question is how Christians should read the Old Testament, not whether Thomas's philosophical interests generated non-Trinitarian theology.[8]

For Thomas, the history of God's self-revelation begins with Moses at the burning bush (Exodus 3:14: 'I am Who I am'). It culminates in the revelation of the three divine persons in the New Testament. Thomas maintained (explicitly, here, against Bonaventure), that it is wrong 'first to posit the Father as God and then to study His paternity', giving as his reason the fact that 'the Father is such only in his relationship to the Son

and the Holy Spirit: "No one knows the Father except the Son"'.
Thomas spells this out thus:

> There are three ways of having knowledge of God: the first is through
> Christ, in the sense that God is the Father of the only begotten and con-
> substantial one, as well as the rest of the knowledge which Christ taught
> about God the Father and Son and Holy Spirit, as regards unity of essence
> and eternity of persons; this is solely a matter of faith, never explicitly
> believed in the Old Testament except only by minors; secondly, God alone
> is to be worshipped and this was also (*etiam*) believed by the Jews; and
> thirdly there is one God and this is known also by the philosophers them-
> selves, and is not a matter of faith.[9]

His conception of God is phased, so to speak: God as creator of whose
existence the wisdom-seekers of the ancient world have knowledge; God
as the Lord whom the people of the Law were commanded to worship;
and God as the Trinity, of whom knowledge has been communicated by
Christ to the apostles.

Given that he spells nothing of this out in the questions on the unity
of the divine essence in the *Summa Theologiae*, and that few students
read anything else, one can scarcely be blamed for failing to understand
that when he thinks of the 'unity of the divine essence', he has in mind
Deuteronomy 6:4: 'Hear, O Israel: The Lord our God is one Lord'. He
cites this when he reaches the question on the unity of God (ST 1.11.3),
but nothing in the *Summa* compares with the emphasis in, for example,
the *De articulis fidei*.[10]

This opens with a strong statement about the unity of the divine
essence, citing Deuteronomy 6:4, and arguing that it should be understood as excluding five erroneous views: the polytheism of the pagans
(citing Exodus 20:3); the dualism of the Manichees (Isaiah 45:5–7); the
anthropomorphites, who believed that the deity is physical (John 4:24,
Isaiah 40); the Epicurean doctrine (as Thomas believes) denying that God
has providential care for creatures (1 Peter 1:3–9); and fifthly the the
doctrine of the 'gentile philosophers' who believe that God can do only
what is anyway predetermined (against whom he cites Psalm 134 (135),
with its emphasis on divine freedom).

But the warning issued by Chenu remains indispensable. However
charged with metaphysical language, the questions on the one God have
to do with the God of Abraham, Isaac, and Jacob, who will send Christ,
not the god of Aristotle's *Physics*. We have to hold on to the religious
character of the text and not reduce it to a deistic theodicy.[11] In other
words, Chenu was allowing, 50 years ago, that many standard Catholic
courses on the unity of the divine nature, in the post-Enlightenment and

anti-Modernist apologetics of Leonine Thomism, amounted to little more than such deism.

The Argument from the Divine Essence

Wolfhart Pannenberg is right: Thomas derives a good deal about God in the course of considering 'the things pertaining to the divine essence' (ST 1.2 prologue).

Briefly, the account goes as follows. God's existence in the world is not obvious. On the other hand, that God exists, as beginning and end of all things, is not solely a matter of faith. God revealed himself to Moses; inferences from the nature of the world confirm the immanent activity of the one whom everyone calls 'God' (ST 1.2.1–3).

We cannot know of God what he is but only what he is not; so we begin by denying of God the marks of the creaturely condition. This results in the doctrine of the divine simplicity: in God there is no real distinction between his essence and his existence (ST 1.3). There is no imperfection about God (1.4). Perfection of being implies perfection of goodness (1.5); so God is the sovereign Good (1.6). God is not finite (1.7); thus God is in everything, 'not as a part or a property but like the agent in an action' (1.8). God is not subject to being changed by anything external to himself (1.9). God is not subject to time or temporal change (1.10). God is one, unique, singular: otherwise something would be added to God, from outside so to speak, constraining him (1.11).

Given this entirely negative description of God, how is God to be known and named by creatures such as we are (1.12–13)? In this life, Thomas thinks, we never know God as he is. That happens only in the beatific vision (1.12.1, citing 1 John 3:2). As we have seen, Thomas's theology is dominated by the promise of eschatological bliss.

What is possible in this life, by reasoning, is that we may come to know of God that he exists, as well as what must be appropriate to God as 'first cause of all things transcending all he has caused' (1.12.12). That is to say, knowledge of God by using our heads comes from thinking about his relationship to creatures: thus God as First Cause, not any part of what he has caused; and, far from this being a defect on his part, it shows his transcendence.

What more is provided by Christian revelation? Even with the benefit of revelation, Thomas thinks, we know nothing of God as he is in himself. In faith, hope and charity, we are at best always united to God as to one unknown. Yet we do have some more knowledge of God by revelation, such as the information that God is both one and three (disclosed by Jesus, Thomas assumed). Moreover, God has shown us more

– and more remarkable – effects, though the example Thomas offers, disappointingly and instructively, is the Holy Spirit's appearing in the form of a dove at Christ's baptism (1.12.13) – whereas one might have thought of Christ's humanity or the sacraments or martyrdom, to keep to disclosures of divine agency that are acknowledged elsewhere in Thomas's theology.

Given that, even in the economy of revelation, we never know God as he is, it might seem useless to try to say anything positive about him. Thomas cites Denys, the principal conduit of Eastern theology as he thinks, arguing however that when he says that God is 'beyond naming', what Denys means is that God as he is in himself is beyond anything we understand or intend (1.13.1). Thomas is no doubt putting a favourable gloss on Denys's extravagant apophaticism.

We might be tempted to follow Rabbi Moses ben Maimon, the exponent of Judaism whom Thomas greatly respected, into maintaining (as Thomas thinks) that when we say that God is good we mean only that God is not evil, or that God is cause of goodness in things; what sounds like an affirmation would really only be another negation (1.13.2).

Against these radical proposals, Thomas simply declares that this is not what people mean when they speak of God. We speak of God as we know him: since we know God from creatures, we can speak of him only as they represent him. 'Any creature, in so far as it possesses any perfection, represents God and is like God, for God, being simply and universally perfect, has pre-existing in himself the perfections of all his creatures' (ST 1.13.2). Thus, we predicate of God perfections we are familiar with in ourselves – meaning them, however, 'in a higher way than we understand'.

Indeed, the perfections we find in creatures (goodness, life and the like) are attributed more appropriately to God (1.13.3), since these realities belong primarily to God and only secondarily to creatures.[12]

Yet, though we never mean anything of God and ourselves in exactly the same sense, it does not follow that what we say is simply ambiguous. There is a way we use words which is neither univocal nor equivocal; we often speak analogically. Thomas does not seem to think there is anything remarkable about this, or that it requires any explanation in terms of a 'theory' of analogy. Using words analogically, he clearly thinks, is a perfectly familiar procedure.

On the other hand, despite claims by some readers that he is only commenting on the way that we use certain words, he explicitly grounds this everyday analogical use of perfection words in respect of God on the real relationship that creatures have towards God as source and the cause of being.[13]

God: Noun or Verb?

Thomas next considers whether the word 'God' is a noun or a verb. The etymologizing is so fanciful that modern readers are not inclined to pay much heed to this question. Yet, given the determination to see Thomas's God as a static entity, it is worth noting that he takes seriously the thought that the word 'God' might actually be better regarded grammatically as a verb.

According to John Damascene, as always taken very seriously, the Greek word *theos* is derived from the verb *thein*, to take care of things; or from *aithein*, to kindle; or from *theasthai*, to contemplate – but whichever it is, the word seems to designate not a thing (*natura*) but an activity (*operatio*).

The word for God, in Greek and Latin, that is to say, seems to designate not an entity but a process, not an object but a happening.

These etymologies are, of course, quite fanciful. Yet, since scholars now believe that the word '*theos*' and its cognates '*deus*' and 'deity' derive from the Sanscrit verb *di*, to gleam, the suggestion remains that the word 'deity' functions more like a verb than a noun, as if it designated not a being but a doing.

Thomas is happy to agree that the word for God, like many words, as he thinks, comes from what the thing in question does or effects. His example is also fanciful: the word *lapis* (stone) derives from *laedere pedem*, meaning to hurt one's foot. Analogously, the word for God is an 'operational word', a 'doing word', in the sense that (as Denys says) 'deity is what takes care of everything by providence and perfect goodness' (ST 1.13.8). Yet, though allowing that it is from such divine activity that the word for God is derived, Thomas simply notes, as a conclusive argument against the suggestion that God might be more like an activity than an entity, that in fact we use the word to mean the divine nature, God as a 'substance'. He seems to assume that we shall not disagree.

He Who Is

The argument continues as follows. We are likely to think that the word 'God' is reserved for naming God alone; but again usage shows that others besides God are called 'gods' (1.13.9). If God has a proper name, naming God and God alone and not extendable to any other particular (*suppositum*), then it has – 'perhaps' – to be the Tetragrammaton, the Hebrew name of God that is transliterated as YHWH (1.13.9).[14]

Thomas returns to the analogical use of the word 'God' (ST 13.10). When Christians say 'That idol is not God' and pagans say 'It is', it seems that they are contradicting one other; the word 'God' is being used in exactly the same sense by both parties, otherwise there could be no possibility of contradiction. On the other hand, Thomas objects, people don't mean anything when they don't know what they are talking about. Pagans have no knowledge of the true God; thus, when they say their idol is 'God' they do not mean the true God; whereas when Catholics say 'God is one', they mean the true God – which shows that the word 'God' is used equivocally of the true God and of the idolaters' god. Either the word 'God' has the same meaning for everyone, and thus is used univocally; or only Christians use it properly, pagans simply misapply it, the word is ambiguous or equivocal.

As Thomas repeats, neither Catholics nor pagans know the nature of God as he is in himself. They can both have knowledge of God as cause of things, transcending them and radically different from them. To that extent, when pagans attribute the creation of life (say) to what Christians would call an idol, they can be taking the word 'God' in the same sense as the latter when they deny that the idol is God. Someone who knew God under no description whatsoever – not even as cause of things – would not be using the word 'God' 'except perhaps as when we use words of whose meaning we are ignorant' (ST 1.13.10). They would be uttering the word meaninglessly.

On the other hand, Thomas contends, when we (Christians) allow that an idol may be called a 'god', we take the word to mean something that the pagans suppose to be the true God but which, of course, we know not to be so. Thus we do not use the word with exactly the same meaning, we use it analogically – obviously, Thomas says, again expecting us to agree, without any explanatory theorizing. This is just how we use the word.

This brings us to the key article (1.13.11): the most appropriate name for God is 'He Who Is', as revealed to Moses at the Burning Bush (Exodus 3:14). First, things are ordinarily named from their 'form' – how they look. But God has no 'form': referring us to the doctrine of divine simplicity (ST 1.3.4), Thomas says that God, since his existing and his nature are identical, is simply 'existing' – *ipsum esse*: designatable, then, by the infinitive of the verb 'to be'.[15] Secondly, while we cannot know God in himself in this life, and thus any way we have of thinking of him is only a way of failing to know him as he is in himself, the less determinate, the more general and simple our way of speaking of him, the better – which is why John Damascene says that 'He Who Is' is the first of all the names by which to describe God: 'for he comprehends all in himself, he has his existence as an ocean of being, infinite and indeterminate'.[16]

The identification of God as 'He who is', far from being specific to Thomas Aquinas, is a move that he makes explicitly in the footsteps of John Damascene, assumed as always to be the bearer of the theology of the undivided Church.

Again, however, Thomas declares that the Tetragrammaton is even more appropriate – to mean 'the incommunicable and, if we are allowed to speak like this, the singular substance of God' (1.13.11).

The God so far described is evidently not merely the God of the wisdom-seekers of the ancient world, let alone of philosophers in the modern sense. The God who is describable in the infinitive verb 'to be' is the God who revealed himself to Moses and whose most appropriate name is the Tetragrammaton.

Conceiving God not as 'life force' but, even more comprehensively, as 'sheer existing', might seem a pretty awesome and unnerving thought. One might be tempted to think, when one recalls that Thomas chanted the Psalms every day of his life, or when one considers his commentary on the Book of Job, that the description of God as 'He who is' (inherited ultimately from Philo of Alexandria) is not such an inappropriate rendering, in less anthropomorphic language, of the God invoked in the liturgy, who responds to Job out of the whirlwind.

Interestingly, while Barth allows that God may be described as 'the fully existent One', he regards this as 'perhaps a very intensive, yet to some extent also a very slender, not to say impoverished and spectral being', becoming 'living for us', acquiring 'abundance of life, vividness and palpable reality, only as he enters into relation with us, as there stands over against him a world and especially man in his manifold movement, in relation to which he himself acquires movement'.[17]

Once again, at another hermeneutic crux, Barth opts for an understanding of God as 'living', rather than simply 'being', and attributes God's being alive, revealingly, principally to the way that he 'acquires movement' in relation to us. For Thomas, God is the activity of sheer being, whether or not that being is shared with us. It is certainly not in virtue of any relation to us that Thomas's God owes his 'vividness and palpable reality'. That would have seemed much too anthropocentric a doctrine, reopening Thomas's fears of conceptions of God which place God at the creature's disposal.

More Event than Entity

Clearly, Thomas is unwilling to collapse the concept of an agent into that of action (ST 1.13.8). Yet, once the concept of the divine substance is subjected to the appropriate negative analysis, and is identified as *esse subsistens*, it surely means that God's nature *is* activity – though activity with a certain 'subsistency'. God is not a substance with accidents, a subject with properties, an agent capable of activities that occasionally express but never totally realize himself (as created agents like us are). In God, being, knowing, loving and creating are identical (the doctrine of divine simplicity); yet this activity has at the same time something of the character of a substance.

In short, the risk for Thomas is not to reify God as a static and motionless entity, but rather, just the opposite, to make so much of the divine essence as activity, denying the distinction between agent and agency, that God becomes sheer process, *perpetuum mobile*. Thomas's God, anyway, is more like an event than an entity.

Once we have in place an account of the one being of God, the 'divine substance', Thomas proceeds to consider the 'activity' of this 'substance' (1.14 prologue). He takes it for granted that this 'substance' is an agent. He distinguishes between two kinds of operation, one that remains in the agent, and one that goes out to produce an external effect. He will consider the latter under the heading of God's power (1.25); but first he considers God's knowledge and will, immanent activities: 'for knowing is in the one who knows, and willing is in the one who wills'.

The divine substance is intelligent (1.14.1) and self-conscious (1.14.2 and 3); indeed, God's act of knowing is his substance (14.4). God sees everything: 'All things are naked and open to his eyes' (14.5 and 6); God's knowing is not discursive, like ours (14.7). God is truth (1.16). Knowing is a kind of living, so the consideration of the divine being as always actually knowing concludes with a note on the divine life (1.18).

Since any one with a mind also has a will, as Thomas thinks, he next considers divine willing (1.19), loving (1.20), justice and mercy (1.21), divine providence (1.22), and predestination (1.23), rounding the discussion off with a note on the Book of Life (1.24) – balancing knowing as living (1.18), somewhat artificially, no doubt.

Having thus considered the divine 'substance' as intrinsically and internally knowing and loving – actually, actively and repletely knowing and loving, not merely possessing cognitive and volitional capacities that may or may not be exercised – Thomas moves to the question of God's activity as bringing about an effect external to himself (1.25). We return to the conception of God as *actus purus*, acting on others but in no way open to being worked upon by anything or anyone else (1.25.1). Thomas's fear, as always, is that God is conceived as being at our disposal, manipulable and controllable by creatures. God is not an agent in the same way as creatures (1.25.2); God can do whatever is absolutely possible (25.3), which therefore excludes undoing the past

(25.4); God can create another world better than this world (25.5), yet he cannot make this world as it stands unrecognizably better than it is (25.6).

The main point of the question is that God's power, in the sense of his ability to act, is identical with his mind and his will: the doctrine of divine simplicity again, though not mentioned explicitly. In creatures such as ourselves, ability to act on something else, like our minds and our wills, is in our nature, and a constituent part of our nature; but agency, thought, and choice are not our nature as such. There is more to our being than our powers of reason and will; there is nothing 'more' to the divine being than actually understanding and loving.

Divine Beatitude

The divine nature or essence, then, this always actually being which is always actually knowing and willing and doing, is also (as Thomas now discloses) sheer bliss (ST 1.26). Though this is the climax of his treatment of the oneness of the divine nature, and the bridge to his discussion of the trinity of persons *in divinis*, he does not announce it in his agenda (1.14 prologue): a rare omission.

This is not a topic which Thomas frequently discussed: apart from *Contra Gentiles* book 1, 100–2, and in connection with 1 Timothy 6:15, the only other discussion is in the *Sentences* commentary book 2, very sketchily.

'God is blessed', Thomas quotes from 1 Timothy 6:15. To be blessed, he explains, is 'the ultimate good possessed by a spiritual being, aware of its own completion in the good that it possesses, and who, whatever happens, is master (*domina*) of its own activities' (1.26.1).

In one sense, obviously, this sounds remarkably like the self-possession aimed at in ancient Greek and Roman philosophy. Indeed, the two objections Thomas raises against attributing bliss to God come, significantly, from Boethius's *De Consolatione Philosophiae* and Aristotle's *Ethics*: contentment is having everything one wants, happiness is earned, respectively. In another sense, of course, as often happens with ancient wisdom, the basic idea is also quite familiar in ordinary life: people are, or would be, happy in themselves, we might say, if they had richly stocked minds and unimpeded control of whatever they want to do. What else is it like, for a person to be content?

Thomas returns to the theme of divine bliss, at the beginning of the *secunda pars*, the lengthy consideration of the movement of the moral agent towards God precisely as beatitude: 'There is bliss in God, because his very being is identical with his doing, thereby enjoying no other than himself (*in Deo est beatitudo, quia ipsum esse ejus est operatio ejus, qua non fruitur alio, sed seipso*)' (ST 1–2.3.2). God's being is his doing: not the doing which is creating the world but the doing internal to the Godhead. Diverging from what we have just seen Barth suggesting, Thomas insists that the doing which is the being that is the divine bliss is precisely not the doing which is bringing us about but simply God's being in and as God is. 'God is bliss, by nature (*Deus est beatitudo per essentiam suam*)' (1–2.3.1).[18]

There is nothing arcane about this thesis. On the contrary, Barth himself notes it as a commonplace, citing in support his favourite Calvinist scholastic Amandus Polanus (1561–1610), going on himself to say, however, that God 'finds no enjoyment in his self-enjoyment', which is why, though he 'does not need us', God 'turns to us in the overflow of the perfection of his essence and therefore of his loving, and shares with us, in and with his love, his blessedness'. While Barth insists that there is no 'need' or 'want' in God's self-enjoyment, the claim that sharing his blessedness with us human beings shows that God finds 'no enjoyment in his self-enjoyment' would have seemed paradoxical to Thomas. Indeed, given Thomas's frequently repeated opposition to any suggestion that God was not perfectly happy without enjoying 'fellowship with us', Barth's remark would have seemed unhelpful. As above, it veers close to making God dependent on us.[19]

To say that God's very existing is a doing, including actually knowing and actually loving, and that this is bliss (an activity, of course, not a state, cf 1–2.3.2), takes us to the other extreme from the static entity of 'classical theism'. To repeat, God, for Thomas, is not even an agent with capacities to know and love. God is nothing other than ceaseless and total actualizations of being, knowing, and loving – utter bliss.[20]

Persons

So much for Thomas's account of the unity of the divine nature. Having considered the implications of monotheistic faith he does not rush headlong into talk of the divine persons. According to traditional Christian faith, of course, the one God is a trinity of persons. As modern theologians immediately warn, the word 'person' has changed its meaning significantly over the centuries. Some might say that the meaning the word naturally has in modern Western culture is irrelevant or even opposed to what it means in discourse about God as Trinity. Thomas begins, anyway, from what he supposes to be the New Testament basis of the belief that in God there are three persons – in the words of Jesus: 'I have come forth from the Father' (John 8:42).

In ordinary usage today, 'person' is co-extensive with 'human being'. If asked, most people would say that a person is an individual human being (man, woman or child), as distinguished from a thing or an animal. Philosophy students will no doubt insist that a person has to be a self-conscious or rational being (a sense that appears in the mid-seventeenth century, according to the *Oxford English Dictionary*; it is certainly familiar to the philosopher John Locke). Thomas holds, with Boethius, that the word 'person' cannot be used of God in its original sense, as a role in a drama (ST 1.29.3). He is happy to accept Boethius's definition of a person as 'an individual substance of a rational nature (*rationalis naturae individua substantia*)', and to employ it in Trinitarian discourse, provided that we exclude discursivity from 'rational', and speak rather of 'intellectual'; understand 'individual' as meaning 'incommunicable', thus unique and incapable of being replicated; and understand 'substance' as 'self-grounded existing' (1.29.3). Of course, as Thomas keeps insisting, this concept of person applies in discourse about God only analogically (ST 1.13.5; 1.29.3).

The language sounds abstract; but what it means is recognizably in continuity with the concept of a person as a human being: unique ('incommunicable'), shaped by memory and reflection ('intellectual') and relational ('substance', properly understood).

But this is another hermeneutic crux. For many theologians, the definition of person which Boethius coined and which Thomas inherited is the expression of 'an individualistic and a substantialist understanding of personhood, which carries an implicit reduction of any relational aspect to the person'.[21] So long as readers are determined to understand the concept of substance as excluding personhood and relationality there is of course no way for them to interpret Thomas differently.

God as Trinity

If we want to grasp Thomas's theology of the Trinity, the first move is to see that he gets to talking of persons at all only by way of talking first of processions (1.27) and secondly of relations (1.28). For him, talk of 'processions', far from being second-order abstraction, is rooted in what he assumes Jesus himself actually said.

Thomas claims, indeed treats it as an axiom, that it is possible to work out whatever is implied by the unity of the divine essence by natural reasoning, whereas this is not possible as regards what concerns the distinction of persons (ST 1.32.1). Yet, given the historical dispensation of the New Covenant and thus the revelation of God as Trinity, we can work out something of what it means. We can discover prefigurings in the Old Testament and elsewhere (1.32.1). In brief, now that we have the doctrine of God as Trinity, granted by divine revelation, we can see that pre-Christian seekers after wisdom had inklings of the doctrine: Thomas lists Aristotle, the Platonists, Pharoah's magicians and Hermes Trismegistus, in short a ragbag of what thirteenth-century Paris knew of ancient literature – nothing in this bizarre list being, however, at all substantial, Thomas argues (1.32.1).

Given, on the other hand, that we have been brought to see, principally by the logic of negative theology and not by detailed biblical documentation, that God is best described in a cluster of verbs, as actually being which is also actually knowing and actually loving, we cannot be very surprised to hear that there are, within the Godhead, 'forthcomings' or 'processions', first of intellection (27.1) and secondly of love (27.4). Indeed, just as Wolfhart Pannenberg says, with this account of the one being of God as this self-knowing and self-loving subsistent activity of existing, Thomas takes us, by conceptual analysis, to the brink of discovering the triune God who is supposedly revealed only to believers in the New Testament dispensation.

This is another hermeneutic crux. On the one hand, with Pannenberg, we may assume that Thomas is working out what can be said about God purely philosophically, bracketing out all biblical knowledge of God, leading us step by step to knowledge of the philosophers' God who then, in an unexpected supplement, turns out to be the Christian God. On the other hand, if Thomas takes for granted the Christian and thus Trinitarian dispensation and, furthermore, that reasoning correctly about God will never conflict with properly understood faith, he is perhaps working out, as a theologian, what the one being of God must be like. Perhaps, even, it is not too audacious to suggest that, though Thomas reasons his way to the description of God as sheer act of existing, he presupposes all the time, consciously or otherwise, the Christian doctrine of creation.

After the event, so to speak, the theologian's task is to show that what God is like is not completely unintelligible. Divine intervention is undeserved, unforced, and utterly free, as Thomas keeps insisting, against those he suspects of seeing God as under an obligation or necessity to fulfil himself by creating; but that does not mean, on the other hand, at least when we reflect on it, that God's intervention is arbitrary, gratuitous and totally unintelligible. On the contrary, 'granted the Trinity, there are certain confirmations from the fittingness of things, yet not such as may prove the Trinity of persons conclusively' (1.32.2).

There are truths about God to which we can reason conclusively, such as that God is 'simple': there is no real distinction in God between essence and existence. On the other hand, there are truths about God, such that in God there is distinction of persons, that we could never reason our way to establishing.

In practice, however, the logical analysis of what God must be like is entirely, if unadmittedly, in the context of belief in the difference between creatures and God, while the insistence that the news about God as Trinity is a total surprise must be qualified by the account of God's bliss in self-understanding and self-loving (1.26). Reason is no doubt more to the fore in the reflecting on the one being of God, and the Creed absolutely basic in considering the Trinity; but, whatever Thomas himself supposed, the reasoning in the former is tacitly guided by the Christian doctrine of creation, while the doctrine in the latter, accepted immediately from the Creed, is spelled out in a series of conceptual analyses that are quite as densely and rigorously metaphysical as anything earlier.

Processions

Now, anyway, we have Christian revelation. Thomas takes for granted the New Testament references to God as Father, Son, and Holy Spirit. He starts from Christ's statement that he 'came forth' from the Father (John 8:42): '*Ego ex Deo processi*', in Latin. He at once outlines the two ancient temptations. On the one hand, he thinks that this 'coming forth' is pictured on the model of an effect's being separated from its cause: the Son comes forth from the Father as a very special creature. This yields the 'subordinationism' traditionally ascribed to the fourth-century theologian Arius. On the other hand, this 'procession' is temptingly modelled on what happens when an effect is simply the sign of its cause: the Son would just be a manifestation of deity. This is 'modalism', the other ancient heresy, ascribed to Sabellius, probably a third century Roman theologian. What the doctrine has to secure, Thomas believes, is a real difference between Father, Son, and Spirit, which is not the same as the difference between creatures and God. Modalism and subordinationism, Thomas thinks, are based on the same mistake: each takes 'coming forth' on analogy with a movement towards something external; whereas for Thomas John 8:42 refers to a 'coming forth within God's own self (*processio in ipso Deo*)' (ST 1.27.1).

What the doctrine has to secure is a real difference between Father, Son and Spirit, which is not the difference between creatures and their creator. Arianism and Sabellianism, Thomas contends, are based on the same mistake: taking 'coming forth' on the model of a movement towards something external; whereas Thomas reads John 8:42 as meaning a 'coming forth within God himself (*processio in ipso Deo*)' (1.27.1).

Thomas returns to the experience of giving birth to a thought in order to help free us from picturing 'procession' on the model of physical movement: 'Whenever one understands, by one's very act of understanding, something comes forth within one, namely the concept of the thing understood proceeding from one's awareness of it'.

There is nothing abstruse about this. Of course, he at once reminds us, what happens in our case falls far short of describing what happens in God's. Yet – minds are what we are: *intellectuales substantiae.* We are perfectly familiar with the emergence of a meaningful word which remains inside oneself: '*emanatio intelligibilis, utpote verbi intelligibilis quod manet in ipso* [*intelligente*]'. When we mean something it comes to be in our minds.[22]

'Procession within the Godhead', as the Catholic faith holds, so Thomas considers, is somewhat like this. What 'comes forward' on the model of locomotion is necessarily different from its starting point. In the case of meaning, by contrast, the terminus need not differ from the origin. In fact, the better some object out there in the world is understood, the deeper and more inward the understanding of it is in the person who understands: the more one with the world the mind is, one may say. Since the divine act of understanding is as perfect as could be, Thomas argues, it follows that God's concept of something is completely at one with that of which it is the concept. The concept is both different from, and always one with, that which gives rise to it (1.27.1). In our case, the thought of something is one with the thing – the thing in the world and the thought in one's mind are formally identical; but things in the world and thoughts in the mind constitute totally separate realms of existence – the world is not our creation. Within the divine act of understanding, by contrast, the concept emerges and yet remains one with what generates it: the Word is other than and yet one with God the Father.

What Thomas wants to rule out, as Rowan Williams notes, is the neo-Platonic thought (if this is what it is) that the One comes first, then performs the act of self-knowing, as if optional and supplementary, and so becomes differentiated. The upshot of Thomas's lengthy analysis of the concept of the one God is that differentiation within the Godhead does not unfold in any such way. On the contrary, the act of sheer existing which is Thomas's preferred description of God is always also actual and active understanding and willing. In other words, there is no unitarily conceived primordial being to which knowledge and love may accrue or be ascribed.

In short, according to the world/mind identity thesis, what is conceived in the mind is the object; but since being and meaning are identical within the Godhead, God's conceiving himself as other cannot but remain the same.

According to traditional Christian doctrine, grounded in the Fourth Gospel (as Thomas would think), there is a second 'procession' within the Godhead besides the procession of the Word: namely the 'procession' of Love. On Thomas's account of knowledge, we never 'just' know; rather, we are always also drawn towards what we know. As Thomas writes: 'There is actual understanding when what is understood is in the mind through its likeness; there is actual willing, not because of a likeness of what is willed as such in the person who wills, but because the will in some way tends to what is willed'. In the act of understanding something the subject who understands takes the object, so to speak, into his or her mind: in knowing the world becomes ours. Simultaneously, however, since the mind that knows is never indifferent to what is known, the world and the objects that we see and understand draw us out into valuing them one way or another. The 'going out' which corresponds to the action of the will, as Thomas puts it, is not an assimilation of the world to the self, as happens in acts of knowing, but, on the contrary, the self's being impelled and moved towards something other than itself (ST 1.27.4).

In acts of meaning we take the world into our minds; but these are simultaneously acts of responding to the goodness and desirableness of things, which thus take us out of ourselves into wonder at the world.

It may even be allowed that Thomas's account of how the world attracts the mind is enriched by the doctrine of the second procession within the Godhead: 'will and intellect are so defined that the processions which correspond to the actions of both bear on each other in a certain order; for there is no procession of love except in connection with the procession of the word conceived by the mind; since nothing can be loved by will unless it be conceived in mind' (1.27.3; cf. 1.80.2).

Translating this to the doctrine of the Trinity:

> Now we recognize a certain relatedness of the Word to the source from which it comes, although in God mind and the conception of mind are the same substance. Similarly, though in God will and intellect are the same, nevertheless because the very meaning of love implies an issuing forth from which the mind conceives, the procession of love in God is distinct by its connection with the procession of the Word. (ibid)

There can be no more than two processions within the Godhead, Thomas argues, in what might seem a useless question (1.27.5). But it allows him once again to insist on his concept of God as an intellectual nature – which means knowing and loving. Referring back to what has already been said (1.14.7 and 19.5), Thomas recalls that, again according to the principle of divine simplicity, God understands and wills in a single simple act – and so we may rightly draw *de Deo uno* insights into *de Deo trino* considerations. Here Thomas is arguing against the no doubt attractive speculation that, since multiplicity is richer than unity, there should be an infinite coming forth within the Godhead of thoughts and lovings. On the contrary, he contends, what manifests God's perfect fecundity, abounding fruitfulness, is that in God there is only one perfect word and one perfect love (1.27.5).

Subsistent Relations

What distinguishes the persons within the Godhead is their relationships. As persons we human beings are definable, to a great extent, by our relationships: as parents, children, nationals of this or that country, employers and employees, and so on. Some philosophers would say that the very nature of being a person at all is to be relational. Some theologians say that what the doctrine of God as Trinity reveals is that as persons we too are relationally constituted. Thomas would not have agreed. For him, on the contrary, it is only in the Trinity that persons are entirely constituted by their relationships, in the sense that the divine persons are nothing more (or less) than subsisting relationships (1.29.4). It is only in relationship to one another that they are distinct.

We are not like that. However much we owe to one another, who we are is not constituted by our relationships. Being someone's child or employee never exhaustively establishes one's identity. In God alone are relationship and nature totally identical: 'While relation in created things exists as an accident in a subject, in God a really existing relation has the existence of the divine nature and is completely identical with it' (1.28.2).

Moreover, 'there can be no real relationship in God except founded on action' (1.28.4). Again, there are no real relations within God 'except as based on the actions (*actiones*) according to which there is procession in God, not going outside God but remaining within'. This is, obviously, a key insight. The relations within the Godhead are themselves action-based and dynamic.

This brings us back to 'processions', of which there are only two: 'one corresponding to activity of mind, the procession of the word, and the other to activity of will, the procession of love'. In each case there is the relationship of what comes forth from the source to the source, and also the relationship of the source to what comes forth. The procession of the word within the Godhead is also the Father's 'generating' the Son. The relation of being the source of this generation of the Son is being the Father: fatherhood (*paternitas*); while the relation of the one who comes forth from the source to the source is being the Son (*filiatio*).

The same goes for the procession within the Godhead of the Holy Spirit, except that we have no proper term for this relationship equivalent to speaking of the procession of the Word as the generation of the Son.

The point, anyway, is that, to understand Thomas, we need to try to stop thinking of the Father as a person who happens also to be a father, as a subject in whose existence fatherhood would be an 'accident', thus as a blown-up version of a human being. In human beings there is always a certain lack of identity between who and what we are: between our nature and our roles and relationships. In discourse about God, on the other hand, to speak of the person of the Father is to speak of nothing more or less than the relationship of fathering – a relationship, then, that consists in the action, within the Godhead, by which the Son is born and the Word comes forth.

The Persons as Verbs

To speak of the Father, in short, is to speak of the relation which is the act of fathering. 'Put succinctly and boldly', Thomas Weinandy says, 'the persons of the Trinity are not nouns; they are verbs and the names which designate them – Father, Son and Holy Spirit – designate the acts by which they are defined'.[23]

Weinandy takes as his guide Thomas's reflection on God as pure act of existence, allowing that he will attempt to 'clarify, correct, and even, at times, go beyond what he proposes'. His parsing of the subsistent relations, constitutive of the Trinitarian 'persons', as 'relations fully in act', allows Weinandy to say that the nouns 'Father', 'Son' and 'Holy Spirit', are grammatically verbs – they designate 'the interrelated acts by which all three persons are who they are'. This does not go much beyond Thomas. The persons of the Trinity are subsistent relations, in that they are constituted in the *actions* of being mutually related.

Obviously, Thomas inherited this way of talking. Its origins lie in the work of Gregory Nazianzen, who writes of *ousiodeis scheseis*, 'substantive relations' or 'onto-relations' (Torrance).[24] Augustine takes up the concept (*De Trinitate* 5–7; and often elsewhere): we cannot say the three are substances (that would be tritheism) nor that they are accidents (modalism) – so what about saying they are relations, which are substantial?

As Mascall noted, Augustine's introduction of the concept of subsistent relations is much more important than the famous 'psychological' analogies.[25] Thomas takes up the 'psychological' analogy (ST 1.27.3) – at once to insist that what 'person' means here is 'relation as subsisting' (29.4). There is no property of 'personhood' applicable univocally to Father, Son and Spirit. There is nothing common to the three divine persons except their being divine – their possessing the divine nature – their enjoying the perfections that are identical with the divine nature. What the word 'person' means here is 'a relation in the manner of a substance which is a hypostasis subsisting in the divine nature' (29.4).

God in Verbs

The main point, however, is that Thomas redescribes the God of Christian revelation in terms of *actus purus*: meaning both actuality and activity. Being *is* act.[26]

Usually, of course, the language of God as being is supposed to endorse a concept of God as a static entity, lacking potentiality and therefore lifeless.[27] Indeed, Barth's endeavour to reconceive the Godhead as a self-moved event, as 'being-in-act', is designed to overcome the supposedly Thomist concept of God as a static substance.

Thomas's concept of God as actuality/activity could not be more different. His preferred designation of the one being of God, not by a noun, as a substantive, but by the verb infinitive, as an activity, so to speak, yet activity with a certain 'subsistency'; and his identification of the persons of the Trinity in language grammatically more like verbs than like nouns: as relations always *secundum actiones* – yet with 'subsistency' – yields a very different concept of God from that which is still often ascribed to Thomas.

In Thomas's theology of God as One and Three, as Weinandy shows, the discussion of the unity and the discussion of the Trinity converge, or coincide, in identifying the Christian God first with verbs rather than by nouns – verbs which then have to be qualified as having something of the 'subsistency' that a noun identifies.

In short, Thomas's God is not the perfect being of Greek metaphysics, the supreme entity at the top of a hierarchy of atomistically conceived substances. Rather, redescribing the biblical and liturgical data about God in what is no doubt an extremely strange and even alienating language, Thomas offers a concept of God as subsistent activity/actuality: a triad of action-based subsisting relations.

Non-standard Interpretations

Thomists of conflicting schools have often held back from spelling all this out. Among notable exceptions we should mention David Burrell. Drawing attention to how central the word '*actus*' is, of course analogically employed, throughout Thomas's work, he pinpoints it as 'the master metaphor guiding Aquinas' grammatical treatment of divinity'.[28] Indeed: 'Insistence on God's actuality is the only clue Aquinas will provide for our grasping what it is to be divine'. The plan of the *Summa*, Burrell thinks, is to show how human beings, created by God, find their way to ultimate beatitude by the activities of knowing and loving. These are the activities which provide Thomas with a paradigm for understanding all action, Burrell says. In particular, when he considers divine activity, Thomas models it on the activity of knowing and loving which we find ourselves practising all the time.[29]

Burrell translates Thomas's thesis that God's nature is to exist as follows: 'To be God is to be to-be' (1.3.4). He hyphenates the final 'to-be' to indicate that the infinitive form of the verb is being put to a substantival use, as a predicate nominative.

William J. Hill distinguishes between the word 'being' used as a substantive and thus suggesting 'a static divinity that is a self-enclosed Absolute' and conceiving God as 'Be-ing Itself' – 'the hyphen serving to convey the participial form of the term' – as with Burrell the alternative is process theology – so it turns out that God's being is 'not something static, akin to essence, but a dynamism expressed as actuality'. Thus, Hill goes on, if God is construed as pure actuality, as the fullness of be-ing, rather than as infinite essence or substance, then it follows that divinity is 'a pure dynamism' – there is a 'spontaneous emanation of being into knowing and loving' – so we have relationality at the core of existence – 'the fecundity of the divine essence as a pure dynamism at once self-expressive and self-unitive'.[30]

These are, obviously, somewhat audacious readings, coming from theologians perfectly aware of English-language reserves about 'being', and acquainted also with analytic philosophy. Years before, quite independently, in his book on Barth, Hans Urs von Balthasar already mocked the custom of setting 'act' against 'being', '*Ereignis*' against '*Sein*'.[31] Juxtaposing them as dialectical opposites is 'absurd' – particularly when we recall the Aristotelico-Thomistic description of *ipsum esse subsistens* as *actus*. For Thomas, and by implication for any competent Thomist, God's being was never static but always intrinsically dynamic.

In short, no doubt polemically, Balthasar meets Barth's supposedly innovatory understanding of God's being as event by citing Catholic theologians for whom God was not 'the pure act of Aristotle in contrast to the potentiality of the world', but for whom 'God is act (*Akt*) as power, deed, love, as what appears in the world and its history as absolute event (*das absolute Ereignis*)'.

Much has been made of Barth's introduction of a certain 'actualism' into theology: Balthasar refers us to Maurice Blondel, who effects the revision of the metaphysical concept of a 'nature' to incorporate the dimension of event (*das Ereignishafte*) in his book *Action* as long ago as 1893.[32] He cannot really have believed that Blondel's work was acceptable to many Thomists, even by 1950. He goes on, anyway, to cite books by three remarkable German theologians (seldom quoted in Anglo-American literature), Hermann Schell, Romano Guardini, and especially Michael Schmaus, to document his claim that Roman Catholic theology was well aware of the 'event-like' character of the divine nature.[33] From Schmaus's *Dogmatik* (1949 fourth edition), by far the most widely used textbook in German-language seminaries and theology faculties at the time, he quotes this: God's being is an 'active, doing Being (*actus purus*), purest efficacy, being doing and doing being (*seiendes Tun und tuendes Sein*)'. 'Being and doing completely coincide'. God is 'living consummation (*lebendiger Vollzug*)'.

In short, despite the standard charge that Thomists are still captivated by the picture of the static deity of 'classical theism', Balthasar was documenting in 1951 that, in standard Roman Catholic theology, God's being and doing were understood to be identical: the divine 'nature' is 'pure act' – in effect, Barth's understanding of God on the model of an event.[34]

On the other hand, in the best recent introduction to Barth's work, George Hunsinger lists 'actualism' as the first of the motifs he proposes to guide the reader: 'At the most general level it means that he thinks primarily in terms of events and relationships rather than monadic or self-contained substances'. All across the board, thinking of human beings as well as of God, and in connection with all the standard issues in Christian theology, Barth constantly speaks in terms of occurrence, happening, event, history, decisions and act. When he wants to describe the living God 'in a technical way', as Hunsinger puts it, Barth says that 'God's being is always a being in act'. What this means, negatively, is that 'any attempt to define God in static or inactive terms, as is customary in certain theologies and philosophies, is therefore to be rejected' – naming no names but Hunsinger (alas) very likely has Thomas's God in mind.[35]

Positively, Barth's actualism in regard to God means that, as a being in act, God is 'a being in love and freedom', 'perfectly complete without us', 'alive in the active relations of love and freedom which constitute

God's being in and for itself'. Barth's God, Hunsinger says, is 'the acting subject of this self-constituting, mysterious event' which is 'the active relations of God's Trinitarian self-differentiation'.

Beautifully put, one wants to say, if we are to describe the living God of the biblical dispensation 'in a technical way'. Indeed, all that Hunsinger cites from Barth's technical description of God would apply to Thomas's, except that for Thomas God's mind and wisdom would always be mentioned as well as God's freedom and love. Perhaps, by omission or inadvertence, Hunsinger makes Barth's concept of God sound more voluntarist than it actually is. Thomas's God, anyway, is always doing things 'wisely', 'providing for each being according to its own way of being' (Wisdom 8:1: *suaviter disponit omnia* – one of Thomas's favourite quotations). That God acts wisely, respectfully of creaturely natures, a constant patristic theme, is perhaps less credible nowadays than that God is free with his love, even to the extent of a freedom that runs close to at least seeming arbitrary.

Thomas's Decisive Maxim

More recently, in his excellent *Systematic Theology*, the American Lutheran theologian Robert W. Jenson writes of the history of the doctrine of the Trinity as the 'overcoming' of pagan antiquity's interpretation of being as 'persistence'.[36] The concept of 'being' is not biblical, he notes; we can imagine (just about) a history of Christian doctrine in which the doctrine that God is one remained no more than repeated denial that there is any other god besides the Lord who brought the people out of slavery (Exodus 20:1–2); but since 'being' was a central concept in the pagan theology with which the Christian faith immediately became entangled it was an unavoidable determinant of how the Christian doctrine of the oneness of God actually developed. Once the ancient Greek thinkers put on the agenda the question why there is something rather than nothing, then the question of what is 'just be-ing', hyphenating to bring out the verbal dimension, refuses to go away, whatever certain philosophers maintain: 'the concept of being is incurably theological'. Jenson directs us to Thomas's doctrine of the identity of essence and existence in God: the doctrine of the divine simplicity.

This provides a suitable conclusion for our rehearsal of Thomas's exposition of the doctrine of God. Jenson, unlike the eminent theologians already cited, does not read Thomas as offering nothing but the static deity of so-called classical theism. Admittedly, Thomas's refusal to allow a real distinction in God between essence and existence will not take us all the way; Jenson brings in Gregory of Nyssa to help him devise 'a Trinitarian concept of being itself'. But Jenson's account of 'the being of the one God' greatly illuminates Thomas's doctrine of the identity of essence and existence in God – 'one of intellectual history's most powerful and tantalizing ideas', Jenson remarks, adding that 'at least from the one side', the doctrine is 'also reasonably clear'.[37]

The clear side, Jenson says, is that what it means to be a creature – 'humans and angels and trees and abstract ideas' – is that these beings 'genuinely are', and yet equally plainly they 'have their being from beyond themselves' (citing ST 1.3.4). The doctrine of the real distinction, in any creature, between its nature and its existence, is simply a reformulation of the doctrine of creation. What it is to be created, in the biblical sense, is to be something that need not have existed: to have a nature which does not guarantee or originate its actual existence. For Jenson, the doctrine both locates the radical difference between God and creatures *and* ensures the authentic reality of created beings.

The less clear side, according to Jenson, is what it means to say that there is no such real distinction in God. Some students of Thomas are content to say that denial of the distinction in God implies nothing more than that God is not a creature, and that no more can be said. Jenson wants more: the contention that the essence or nature of God is 'an otherwise unqualified act of existing' is Thomas's 'decisive maxim'. Jenson's interest lies in completing the discussion by examining the doctrine of the Trinity; but he is absolutely clear that Thomas's God is not the god of Plato and Aristotle. 'The fatal error', as he says, 'is to think of God as simply one thing and creatures as another, and then inquire how the second, with its capabilities, can know the first, given its characteristics'. This is likely to tempt us perilously close to 'Mediterranean antiquity': the assumption that God is not radically other. Whatever else is to be said, Thomas is plainly out to save God from being turned into one more entity. The best way to avoid blurring the line between God and the gods will be to remember that God is 'not monadic but triune', Jenson maintains; the biblically revealed doctrine of God as Trinity is his 'dominant concern' throughout. But first he recalls the metaphysical doctrine of the 'convertibility' of the 'transcendentals: being, unity, truth, goodness and beauty'.[38]

God as being, truth, goodness and beauty, is, adjectivally, God as knowable, lovable and enjoyable, as being and one. None of these concepts is properly understood in isolation from the others, Jenson holds. 'God's one being', as knowable, lovable and enjoyable, is thus considered 'in its openness to participation'. In short, it is because God's truth, goodness and beauty are his knowability, lovability and enjoyability, that we begin to conceive God's one being in Trinitarian openness.

This move is both like and unlike Thomas's reflections on the one being of God. His consideration of the divine being as actuality-activity of sheer existing leads him to say that this being is actually-actively self-knowing, self-loving and self-enjoying (ST 1.3–26) – which takes him to the brink of the doctrine of the Trinity. God is knowable, Jenson holds, because and only because he is actually known, in the historical revelation of the biblical tradition. This is Barth's point: talk of the possibility of knowing God prior to and independently of remembering the actual knowledge of God historically vouchsafed leads nowhere – or, worse, generates 'natural theology'.[39] On the other hand, Jenson asks, what else does Thomas's maxim entail? God's essence is his existence (cf ST 1.3): 'there is no form of deity metaphysically or otherwise prior to its actuality'.

Indeed, Jenson cites Thomas's 'decisive maxim' again on his last page: if it is true that God's essence is his existence, then we may say, Jenson thinks, that the exchange between the persons of the Trinity that is God's essence is not other than 'its sheer occurrence as the divine perichoresis'. The doctrine of the 'one being of God', thus understood, brings us to God as an event, an exchange, a conversation, finally to God as 'a great fugue'.

That goes much further than Thomas. He is unlikely ever to have imagined the inner life of the Godhead on analogy with a conversation, let alone as a fugue. We have become vastly more aware of the importance of language and of music. On the other hand, Jenson shows, time and again, how much we can learn from Thomas's concept of God. He certainly has no time for the standard accounts of Thomas's God as a static entity. He is clear that, while Thomas was 'stimulated and helped to his own metaphysical positions' by studying Aristotle, his key insights 'could hardly be less Aristotelian'. In particular, Aristotle could never have accepted the doctrine of divine simplicity. Furthermore, for Jenson, the Five Ways 'occur within a specifically biblical apprehension already in place'; but that is because 'the entire body of Thomas Aquinas' *Summa Theologiae*, encompassing alike the propositions supposed to be available by nature to all humans and those attributed to historically specific revelation alone, is shaped by a narrative of creational-incarnational procession from and return to God'. And that takes us back to Jenson's early work on Thomas: his demonstration of the eschatological character of Thomas's theology: 'while Thomas indeed says that the axioms of theology are theorems of a prior body of knowledge, this turns out to be knowledge that only God and his perfected saints possess (cf ST 1.1.2), to which we therefore can appeal only within the mystery of the church's anticipatory participation in the Kingdom'.[40]

'God's sovereign goodness as we know it now through its effects can be known apart from the Trinity of Persons', Thomas maintains; 'but as known in himself, as seen by the blessed, God cannot be known apart from the Trinity of Persons' (ST 2–2.2.8). Moreover, as he adds, 'it is the mission of the Divine Persons precisely that brings us to beatitude'.

Chapter 12

CONCLUSION

More might be said. I have paid no attention to what Thomas Aquinas says that is now totally unacceptable. I have left aside much that is still of interest: his work on the sacraments as signs of faith, for example.[1] As far as recent reception of his work goes, my principal interest throughout, I have said nothing about Thomist studies in Italian, Spanish, Dutch and Polish, and little enough about current French and German work.[2]

Enough has been said, on the other hand, to display the diversity and incommensurability of the available interpretations of Thomas's work. Returning to the received account in the English-speaking world, we may surely say that it will not do. The proofs of God's existence which come early in the *Summa Theologiae* cannot be transported from their theological context into philosophy of religion courses – arguably, at least.[3] The God with whom Thomas is concerned is, arguably again, not the God of generalized theism but (for better or worse) the God of patristic Christianity. We have to allow for ways of reading Thomas that put him into conversation, so to speak, with Ibn Sina and Moses ben Maimon,[4] and relate him back to John of Damascus and Dionysius the Areopagite, as well as to Augustine of Hippo. The distinction that Thomas saw between Aristotle and 'Platonists', over particular philosophical issues, does not necessarily make him an out and out Aristotelian (whatever that would mean); he owes much more, arguably again, to the likes of Proclus.[5] Given the instabilities of current expositions both of the significance of Christ and of the doctrine of God as Trinity, it seems not unreasonable to recommend some attention to Thomas's accounts.[6] Finally, in the present flood of work in 'virtue ethics', Thomas should not be regarded as mainly or only an exponent of natural law ethics.[7]

The hard question is to account for the rival ways of reading Thomas. The mid-nineteenth-century revival of interest, primarily in his supposedly Aristotelian philosophy, was intended to put it to use in containing and eradicating the supposedly Cartesian/Kantian subjectivist individualism by which Roman Catholic thinkers were then attracted. This use of Thomas, as we saw in chapter 2, remains effective in the context of analytic philosophy. It may, however, soon have to deal with a threat from medieval scholarship: anachronism is always a risk when one calls on earlier thinkers to refute current arguments.[8] Anyway, the standard outsider's view of Thomas owes everything to Leonine Thomism: at worst, 'arid Aristotelianism', at best a combination of natural theology and natural law ethics which satisfies some and repels others.

On the inside, so to speak, among those educated in institutions where Leonine Thomism was all but mandatory, it was being rejected by the 1920s. Initiated by such remarkable interpreters as Pierre Rousselot and Joseph Maréchal, many students of Thomas concluded that Cartesian/Kantian philosophy could not be outwitted by being regarded as a total mistake; rather, Thomas had to be reread in the light of modern philosophical considerations. The 'Copernican revolution' inaugurated by Kant, in his focus on the active role of the knower and the autonomy of the moral agent, turned out, in this rereading, to be anticipated in Thomas's conception of the natural drive of the mind towards truth and being. Far from being a supposedly empiricist epistemology, with the mind being conformed to things in the world, Thomas viewed every act of knowing and choosing as implicitly knowing and choosing the truth and goodness which is the mystery of the divine being. This generated transcendental Thomism.[9] Kant's analysis of experience is 'transcendental', in the sense of getting behind actual experience to lay bare the conditions which make it possible at all. This reading of Thomas disclosed the *a priori* conditions that Thomas took for granted in his understanding of human experience: namely, that in every act of knowing and loving the human being is tacitly and no doubt mostly unwittingly growing closer to (or further away from) God.[10]

In a somewhat different way, theologians of the same generation, notably Henri de Lubac, reconnected Thomas's thought with the patristic tradition: in short, as we saw in chapter 8, retrieving his understanding of the human spirit as created in the divine image and naturally desiring the face-to-face vision of God which of course can be granted only as a gift. This puts an end to the two-storey view of grace and nature, setting the two over against each other, in favour of understanding human life under divine grace as the perfection of human nature. Opponents of this view feared that human nature as always already graced, human reason as always already anticipating beatific vision, and human desire as always already fulfilled in charity, smooths out the tensions and contradictions and risks allowing nature, reason and desire to collapse into grace, faith and charity – or, by naturalizing the latter, turning Christian life into a form of secular humanism.

In his book on Karl Barth, Hans Urs von Balthasar rejected 'sawdust Thomism' in favour of de Lubac's retrieval of Thomas's doctrine of natural desire for God. Balthasar's main concern, however, was to put Thomas's thought back into the context of the entire Western metaphysical tradition, understanding this as repeated disclosure of the divine goodness, truth and beauty, consummated in the self-revelation of God in the Christian dispensation of grace. Above all, as we saw in chapter 5, Balthasar sought to bring out the importance of Thomas's insistence on the distinction in creatures between their nature and their existence, or, rather, on the complete absence of any such distinction in God.

Thomas, we may agree, is a transitional figure: later than the monastic theology and sacramental sense of the world which we find still in the early thirteenth century, earlier than the fourteenth-century developments that opened tensions and contradictions between nature and grace, reason and faith, and so on, leading eventually to the rejection (in the West) of Aristotle and Christian Platonism. It is not easy, nowadays, to believe in the harmony of reason and faith for which the High Middle Ages, or at least Thomas Aquinas, were once celebrated.[11] It remains an option, on the other hand, to take Thomas either as a key figure in the development of modern theology or as primarily a continuator of premodernity. As we saw in chapters 3 and 4, he can be read as inaugurating modern philosophy of religion, but only if his conceptual apparatus, and in particular his understanding of causality and substance, are assumed to anticipate the standard modern view. If, on the other hand, he has a notion of agent causality, and of self-diffusive substance, we find ourselves on a different hermeneutic line altogether.[12]

Similarly, as we saw in chapter 7 with his conception of moral theology as principally an ethics of divine beatitude, and in chapter 9 with his conception of sanctification as deified creaturehood, we are once again reading Thomas in the light of theological traditions he inherited, rather than in that of modern and in particular post-Reformation problems.[13]

Sometimes, no doubt, this or that interpretation must be regarded as simply mistaken. On the whole, however, more complex factors are at play. For those who have been trained in analytic philosophy, and are inclined to accept Frege's principle that 'existence is not a predicate', Thomas's talk of 'Being' will (as Anthony Kenny says) be 'sophistry and illusion'. On the other hand, for those who believe Heidegger's grand narrative about the forgetfulness of Being in the metaphysical tradition, Thomas's talk of 'Being' will either be 'idolatry' or (with Balthasar) the wonderful exception to Heidegger's rule.[14] While there are recent attempts to show that analytic philosophy and hermeneutic/deconstructionist philosophies are not as radically incommensurable as they look, it seems unlikely that students of Thomas from these rival traditions will ever take each other very seriously, let alone come to any common understanding.

Perhaps we should rescue Thomas from philosophy altogether – but then, after all, he *is* a great philosopher, indeed that is one of the sources of the ambivalence of his thought. He is a philosopher and he is a theologian, and we are never going to agree where to put the emphasis.

In short, as some readings of his natural law theory (see chapter 6) seem to show, incommensurable yet equally plausible, Thomas's thought, perhaps over a range of issues, contains within itself the Janus-like ambiguities that generate competing interpretations which can never be reconciled. Working out a doctrine of God and of creation in conjunction with Jewish and Islamic metaphysics, a Latin theologian in the new university environment referring all the time to great monastic theologians of the Eastern Church, a Catholic theologian haunted by Catharist dualism, more concerned to protect the faith of friends in the arts faculty against Islamicized Aristotelianism than to avoid alarming his colleagues in divinity with his Aristotelian insights – all along the line Thomas's work, we may surely say, offers readers today little of the 'synthesis' and 'equilibrium' for which it was widely admired 50 years ago, but, on the contrary, reveals a loose-endedness in its constantly repeated discussions of finally unresolvable problems: 'straw', Thomas called his work, in comparison with the knowledge of God for which he hoped and prayed; sketches, we may say, that he made in the course of his long and involved journeyings.

NOTES

Preface

1 Thomas Aquinas, the Latin form of his name, was universally known as St Thomas in English-language discussion until about 1970; then, especially among philosophers, he became Aquinas; in the most recently published volumes of the critical editions of his works he has become Thomas de Aquino. I shall refer to him as Thomas, in accordance with usage in current American scholarship.

Chapter 1 Life and Times

1 The best biography is by Simon Tugwell, in *Albert and Thomas: Selected Writings* (New York: Paulist Press, 1988); for more detail about Thomas's life, work and reception see M.-D. Chenu, *Toward Understanding Saint Thomas* (Chicago: Regnery, 1964); J.-P. Torrell, *Saint Thomas Aquinas: The Person and his Work* (Washington, DC: Catholic University of America Press, 1966) and Thomas F. O'Meara, *Thomas Aquinas: Theologian* (Notre Dame, IN: University of Notre Dame Press, 1997); for the biographical documents see Kenelm Foster, *The Life of Saint Thomas Aquinas* (London: Longmans, Green, 1958); and for a good sketch outlining Thomas's conflict-marked life see Romanus Cessario, 'Thomas Aquinas: A doctor for the ages', *First Things* 91 (March, 1999): 27–32.
2 References to the *Summa Theologiae* will be incorporated in the text: ST 1–2.48.4 = *Summa Theologiae*, part 1 of part 2, question 48, article 4.
3 See Foster, *The Life of Saint Thomas*: 22: 'To turn from that conventionally impassive countenance to the handwriting of Aquinas – surviving in such abundance – may surprise one by the contrast: "tranquil" is hardly the

word for this furiously rapid script'; and see especially the wonderful essay by Piet Gils, the most expert decipherer of Thomas's appalling writing, *Expositio libri Boetii De ebdomadibus*, vol. 50 (Rome: Commissio Leonina, 1992): 175–209.

4 Frederick II (1194–1250), half German and half Sicilian, grew up in Palermo which remained his base; fluent in Arabic, interested in science, religion and the occult, by 1220 he had the Holy Roman Empire entirely under his control (bad news for the popes); though excommunicated by Pope Gregory IX he went on crusade, did a deal with the Sultan al-Kamil, regained Jerusalem, crowned himself in the Holy Sepulchre church as the new King David; travelled in oriental splendour with Saracen guards; in 1243 secured the election of Pope Innocent IV who then excommunicated and waged war against him even more determinedly than previous popes; for Frederick's court in Palermo see C.H. Haskins, *Studies in the History of Mediaeval Science* (Cambridge, MA: Harvard University Press, 1924): 242–71.

5 For a good account of traditional monastic spirituality see Jean Leclercq, *The Love of Learning and the Desire for God: Study of Monastic Culture* (New York: Fordham University Press, 1961); for Thomas's knowledge of patristic literature see most recently L. Elders, 'Thomas Aquinas and the Fathers of the Church', in Irena Backus (ed.), *The Reception of the Church Fathers in the West* (Leiden: Brill, 1997) but, better, Godefroid Geenen, 'Thomas d'Aquin et les Pères', *Dictionnaire Théologique Catholique* 15 (Paris: Librairie Letouzet et Ané, 1946), cols 738–61.

6 Dominic Guzman (c.1172–1221) was born in Old Castile; canon of Osma cathedral; founded missionary community in Toulouse, then the Order of Preachers (Dominicans, or Black Friars); see F.C. Lehner (ed.) *Saint Dominic: Biographical Documents* (Washington, DC: The Thomist Press, 1964) and M.H. Vicaire, *Histoire de saint Dominique* (Paris: Cerf, 2 vols 1957, 3rd edn revised 1982; English translation by K. Pond, London: Darton, Longman and Todd, 1964).

7 Manichee: follower of Mani, Persian founder of a Gnostic Judeo-Christian religion, put to death in 276; see Steven Runciman, *The Medieval Manichee: A Study of the Christian Dualist heresy* (Cambridge, UK: Cambridge University Press, 1955), Malcolm Lambert, *The Cathars* (Oxford: Blackwell, 1998), Michael Costen, *The Cathars and the Albigensian Crusade* (Manchester: Manchester University Press, 1997) and René Weis, *The Yellow Cross: The Story of the Last Cathars 1290–1329* (London: Viking, 2000); though there is no satisfactory account in English of Catharist theology.

8 The religion is said to have existed in Chinese Turkestan into the tenth century and as the 'Doctrine of Light' flourished in Fukien in the thirteenth century; whether there was direct connection with the Cathars is disputed; doctrines preached in the Byzantine Church by the tenth-century Bulgarian monk Bogomil may have spread to the West (the Cathars were sometimes called bougres): see Bernard Hamilton, 'Wisdom from the east: The reception by the Cathars of eastern dualist texts', in *Heresy and Literacy 1000–1530* ed. P. Miller and A. Hudson (Cambridge, UK: Cambridge University Press, 1994). Bogomilism was almost as great a problem in the Eastern Church as Catharism in the West: repressive measures are recorded

in the twelfth century, including burning at the stake, cf. D. Obolensky, *The Bogomils: A Study in Balkan neo-Manichaeism* (Cambridge, UK: Cambridge University Press, 1948).

9 Albertus Magnus (d. 1280, over 80 years old), taught in Paris and Cologne, and sought to make the complete Aristotelian corpus 'intelligible to the Latins', albeit 'Albertism' is a much more openly and mystically oriented Christian neo-Platonism than 'Thomism': but see Tugwell, *Albert and Thomas*: 3–129.

10 Thomas's three texts are translated by John Procter, *An Apology for the Religious Orders* (London: Sands, 1902) and *The Religious State, the Episcopate, the Priestly Office* (London: Sands, 1902): an important source for understanding how Christ-centred Thomas's theology was all along. For background see D.L. Douie, *The Conflict between the Seculars and the Mendicants at the University of Paris in the Thirteenth Century* (Oxford: Aquinas Papers 23, 1954); and, for much greater detail, see the wonderfully learned and entertaining essays by Michel-Marie Dufeil, collected in *Saint Thomas et l'histoire* (Aix-en-Provence: Centre Universitaire d'Etudes et de Recherches Médiévales d'Aix, Université de Provence, 1991), arguing that in his exchanges with his principal adversary Guillaume de Saint-Amour Thomas hit hard, showing himself 'not to be the 'chitterling' (*andouille*) he is often taken to be', indeed finding he had something of his own to say, which, in refusing Guillaume's 'stubborn traditionalism' as well as Joachimite apocalypticism, was effectively to discover the concept of *history*. While conceding that, even at Vatican II, Thomas was being rejected or endorsed because of his supposed immunity to development, Dufeil contends that Thomas was among the first to be interested in evolution, temporality and history: '*Incluant l'homme, le devenir temporel concret de la création jusqu'au bonheur qui se déchiffre mu de l'intérieur par et vers le moteur de l'Acte Pur – constitue le plan même de sa Somme et le principal foyer de sa réflexion*' (p. 65).

11 See Marjorie Reeves, *Joachim of Fiore and the Prophetic Future* (London: SPCK, 1976).

12 Bonaventure (c.1217–74), by birth Giovanni di Fidanza, Franciscan theologian, Thomas's colleague in Paris; much more reserved about Aristotle.

13 Abu 'Ali al Husain ibn 'Abdallah ibn Sina (990–1037), Avicenna to Thomas, Muslim philosopher, physician to Iranian princes, wrote in Arabic but widely known in Hebrew and Latin translations; at least as significant as Aristotle in Thomas's philosophical development.

14 Following the excellent introduction by Andrew Louth, *Denys the Areopagite* (London: Geoffrey Chapman, 1989), I shall refer to this unknown author as Denys, one of the three or four most significant authorities for Thomas: originally identified or identifying himself with Dionysius the Areopagite (Acts 17:34) he became Pseudo-Dionysius when sixteenth-century scholars contested the identification: a late fifth-century Syrian monk whose neo-Platonist Christianity exercised profound influence on the Church in both East and West.

15 See *Thomas Aquinas: Selected Writings*, edited and translated with an introduction and notes by Ralph McInerny (Harmondsworth: Penguin, 1998),

an excellent selection, including the Inaugural Sermons and *On Being and Essence*.

16   Anicius Manlius Torquatus Boethius (c.480–c.524), Roman senator, charged with treason at the Ostrogothic court in Ravenna, and eventually murdered; main conduit of Aristotle's logical works; best remembered for his *De consolatione philosophiae*: through the love of wisdom the soul attains knowledge of the vision of God, nowhere explicitly mentioning Christ (widely read, Anglo-Saxon translation attributed to King Alfred); see the wonderful study by H. Chadwick, *Boethius: The Consolation of Music: Logic, Theology, and Philosophy* (Oxford: Clarendon Press, 1981).

17   See the excellent English translation in five volumes by Anton C. Pegis et al. (New York: Doubleday, 1955–7; Notre Dame, IN: University of Notre Dame Press, 1975). The best introduction is by R.A. Gauthier (Paris: Editions Universitaires, 1993) but see Thomas S. Hibbs, *Dialectic and Narrative in Aquinas: An Interpretation of the Summa Contra Gentiles* (Notre Dame, IN: University of Notre Dame Press, 1995) and the totally different studies by Norman Kretzmann, *The Metaphysics of Theism* (Oxford: Oxford University Press, 1997) and *The Metaphysics of Creation* (Oxford: Oxford University Press, 1999): a great medievalist and fine philosopher in the analytic tradition, expounding Thomas's natural theology, uncowed by 'Barthian' objections, advocating it as the best instance available even now of an unavoidable intellectual enterprise.

18   There is a serviceable English translation by R.W. Mulligan, J.V. McGlynn and R.W. Schmidt, *On Truth* (3 vols, Chicago: Regnery, 1952–54; reprint Indianapolis, IN: Hackett, 1994); Serge-Thomas Bonino is preparing a French translation with commentary.

19   There is a dated but serviceable English translation by L. Shapcote, *On the Power of God* (3 vols, London: Burnes, Oates and Washboume, 1932–34) and an excellent translation by Jean Oesterle, *On Evil* (Notre Dame, IN: University of Notre Dame Press, 1995).

20   The *Summa Theologiae*, left unfinished, with another volume to write, exists in two English translations: one by Fathers of the English Dominican Province (22 volumes including the index of biblical, patristic and other quotations, London: Burnes, Oates and Washbourne, 1912–36; reprinted Westminster, MD: Christian Classics, 1981), the other edited by T. Gilby and T.C. O'Brien (60 vols, Latin-English, with an excellent index of concepts, topics, etc., London: Eyre and Spottiswoode/New York: McGraw Hill, 1964–73).

21   See the fundamental discussion by Mark D. Jordan, *The Alleged Aristotelianism of Thomas Aquinas*, Etienne Gilson lecture (Toronto: Pontifical Institute of Medieval Studies, 1992).

22   Splendidly translated by Robert Pasnau (New Haven, CT and London: Yale University Press, 1999).

23   Translated by C.I. Litzinger (2 vols, Chicago: Regnery, 1964; reprinted Notre Dame, IN: Dumb Ox Books, 1993); for the dispute about the book's aim and value: see James C. Doig, *Aquinas's Philosophical Commentary on the Ethics: A Historical Perspective* (Dordrecht: Kluwer, 2001).

24 Translated by J.P. Rowan (Chicago: Regnery, 1964; reprinted Notre Dame, IN: Dumb Ox Books, 1995).

25 According to Weisheipl (1983: 332) this must be the work on pneumatics composed by Hero of Alexandria (floreat c.100/150 BC), mathematician and natural philosopher, inventor of many machines using water, including a steam-engine, a fireman's pump and the water jet known as Hero's fountain.

26 The early biographers say little about Thomas's part in assimilating Aristotle's work: for William Tocco, for example, a young friar in Naples when Thomas lived there in 1272–72, the controversies in which Thomas was involved were four: against 'Averroism' (misconceptions of Aristotle); defence of the friars against the bishops and diocesan clergy; the apocalyptic millennarianism of the Fraticelli; and the misguided doctrines of the Greek Church.

27 See St Thomas Aquinas, *Commentary on the Book of Causes* translated by Vincent A. Guagliardo and others (Washington, DC: The Catholic University of America Press, 1996). The discovery of Thomas's participationist metaphysics by Cornelio Fabro (1939) and Louis Bertrand Geiger (1942) instigated acrimonious conflicts over Thomas's 'Aristotelianism'; Henri Dominique Saffrey's edition of Thomas's commentary on the *Liber de causis* (Fribourg: Société Philosophique, 1954) led by the 1980s to the view now dominant outside English-language approaches to Thomas that his thought is best interpreted as neo-Platonic; see the informative and entertaining study by Wayne Hankey, 'Denys and Aquinas: Antimodern cold and postmodern hot', in *Christian Origins: Theology, Rhetoric and Community* edited by Lewis Ayres and Gareth Jones (London: Routledge, 1998): 139–84; and Cristina D'Ancona Costa, 'Historiographie du platonisme médiéval: le cas de saint Thomas', in *Saint Thomas au XXe siècle*, edited by Serge-Thomas Bonino (Paris: Editions Saint-Paul, 1994): 198–217.

28 Ibn Rushd (1126–98), Muslim philosopher, born in Cordoba, physician at the court of Marrakesh; Latin translations of his Arabic expositions of Aristotle's Greek were immensely influential in medieval Latin theology.

29 At least three English translations exist; see Ralph McInerny's *Aquinas Against the Averroists: On There Being Only One Intellect* (West Lafayette, IN: Purdue University Press, 1993) with excellent notes.

30 Translated together with texts by Siger of Brabant and Bonaventure by C. Vollert et al. (Milwaukee: Marquette University Press, 1964).

31 See Daniel A. Callus, *The Condemnation of St Thomas at Oxford* (Oxford: Aquinas Papers, 1955); Tugwell, *Albert and Thomas*: 237ff.

32 Peter of Spain, who studied at Paris in the late 1220s, composed a treatise on logic that was eventually printed and remained in print well into the seventeenth century; taught and practised medicine; took the title John XXI though there was no John XX; killed when the ceiling of a newly constructed apartment fell on him, eight months into his pontificate.

33 Edward Grant, 'The effect of the Condemnation of 1277', in *Cambridge History of Later Medieval Philosophy* (Cambridge, UK: Cambridge University Press, 1982): 537–9.

34 Etienne Gilson, *Christian Philosophy* (London: Sheed and Ward, 1953): 406.
35 David Piché, *La Condamnation parisienne de 1277*: translation, introduction and commentary (Paris: Vrin, 1999): a richly documented introduction to what many regard as the greatest intellectual event of the thirteenth century, and also to the plethora of modern (often conflicting) interpretations of its significance.
36 Hans Urs von Balthasar, 'On the tasks of Catholic Philosophy in our time', *Communio* 20 (1993): 147–87 (quotation in text p. 173) but originally in *Annalen der Philosophischen Gesellschaft der Innerschweiz* 3 (1945): 1–38.
37 Henri de Lubac, *Surnaturel: Etudes historiques* (Paris: Aubier, 1946): 435–6.
38 *Letters of Etienne Gilson to Henri de Lubac*, annotated by Henri de Lubac (San Francisco: Ignatius Press, 1988): 23–4 (letter dated July 8, 1956).
39 Serge-Thomas Bonino, 'Thomistica', *Revue Thomiste* 97 (1997): 563–603, esp. 563.

Chapter 2   Overcoming Epistemology

1 I take Roger Scruton, *From Descartes to Wittgenstein* (London: Routledge, 1981) as the best introduction to what English-speaking philosophers understand as modern philosophy; Frank B. Farrell, *Subjectivity, Realism and Postmodernism: The Recovery of the World* (Cambridge, UK: Cambridge University Press, 1994) tells much the same story but relates modern philosophy to its roots in medieval theology; Richard Popkin, in a series of works since *The History of Scepticism from Erasmus to Spinoza* (Berkeley, CA: University of California Press, 1979) shows the extent to which scepticism issues from Christian divisions: with appeals to infallible biblical revelation sabotaged at the Reformation by conflicting interpretations, theologians began to look elsewhere for certainty (Descartes, after all, addressed the *Meditations* to the Dean and Doctors of the Sacred Faculty of Theology of Paris, in 1641, hoping to persuade them that he had arguments for God).
2 Alasdair MacIntyre, *Three Rival Versions of Moral Enquiry: Encyclopaedia, Genealogy, and Tradition* (London: Duckworth: 1990; all quotations in text pp. 73–5); *First Principles, Final Ends and Contemporary Philosophical Issues* (Aquinas lecture, 1990), in *The MacIntyre Reader*, edited by Kelvin Knight (Cambridge, UK: Polity Press, 1998); and 'Natural law as subversive: The case of Aquinas', *Journal of Medieval and Early Modern Studies* 26 (1996): 61–83.
3 Joseph Kleutgen (1811–83), born in Westphalia, entered the Society of Jesus in 1834, and was probably the most influential Catholic theologian in the nineteenth century, though there is no study or biography and he does not have an entry in the *Oxford Dictionary of the Christian Church*, 3rd edn., 1999; he had a hand in drafting the decrees of the First Vatican Council (1869–70), and the papal encyclical *Aeterni Patris* (1879), but is mentioned

here because of *Die Theologie der Vorzeit* (3 vols 1853–60; 2nd edn 8 vols 1867–74) and especially *Die Philosophie der Vorzeit* (2 vols 1860–3), soon translated into Italian and French.

4   Francisco Suárez (1548–1617), Spanish Jesuit theologian/metaphysician, immensely influential on Protestant as well as Catholic thinkers; his *De Legibus* expounded the principles of natural/international law; copies of his *Defensio fidei*, directed against Anglicanism, were burned in London.

5   Leo XIII, *Aeterni Patris*.

6   A sketch is provided by Aidan Nichols, *Catholic Thought Since the Enlightenment: A Survey* (Pretoria: University of South Africa Press, 1998). For Thomism in particular see Gerald A. McCool, *Catholic Theology in the Nineteenth Century: The Quest for a Unitary Method* (New York: Seabury Press, 1977) republished as *Nineteenth-Century Scholasticism* (New York: Fordham University Press, 1989); P.J. FitzPatrick, 'Neoscholasticism' in *The Cambridge History of Later Medieval Philosophy*, edited by Norman Kretzmann et al. (Cambridge, UK: Cambridge University Press 1982): 838–52; James Hennesey, 'Leo XIII's Thomistic revival: A political and philosophical event', *Journal of Religion* 58 (Supplement, 1978): 185–97, and especially Wayne J. Hankey, 'Pope Leo's purposes and St Thomas' Platonism', in *S. Tommaso nella storia del pensiero*, edited by A. Piolanti (Vatican City: Libreria Editrice Vaticana, 1982): 39–52; 'Making theology practical: Thomas Aquinas and the nineteenth century religious revival', *Dionysius* 9 (1985): 85–127.

7   R.P. Phillips, *Modern Thomistic Philosophy: An Explanation for Students, vol 2: Metaphysics* (Westminster, MD: The Newman Press, 1957, 7th printing), first published 1935; the product of many years of teaching philosophy at St John's Seminary, Wonersh, Surrey.

8   Cornelius Ernst (1924–77): papers collected in *Multiple Echo: Explorations in Theology*, edited by Fergus Kerr and Timothy Radcliffe (London: Darton, Longman and Todd, 1979).

9   Ludwig Wittgenstein, *Philosophical Investigations* (Oxford: Blackwell, 1953): 178.

10 Roger Pouivet, *Après Wittgenstein, saint Thomas* (Paris: PUF, 1997), dealing also with Anthony Kenny, *Acts, Emotion, and Will* (London: Routledge and Kegan Paul, 1963) and *The Metaphysics of Mind* (Oxford: Oxford University Press, 1989): '*un compendium de thomisme wittgensteinien*'; among much else; G.E.M. Anscombe, *Intention* (Oxford: Blackwell, 1957); P.T. Geach, *Mental Acts* (London: Routledge and Kegan Paul, 1957).

11 See for example Panayot Butcharov, *Skepticism in Ethics* (Bloomington: Indiana University Press, 1989), and *Skepticism about the External World* (Oxford: Oxford University Press, 1998); and P.F. Strawson, *Skepticism and Naturalism: Some Varieties* (London: Methuen, 1985).

12 Gilbert Ryle, *Concept of Mind* (London: Hutchinson, 1949); Stanley Cavell, *The Claim of Reason: Wittgenstein, Skepticism, Morality and Tragedy* (Oxford: Oxford University Press, 1979): 468–496.

13 Donald M. MacKinnon, *A Study in Ethical Theory* (London: A and C Black, 1957): 79–90 (quotations in text pp. 80, 89–90); these chapters might be

the script, except that he never used notes, of the lectures MacKinnon gave at the University of Aberdeen in winter 1950–1.

14 Amazingly, this refers to the Dominicans then at Blackfriars, Oxford; for an account see Aidan Nichols, *Dominican Gallery: Portrait of a Culture* (Leominster: Gracewing, 1997).

15 R. Cant, 'Recent tendencies in theological writing', *Church Quarterly Review* 142 (1946): 370–1. Oddly, Cant does not mention Eric L. Mascall, though *He Who Is: A Study in Traditional Theism* (London: Longman, Green, 1943) already established him as the most eminent Thomist in the Church of England. It was remarkably perceptive of Hoskyns to see the parallels between Maritain's Thomism and Barth's anti-Liberal Protestantism as early as 1928.

16 Eberhard Busch, *Karl Barth: His Life from Letters and Autobiographical Texts* (London: SCM, 1976): 243.

17 Cf. Jacques Maritain, *Three Reformers: Luther-Descartes-Rousseau* (London: Sheed and Ward, 1928, 1950).

18 Karl Barth, *Church Dogmatics*, I/1, translated by G.W. Bromiley and T.F. Torrance (Edinburgh: T. & T. Clark, 1957–75): 195.

19 Ibid., III/1: 350–62.

20 Martin Heidegger, *Being and Time*, translated by J. Macquarrie and E. Robinson (Oxford: Blackwell, 1973): 202–6.

21 Christopher Gill, *Personality in Greek Epic, Tragedy, and Philosophy: The Self in Dialogue* (Oxford: Clarendon Press, 1996): an immensely rich and instructive book.

22 In effect, Thomas's claim that self-knowledge rests on reflective knowledge of one's acts anticipates Wittgenstein's argument against the possibility of a private language, *Philosophical Investigations* §243 ff.

23 But see Phillip Cary, *Augustine's Invention of the Inner Self: The Legacy of a Christian Platonist* (Oxford: Oxford University Press, 2000): criticizing Augustinian inwardness explicitly in light of Luther's and the 'standard Roman Catholic view' that 'we can never cling too tightly to external means of grace such as the sacraments and the Gospel of Christ' (p. 143).

24 See *New Blackfriars* 80 (1999): 157–216 with bibliography.

25 Charles Taylor, *Philosophical Arguments* (Cambridge, MA: Harvard University Press, 1995): 3.

26 Hilary Putnam, *Word and Life* (Cambridge, MA: Harvard University Press, 1994): 282; John McDowell, *Mind and World* (Cambridge, MA: Harvard University Press, 1994); and John Haldane, 'On coming home to (metaphysical) realism', *Philosophy* 71 (1996): 287–96 and 'The life of signs', *The Review of Metaphysics* 47 (1994): 451–70, in which, among much else, Haldane, perhaps mischievously, compares McDowell's Wittgensteinian view of the mind's place in the world with the view attributed to Meister Eckhart (c.1260–c.1328): intellect as 'a deprivation of being – always ready to be filled by one thing or another and to be wholly informed by the nature of its object so long as this is present'.

27 Norman Kretzmann, 'Philosophy of mind', in *The Cambridge Companion to Aquinas*, edited by Norman Kretzmann and Eleonore Stump (Cambridge, UK: Cambridge University Press, 1993): an excellent collection on Thomas

as a philosopher: Jan Aertsen on the historical setting, Joseph Owens on Aristotle, David Burrell on the Islamic and Jewish connections, John Wippel on metaphysics, Scott MacDonald on theory of knowledge, Ralph McInerny on ethics, Paul Sigmund on law and political theory, Mark Jordan on philosophy and theology, and Stump on philosophy and biblical commentary.

28 Bernard Lonergan, *Verbum: Word and Idea in Aquinas*, edited by David B. Burrell (Notre Dame, IN: University of Notre Dame Press, 1967), reprinting articles in *Theological Studies* 1947–9.

29 Franz Brentano (1838–1919): a Catholic priest who left the Church in 1879; the chief conduit of medieval scholastic philosophy into modern philosophy, in particular he revived the notion of intentionality: ideas are not self-generating but always about something; famously, his best known book set the 17-year-old Heidegger off on his *Denkweg*.

30 In 1965, in a brief review of the first volumes of the new translation of the *Summa Theologiae*, Anscombe wondered whether the confusions of modern philosophy might not be so intractable that we should survey 'the obscurities of the scholastic *esse intelligibile*, whose actuality is the same thing as the actual occurrence of a thought of such-and-such, with a not totally unfavourable eye'; see G.E.M. Anscombe, *Collected Papers, vol I From Parmenides to Wittgenstein* (Oxford: Basil Blackwell, 1981): p. 85.

Chapter 3   Prolegomena to Natural Theology

1 Barth, *Church Dogmatics*, I/1 preface (dated 1932). Defending himself with characteristic panache against charges of 'crypto-Catholicism', based (he says) on his regarding early church doctrine as normative as well as being willing to quote Anselm and Thomas 'without horror', and above all on his belief in the doctrine of the Trinity and 'even that of the Virgin Birth', Barth insists: 'I regard the *analogia entis* as the invention of Antichrist, and I believe that because of it it is impossible ever to become a Roman Catholic, all other reasons for not doing so being to my mind short-sighted and trivial'; 'exploitation of the *analogia entis*' is 'legitimate only on the basis of Roman Catholicism', displaying 'the greatness and misery of a so-called natural knowledge of God in the sense of the Vaticanum' (i.e. Vatican I, 1869–70); Karl Barth, *Church Dogmatics*, translated by G.W. Bromiley and T.F. Torrance (Edinburgh: T & T Clark, 1957–75).

2 Colin E. Gunton, *Becoming and Being: The Doctrine of God in Charles Hartshorne and Karl Barth* (Oxford: Oxford University Press, 1978): 1.

3 T.F. Torrance, *Karl Barth, Biblical and Evangelical Theologian* (Edinburgh: T&T Clark, 1990; quotations in text pp. 183–6).

4 In June 1933, Karl Eschweiler, a well known neo-Thomist theologian at the time, cited the 'Catholic truth that the grace of divine faith, in the German people, does not destroy their divinely created natural talents, but presupposes them', specifically in support of Nazi racial policies and even the sterilization law of 14 July 1933, for which indeed he was censured by the

Vatican; again in July 1933, Michael Schmaus and Karl Adam, much more important theologians, appealed to the axiom to justify a benign view of the continuity between National Socialism and Catholicism; see Robert Anthony Krieg, *Karl Adam: Catholicism in German Culture* (Notre Dame, IN: University of Notre Dame Press, 1992): 114–20.

5 For the text see *Decrees of the Ecumenical Councils*, vol. 2, edited by Norman P. Tanner (London: Sheed and Ward, 1990): 804–11 (all quotations in text chapter 8).

6 Colin E. Gunton, *Theology Through the Theologians* (Edinburgh: T & T Clark, 1996).

7 For emanation see John Inglis, 'Emanation in historical context: Aquinas and the Dominican response to the Cathars', *Dionysius* 17 (1999): 95–128.

8 Karl Barth, *Dogmatics in Outline* (London: SCM Press, 1949): chapter 8; the text of the wonderful lectures Barth gave in 1946 in the ruins of Bonn to students from all faculties.

9 Adolf Harnack (1851–1930, von since 1914), through his immense and immensely influential if perhaps not now much read *Lehrbuch der Dogmengeschichte* (1886–9, *History of Dogma*, 7 vols, 1894–9), persuaded Protestant theologians, as well as philosophers like Heidegger and more recently many Catholic theologians, that, in patristic and medieval theology, 'primitive Christianity' was corrupted by Greek metaphysics ('Hellenization').

10 My licentiate dissertation at Le Saulchoir in 1964, typically, was a rehash of Thomas's teaching on secondary causality.

11 David Braine, *The Reality of Time and the Existence of God* (Oxford: Clarenden Press, 1988): 3.

12 To Braine's list, I add J.L. Austin, 'A plea for excuses', delivered in 1956, reprinted in *Philosophical Papers* (Oxford: Oxford University Press, 1970): 202.

13 Jonathan Barnes, *Aristotle* (Oxford: Oxford University Press, 1982): 46.

14 Such as the classical discussion by Joseph de Finance, *Etre et agir* (Paris: Beauchesne, 1945; Rome: Librairie Editrice de l'Université Grégorienne, 1960).

15 For a start see essays from 1952 onwards, collected in W. Norris Clarke, *Explorations in Metaphysics: Being-God-Person* (Notre Dame, IN: University of Notre Dame Press, 1994). For doubts that the concept of substance has always to be characterized as inert, static, etc., and that classical theism therefore necessarily suffers from 'substantialist metaphysics' see William Alston, 'Substance and the Trinity', in *The Trinity*, edited by Stephen Davis and others (Oxford: Oxford University Press, 1999): 179–201.

Chapter 4   Ways of Reading the Five Ways

1 Parts of this chapter appear in 'Theology in philosophy: Revisiting the Five Ways', *International Journal for Philosophy of Religion* 50 (2001): 115–30.

2 *Dictionnaire de Théologie Catholique*, vol. 4 (Paris: Letouzet et Ané, 1939): col. 932–5.

3 Henri de Lubac, *De la connaissance de Dieu* (Paris: Editions du Temoignage Chrétien, 1941), revised and greatly expanded as *Sur les chemins de Dieu* (1956), translated as *The Discovery of God* (London: Darton, Longman and Todd, 1960), with a postscript explaining that, whatever critics held, the original edition, which never claimed to deal with all the classical problems in 'natural theology' and was not offered as a 'substitute', is entirely consistent with the 'traditional philosophy' required of Roman Catholic theologians by the papal encyclical *Humani generis* (1951), and, far from criticizing Thomas in the light of patristic tradition, is only throwing into relief the traits in which that tradition finds him its best witness.

4 *La nouvelle théologie*: the label given by Thomists who interpreted Thomas in the light of his sixteenth and nineteenth-century expositors to the generation of mostly French and Jesuit scholars who reread Thomas in the light of the theology he inherited. See Aidan Nichols, 'Thomism and the *nouvelle théologie*', *The Thomist* 64 (2000): 1–19.

5 *Revue des Sciences Philosophiques et Théologiques* 38 (1954): 268.

6 Gilson, *Being and Some Philosophers* (Toronto: Pontifical Institute of Medieval Studies, 1949): 214–15.

7 Gilson, *L'Etre et l'Essence* (Paris: J. Vrin, 1948): 175–6.

8 M.D. Chenu, 'Vérité évangélique et métaphysique wolfienne à Vatican II', *Revue des Sciences Philosophiques et Théologiques* 57 (1973): 632–40.

9 This essay was placed on the Index of Prohibited Books in 1942 at the instigation of Garrigou-Lagrange, so Chenu believed; it was republished in 1985: Marie-Dominique Chenu, *Une école de théologie: le Saulchoir* (Paris: Cerf, 1985) with valuable commentaries by Giuseppe Alberigo, Etienne Fouilloux, Jean Ladrière and Jean-Pierre Jossua.

10 John of Damascus (c.655–c.750): of rich Christian family, held an important post at the court of the Caliph, resigned c. 725 to become a monk at St Sabas near Jerusalem; his *De Fide Orthodoxa* treats the main Christian doctrines; in a somewhat inadequate Latin translation it was one of Thomas Aquinas's principal authorities; the medievals did not know that it was largely compiled from the writings of earlier monks of Palestine but since they did not have modern ideas about plagiarism this fact would only have increased the text's authority for them.

11 See Alvin Plantinga (ed.), *The Ontological Argument from St Anselm to Contemporary Philosophers* (London: Macmillan, 1968).

12 In citation of Psalms I refer to the numbering given in Catholic versions & the Bible, with the numbering in Protestant versions given in brackets.

13 Whatever is, is (in principle) unifiable, intelligible, lovable and aesthetically enjoyable: a traditional metaphysical doctrine recently put to good use theologically, in connection with Aquinas, by R.W. Jenson, *Systematic Theology, vol. 1 The Triune God* (Oxford: Oxford University Press, 1997): 225–36.

14 Joseph A. Fitzmyer, in *New Jerome Biblical Commentary* (London: Geoffrey Chapman, 1989: 835–6).

15 John Ziesler, *Paul's Letter to the Romans* (London: SCM Press, 1989): 77–8.

16 J.C. O'Neill, *Paul's Letter to the Romans* (London: Penguin Books, 1975): 41.

17 Karl Barth, *The Epistle to the Romans*, translated from the sixth edition by Edwyn C. Hoskyns (London, Oxford, New York: Oxford University Press, 1933): 46.

18 Douglas A. Campbell, 'Natural theology in Paul? Reading Romans 1. 19–20', *International Journal of Systematic Theology* 1 (1999): 231–52.

19 Karl Barth, *Church Dogmatics*, II/1, (Edinburgh: T. & T. Clark, 1957): 127.

20 Eugene F. Rogers Jr., *Thomas Aquinas and Karl Barth: Sacred Doctrine and the Natural Knowledge of God* (Notre Dame, IN: University of Notre Dame Press, 1995; quotations in text pp. 7, 5).

21 T.C. O'Brien, in St Thomas Aquinas, *Summa Theologiae, vol. 31, Faith* (London: Eyre and Spottiswoode, 1974): 44–5; one may draw attention to an earlier paper, dating from 1964, on the nature of so-called natural theology: 'Philosophy in the seminary', in Cornelius Ernst, *Multiple Echo: Explorations in Theology* (London: Darton, Longman and Todd, 1979): 126–36.

22 Victor Preller, *Divine Science and the Science of God: A Reformulation of Thomas Aquinas* (Princeton, NJ: Princeton University Press, 1967): 228–30.

23 Timothy McDermott, introduction to St Thomas Aquinas, *Summa Theologiae, vol. 2 Existence and Nature of God* (London: Eyre and Spottiswoode, 1964).

24 Eric L. Mascall, *He Who Is: A Study in Traditional Theism* (London: Longman, Green, 1943, revised 1966): 80–82.

25 Edward Sillem, *Ways of Thinking About God* (London: Darton, Longman and Todd, 1961; quotations in text from pp. 30, 14, 29, 60–1).

26 *Super Evangelium S. Ioannis Lectura* ed Raphael Cai (Turin and Rome: Marietti, 1952) §2: the 'most effective way' (*via efficacissima*) of attaining knowledge of God is by God's authority; the evidence of teleology in the universe and thus of a governing authority is confirmed in the Word of God, at Psalm 88:10 (89:9): 'Thou rulest the raging of the sea' (etc). The four 'modes' in which the philosophers of antiquity came to knowledge of God (teleology, mutability, participation, truth) are all confirmed in Scripture, especially the Psalms, but now also in the Prologue to the Fourth Gospel, so Thomas contends.

27 L. Elders, 'Justification des "cinq voies"', *Revue Thomiste* 61 (1961): 207–25.

28 Jacques Maritain, *Approches de Dieu* (Paris: Alsatia, 1953), translated as *Approaches to God* (London: George Allen and Unwin, 1955): 3–6.

29 Starting, for example, with Brian Davies, *Thinking about God* (London: Geoffrey Chapman, 1985); or David Braine, *The Reality of Time and the Existence of God: The Project of Proving God's Existence* (Oxford: Clarendon Press, 1988).

Chapter 5   Stories of Being

1 Anthony Kenny, *Aquinas* (Oxford: Oxford University Press, 1980): 60.

2 Jacques Maritain, *Distinguish to Unite, or The Degrees of Knowledge* (Notre Dame: University of Notre Dame Press, 1995): 245; the original French appeared in 1932.

3 John Paul II, 'Perennial philosophy of St Thomas for the youth of our times', *Angelicum* 57 (1980): 139–41.

4 A.E. Taylor, *Elements of Metaphysics* (London: Methuen, 1903, often reissued).

5 G.K. Chesterton, *Saint Thomas Aquinas* (London: Hodder and Stoughton, 1933, often reissued): chapter 6.

6 Kenny, *Aquinas*: 60; J.L. Austin, *Sense and Sensibilia* (Oxford: Oxford University Press, 1962): 68.

7 For a good account see Brian Davies, 'Classical theism and the doctrine of divine simplicity', in *Language, Meaning and God: Essays in Honour of Herbert McCabe*, edited by Brian Davies (London: Geoffrey Chapman, 1987): 51–74; or Katherin A. Rogers, *Perfect Being Theology* (Edinburgh: Edinburgh University Press, 2000): chapter 3; but see also Christopher Hughes, *On a complex theory of a simple God* (Ithaca, NY: Cornell University Press, 1987), who finds the whole idea and ST 1.2–11 'entirely unintelligible'.

8 Plato, *Theaetetus* (155 d): 'philosophy has no other starting-point than the experience of wonder'; Aristotle *Metaphysics* (982 b 12 sq): 'it is from a feeling of wonder that human beings start now, and did start in the earliest times, to practise philosophy'; philosophy as the love of wisdom originates and is motivated by an experience of wonder which, at this stage, is barely distinguishable between religious awe and proto-scientific inquiry; this is, anyway, the tradition in which Thomas stands.

9 The Latin is so neat as to be almost untranslatable: *divina essentia unitur intellectui creato, ut intellectum in actu, per seipsam faciens intellectum in actu.*

10 Etienne Gilson (1884–1978) was never exposed to seminary Thomism, but was taught at the Sorbonne by Bergson, which familiarized him from the start with anti-Cartesian and anti-rationalist philosophy. Advised by Lucien Lévy-Bruhl (a Jewish philosopher, like Bergson), he devoted his post-graduate research to investigating Descartes's debt to medieval philosophy. His doctoral thesis, published in 1913, dealt with divine and human freedom, maintaining that Descartes freed God's will by denying final causality to nature. Connected with this, he published work demonstrating the continuity between Descartes, 'father of modern philosophy' and medieval thought, as well as the widely acknowledged discontinuity. Gilson believed that the Modernist crisis in the Roman Catholic Church was rooted in understandable opposition to a rationalistic version of Leonine Thomism.

11 The Gifford lectures, which Gilson delivered in French, 1931–2, appeared in English as *The Spirit of Mediaeval Philosophy* (London: Sheed and Ward, 1936). Gilson dedicated the book to John Laird, an admirer of Thomas

Aquinas and presumably the instigator of the invitation to Gilson to give the lectures. Judging by his own Gifford Lectures (1940–1), Laird no doubt appreciated Gilson's mockery of Bréhier's assertion that New Testament Christianity was 'altogether unspeculative' – though one wonders whether all the devout Presbyterians in the audience were amused. Quotations in text are from pp. viii. 11, 51.

12 Interestingly, in the finest recent work by a medievalist who was also in the analytic philosophy tradition, Norman Kretzmann heads a paragraph 'The metaphysics of Exodus', making no reference to Gilson, but contending that when he quotes Exodus 3:13–14, Thomas interprets the verse, 'not implausibly', 'as the Lord's revealing "that God's very being is his essential nature" ' – citing *Summa Contra Gentiles* 1.22: 'No doubt biblical scholarship would dismiss Aquinas's interpretation, even as applied to the Latin text of the passage' – but Kretzmann goes on 'I'm in no position to defend it as an interpretation, though I can imagine, and perhaps even share, the intellectual satisfaction he seems to have felt on seeing the connection between the abstrusest sort of metaphysical thesis and the epiphany of the burning bush'. Much more work remains, Kretzmann concedes, before Thomas can identify the First Cause with 'God'; but in recognizing the metaphysical thesis of God as *ipsum esse subsistens* in the 'sublime truth' of Exodus 3 Thomas 'makes a noteworthy advance in that direction'. See *The Metaphysics of Theism: Aquinas's Natural Theology in Summa contra gentiles I* (Oxford: Oxford University Press, 1997): 127–8.

13 Etienne Gilson, *God and Philosophy* (New Haven, CT: Yale University Press, 1941): 143. See also pp. 63, 65, 68.

14 Thomas de Vio (1469–1534), Gaetano or Cajetan from his birthplace, Master of the Order of Preachers 1508–18; sent to reason with Luther in 1518; composed his commentary on Thomas's *Summa Theologiae* before turning to biblical exegesis in quite a Renaissance Humanist style.

15 *On Truth* (*De veritate*): 22.2.

16 Cited by L.K. Shook, *Etienne Gilson* (Toronto: Pontifical Institute of Medieval Studies, 1984): 335.

17 John F.X. Knasas, *New Blackfriars* 81 (2000): 400–8; the encyclical *Fides et Ratio* was issued in 1999; a lengthy case has been made out for the futility of Gilsonian Thomism, not from an analytic-philosophical perspective but from that of neoplatonic scholarship, see Wayne J. Hankey, 'From metaphysics to history, from Exodus to neoplatonism, from scholasticism to pluralism: The fate of Gilsonian Thomism in English-speaking North America', *Dionysius* New Series 16 (1998): 157–88; but for a much more positive appreciation see 'Autour d'Etienne Gilson: Etudes et documents,' *Revue Thomiste* 94 (1994): 355–553, essays by Géry Prouvost, Yves Floucat, E.H. Wéber, C.G. Conticello and Serge-T. Bonino.

18 M. Heidegger, *An Introduction to Metaphysics* (New Haven, CT: Yale University Press, 2000): 6.

19 You don't have to be Roman Catholic: Heidegger's story of being is taken seriously in one of the most important books by a Lutheran theologian,

Eberhard Jüngel, *God as the Mystery of the World: On the Foundation of the Theology of the Crucified One in the Dispute between Theism and Atheism* (Edinburgh: T. & T. Clark, 1983).

20 Rightly or wrongly, the history of the self-gift/self-withholding of Being in Heidegger's story is difficult to distinguish from a secularization of the presence/absence in history of a voluntaristically conceived God.

21 M. Heidegger, *Identity and Difference* (New York: Harper and Row, 1969): 72 (the product of a seminar on Hegel 1956–7).

22 M. Heidegger, *The Principle of Reason* (Bloomington, IN: Indiana University Press, 1991): 63 (from lectures in 1955–6).

23 Reiner Schürmann, *Heidegger on Being and Acting: From Principles to Anarchy* (Bloomington, IN: Indiana University Press, 1987).

24 M. Heidegger, *Poetry, Language, Thought* (New York: Harper Collins, 1971): 180 (from a lecture given in 1950): here again, whatever the talk of the world's worlding, the reference to the impossibility of saying anything about the simpleness (*das Einfache*) of the world cannot but remind one of Thomas's doctrine of the divine *simplicitas*.

25 Gustav Siewerth, *Das Schicksal der Metaphysik von Thomas zu Heidegger* (Einsiedeln: Johannes Verlag, 1959); J.B. Lotz, *Martin Heidegger und Thomas von Aquin: Mensch, Zeit, Sein* (Pfullingen: Neske, 1975); Bernhard Welte, 'La Métaphysique de saint Thomas d'Aquin et la pensée de l'être chez Heidegger', *Revue des Sciences Philosophiques et Théologiques* 50 (1966): 601–14, reprinted in *Zeit und Geheimnis* (Freiburg: Herder, 1975).

26 Karl Rahner, the other great German-speaking Catholic theologian of the twentieth century, attended Heidegger's classes in 1934–6, but, according to Thomas Sheehan, in his remarkable book *Karl Rahner: The Philosophical Foundations* (Athens, OH: Ohio University Press, 1987: 316–7), though Rahner made a start in the first edition of his *Geist in Welt: zur Metaphysik der endichen Erkenntis bei Thomas von Aquin* (Innsbruck: F. Rauch, 1939), he did not go far enough:

> Rahner recaptured a hidden theme in Aquinas that is finally only a transcendentalized Aristotelianism. But Rahner did not go deep enough into the pre-philosophical roots of Aristotle (I mean the archaic Greeks) or into the pre-theological roots of Aquinas (I mean Jesus). To have taken those further steps would have meant a decisive move out of metaphysics as natural theology, the rational search for the stable ground of all that is. Instead, Rahner . . . delivered the possibility of regrounding theological metaphysics on a transcendental-anthropological base, even a kinetic base, but one which finally did not undo the ontology of identity that is the heritage of Western thought since Plato.

27 Moreover, in the introductory note to the final volume of his *Theo-Drama* Balthasar claims that he has only been 'following Aquinas', in trying to build theology 'on the articles of faith (and not vice versa)' – 'on the Trinity, the Incarnation of the Son, his Cross and Resurrection on our behalf, and his sending of the Spirit to us in the apostolic church and in the *communio sanctorum*'; he refers us to the 'celebrated prologue to the *Sentences*' in

which Thomas makes 'lucidly clear' his commitment to a Trinitarian doctrine of creation – in both instances, no doubt, remonstrating with Rahner's thesis about Thomas's somewhat non-Trinitarian theology, cf. *Theo-Drama: Theological Dramatic Theory Vol. V: The Last Act* (San Francisco: Ignatius Press, 1998): 14, 61–2.

28 Balthasar, *The Glory of the Lord*, Vol. V (Edinburgh: T. and T. Clark, 1991): 429–50 (German original 1965).

29 *Ibid.*, Vol. IV: 280–313.

30 *Ibid.*: 16 n. 4.

31 Hans Urs von Balthasar, *Prayer* (London: Geoffrey Chapman, 1961, German original 1957).

32 *The Glory of the Lord*, Vol. IV: 393, 406, 407.

33 C.J.F. Williams, *What is Existence?* (Oxford: Clarendon, 1981) and *Being, Identity, and Truth* (Oxford: Clarendon Press, 1992); it should be noted that his Fregean objections to Thomas's doctrine of God did not prevent Williams from being a devout Catholic. See Brian Davies, 'Aquinas, God, and Being', *The Monist* 80 (1997): 500–20 for a good attempt, after Frege, to save Thomas's doctrine. Dedicated to the memory of C.J.F. Williams, Barry Miller, *The Fullness of Being: A New Paradigm for Existence* (Notre Dame: University of Notre Dame Press, 2002), argues, entirely from within an analytic perspective, that the Frege–Russell–Quine claim 'existence is not a predicate' is seriously awry.

34 The Septuagint, supposedly translated by 72 scholars for the great library at Alexandria in mid-third-century BCE was clearly virtually complete as we have it by 132 BCE; while the Hebrew is often followed in New Testament citations, rather than the Greek, the Septuagint was the standard version of the Old Testament for the Christian Fathers down to the later fourth century; it remains the canonical text in the Eastern Orthodox Church, and certainly greatly influenced Latin theology until the sixteenth century.

35 Cf. Raymond E. Brown, *The Gospel According to John* (London: Geoffrey Chapman, 1971), Appendix IV: *Ego Eimi* – 'I am', pp. 533–8.

36 For example, in *Enarrationes in Psalmos*, 101.

37 I cite the Douay version (1609); the Latin goes as follows: '*In pace in idipsum dormiam et requiescam, quoniam tu, Domine, singulariter in spe constituisti me*'; King James (1611), being from Hebrew, neither has the self's being singularly constituted in hope nor the selfsame as the one in whom one falls asleep: 'I will both lay me down in peace, and sleep; for thou, Lord, only makest me dwell in safety'; the highlight of compline during Lent in the Dominican liturgy was the cantor's singing the '*In pace*'.

38 Alain de Libera, 'L'Etre et le bien: Exode 3.14 dans la theologie rhenane', in Alain de Libera and Emilie Zum Brunn, *Celui qui est: Interpretations juives et chrétiennes d'Exode 3.14* (Paris: Editions du Cerf, 1986): an excellent collection, perhaps even better than *Dieu et l'Etre: Exégèse d'Exode 3.14 et de Coran 20, 11–24* (Paris: Editions du Cerf, 1978).

39 Paul Ricoeur and André LaCocque, *Thinking Biblically: Exegetical and hermeneutical Studies* (Chicago: University of Chicago Press, 1998).

40   For two excellent essays on Exodus 3:14 see Richard Kearney, 'The God
     Who May Be' and Jean Greisch, ' "Idipsum": Divine Selfhood and the
     Postmodern Subject', in *Questioning God*, edited by John D. Caputo, Mark
     Dooley, and Michael J. Scanlon (Bloomington IN: Indiana University Press,
     2001).

Chapter 6   Natural Law: Incommensurable Readings

1   Jeffrey Stout, 'Truth, natural law, and ethical theory', in *Natural Law Theory:
     Contemporary Essays*, edited by Robert P. George (Oxford: Clarendon
     Press, 1992): 71–102, an excellent essay in a first-rate collection, with
     chapters by Joseph Boyle, Robert P. George, and Russell Hittinger on
     natural law, practical reasoning, and morality, as well as on natural law
     and legal theory by Neil MacCormick, John Finnis, Jeremy Waldron and
     Michael S. Moore, natural law, justice, and rights by Hadley Arkes and
     Lloyd L. Weinreb, and on legal formalism by Joseph Raz and Ernest J.
     Weinrib; Vernon Bourke, 'Is Thomas Aquinas a natural law ethicist?', *The
     Monist* 58 (1974): 66.
2   A.P. d'Entrèves, *Natural Law: An Introduction to Legal Philosophy*
     (London: Hutchinson, 1951, revised 1970): 42, 49; whether Hooker had
     this much importance, or was even much read, before John Keble
     brought out his edition of the Works in 1836, is debatable; for more on the
     continuity of Anglicanism with the pre-Reformed Church see d'Entrèves,
     *The Medieval Contribution to Political Thought: Thomas Aquinas,
     Marsilius of Padua, Richard Hooker* (London: Oxford University Press,
     1939).
3   D.J. O'Connor, *Aquinas and Natural Law* (London: Macmillan, 1967); out
     of print, not listed in recent bibliographies, but still much consulted in phi-
     losophy department libraries, no doubt in the absence of anything else as
     lucid and short.
4   Michael Keeling, *The Mandate of Heaven: The Divine Command and the
     Natural Order* (Edinburgh: T. and T. Clark, 1995): 17.
5   Ibid, p. 203. Whether the Greek Fathers understood *perichoresis* in the
     Trinity as dancing depends on conflating an omega and an omicron.
6   H.O. Mounce in Brian Davies (ed.), *Philosophy of Religion: A Guide to the
     Subject* (London: Cassell, 1998): 270 ff.
7   Jacques Maritain, *The Rights of Man and Natural Law* (London: Bles,
     1944), *The Person and the Common Good* (London: Bles, 1947), *Man and
     the State* (Chicago: University of Chicago Press, 1951).
8   Oliver O'Donovan, *Resurrection and Moral Order: An Outline for Evan-
     gelical Ethics*, 2nd edn. (Leicester: Apollo, 1994): 87.
9   Apollinarius (c.310–c.390) denied that Christ had a human mind or soul;
     the view that Barth's doctrine of Christ's divinity diminishes his humanity
     to this extent seems rather implausible.
10   Michael S. Northcott, *The Environment and Christian Ethics* (Cambridge,
     UK: Cambridge University Press): 135.

11 R. Hittinger, 'Natural law and Catholic moral theology' in *A Preserving Grace: Protestants, Catholics, and Natural Law*, edited by Michael Cromartie (Washington, DC: William B. Eerdmans, 1997): 1–30, quotations in text pp. 11–12, 16.

12 Servais Pinckaers, *The Sources of Christian Ethics* (Washington, DC: Catholic University of America Press, 1995).

13 Pamela M. Hall, *Narrative and the Natural Law: An Interpretation of Thomistic Ethics* (Notre Dame, IN: University of Notre Dame Press, 1994).

14 Thomas's discussion of law in the *Summa Theologiae*, as J. Tonneau, 'The teaching of the Thomist Tract on Law', *The Thomist* 34 (1970): 11–83, demonstrates, is pervaded by biblical allusions: even in 1–2.90–97 there are 64 references to Scripture, compared with 48 to Aristotle and 35 to Augustine; in 90–108 there are 724 to Scripture, 96 to Aristotle, 87 to Augustine, 5 to Denys; the references are especially to Deuteronomy, Psalms, the Wisdom books, Isaiah, Ezechiel, Hosea, Job, Jeremiah; and, of course, as Tonneau notes, when Thomas writes of 'reason' (*ratio*), he thinks implicitly of *logos* with the divine *Logos* in the background, and not of 'reason' as philosophers think of it since the Enlightenment; the whole discussion is conducted as polemic with Pelagianism; and the questions on grace should not be treated as a complete treatise *de gratia*; they contain very little about illumination, adoption and divinization.

15 M.D. Chenu, 'L'Ancien Testament dans la théologie médiévale', in his splendid collection *La Théologie au douzième siècle* (Paris: Vrin, 1957), covering the twelfth-century Renaissance, the discovery of nature and history, Platonism, the work of Boethius, symbolism and allegory, the 'evangelical revival', the entry of Greek patristic theology, etc., by far the best introduction to the background to Thomas Aquinas's thought, partly translated as *Nature, Man, and Society in the Twelfth Century: Essays on New Theological Perspectives in the Latin West* (Chicago: University of Chicago Press, 1968, reprinted Toronto: University of Toronto Press, 1997).

16 The best book here is W.G.B.M. Valkenberg, *'Did Not Our Hearts Burn?': Place and Function of Holy Scripture in the Theology of St Thomas Aquinas* (Utrecht: Thomas Institute, 1990).

17 See Beryl Smalley, 'William of Auvergne, John of La Rochelle and St Thomas Aquinas on the Old Law', in *St Thomas Aquinas: Commemorative Studies*, edited by A.A. Maurer, vol. 2 (Toronto: Pontifical Institute of Medieval Studies, 1974): 11–71; her pioneering book *The Study of the Bible in the Middle Ages* (Oxford: Oxford University Press, 1940), remains indispensable.

18 Anthony J. Lisska, *Aquinas's Theory of Natural Law: An Analytic Reconstruction* (Oxford: Clarendon Press, 1996).

19 Ibid., pp. 167–8. Lisska sides with Henry Veatch in his criticism of the 'Cartesianism' that distorts the 'revisionist Thomism' represented by the work of John Finnis, Germain Grisez, and others: one more version of Thomism, much contested, and regrettably much too large a subject to be discussed here.

20 Lisska, *Aquinas's Theory*, p. 81. Columba Ryan, 'The traditional concept of natural law', in *Light on the Natural Law*, edited by Illtud Evans (London: Burns & Oates, 1965).

21 John Bowlin, *Contingency and Fortune in Aquinas's Ethics* (Cambridge, UK: Cambridge University Press, 1999).

22 Thomas Aquinas, *Collationes in Decem Praeceptis*, edited with introduction and notes by J.P. Torrell, *Revue des Sciences Philosophiques et Théologiques* 69 (1985): 5–40, 227–63.

23 Ulrich Kühn, *Via Caritatis: Theologie des Gesetzes bei Thomas von Aquin* (Göttingen: Vandenhoeck & Ruprecht, 1965); Hampus Lyttkens, *The Analogy Between God and the World: An Investigation of its Background and Interpretation of its Use by Thomas of Aquino* (Uppsala: Lundequistka Bokhandeln, 1953); Per-Erik Persson, *Sacra Doctrina: Reason and Revelation in Aquinas* (Oxford: Blackwell, 1970; Swedish original 1957); Thomas Bonhoeffer, *Die Gotteslehre des Thomas von Aquin also Sprachproblem* (Tubingen: Mohr, 1961); Hans Vorster, *Das Freiheitsverständnis bei Thomas von Aquin und Martin Luther* (Göttingen: Vandenhoeck & Ruprecht, 1965).

24 Kühn, *Via Caritatis*, pp. 30–43, 252–8.

25 On Luther and natural law see Antti Raunio, 'Natural law and faith: The forgotten foundations of ethics in Luther's theology', in *Union with Christ: The New Finnish Interpretation of Luther*, edited by Carl E. Braaten and Robert W. Jenson (Grand Rapids, MI: Eerdmans, 1998): 96–124.

Chapter 7   Theological Ethics

1 See Stanley Hauerwas, 'On doctrine and ethics', in *The Cambridge Companion to Christian Doctrine*, edited by Colin E, Gunton (Cambridge, UK: Cambridge University Press, 1997): 21–40; reprinted in *Sanctify Them in the Truth: Holiness Exemplified* (Edinburgh: T.&T. Clark, 1998).

2 James Gustafson, *Ethics from a Theocentric Perspective*, vol. 2: *Ethics and Theology* (Chicago: University of Chicago Press, 1984): 42–6.

3 For a good example see D.M. MacKinnon, *A Study in Ethical Theory* (London: Adam & Charles Black, 1957): pretty much the lectures he delivered in 1950–1, not that he spoke from notes let alone a text; while referring to Aristotle's *Metaphysics*, he shows no interest in 'virtue ethics'.

4 For a good introduction see *Virtue Ethics*, edited by Roger Crisp and Michael Slote (Oxford 1997), opening with Anscombe's essay and reprinting important contributions by Bernard Williams, Iris Murdoch, Alasdair MacIntyre, John McDowell and Philippa Foot among others. For 'divine command ethics' see Paul Helm (ed.), *Divine Commands and Morality* (Oxford: Oxford University Press, 1981); G.E.M. Anscombe, 'Modern Moral Philosophy', *Philosophy* 33 (1958); reprinted in *Collected Philosophical Papers*, vol. 3 (Oxford: Basil Blackwell, 1981): 26–42.

5 'If anyone says that Jesus Christ was given to men by God as a redeemer to trust, and not also as a lawgiver to obey, let him be anathema', Council of

Trent 1545–1563 Session 6, Decree on Justification 13 January 1547 cf. *Decrees of the Ecumenical Councils,* edited by Norman P. Tanner (London: Sheed and Ward, 1990): 678. The worry was that some believed that being justified they were free from keeping the commandments: antinomianism, perhaps represented by Johann Agricola (c.1494–1566), who fell out with Luther over precisely this issue, and Anabaptists, vehemently denounced by Luther. Anscombe goes somewhat awry as regards the Reformation in general, but see James Hogg, *The Private Memoirs and Confessions of a Justified Sinner* (1824), a remarkable novel exploring the psychology of one of God's elect who comes to believe that no sin can affect his destiny.

6   To mention only a few: Stanley Hauerwas, *Character and the Christian Life* (San Antonio, TX: Trinity University Press, 1975); Alasdair MacIntyre, *After Virtue* (Notre Dame, IN: University of Notre Dame Press, 1981); Jean Porter, *The Recovery of Virtue: The Relevance of Aquinas for Christian Ethics* (London: SPCK, 1990); James Keenan, *Goodness and Rightness in Thomas Aquinas's Summa Theologia* (Washington, DC: Georgetown University Press, 1992); Daniel Mark Nelson, *The Priority of Prudence: Virtue and Natural Law in Thomas Aquinas and the Implications for Modern Ethics* (University Park, PA: State University of Pennsylvania Press, 1992); Daniel Westberg, *Right Practical Reason: Aristotle, Action and Prudence in Aquinas* (Oxford: Clarenden Press, 1994); Joseph J. Kotva, Jr., *The Christian Case for Virtue Ethics* (Washington, DC: Georgetown University Press, 1996); Romanus Cessario, *Christian Faith and the Theological Life* (Washington DC: Catholic University of America Press, 1996); Hayden Ramsay, *Beyond Virtue: Integrity and Morality* (London: Macmillan, 1997); Denis J. M. Bradley, *Aquinas on the Twofold Human Good: Reason and Human Happiness in Aquinas's Moral Science* (Washington DC: Catholic University of America Press, 1996); and Rufus Black, *Christian Moral Realism: Natural Law, Narrative, Virtue, and the Gospel* (Oxford: Oxford University Press, 2001).

7   P.T. Geach, *The Virtues* (Cambridge: Cambridge University Press, 1977): 164–5.

8   Mark Jordan, *Ordering Wisdom: The Hierarchy of Philosophical Discourses in Aquinas* (Notre Dame, IN: University of Notre Dame Press, 1986): 147.

9   Leonard Boyle, *The Setting of the Summa Theologiae of Saint Thomas* (Toronto: Pontifical Institute of Mediaeval Studies, 1982): 16.

10   See James C. Doig, *Aquinas's Philosophical Commentary on the Ethics: A Historical Perspective* (Dordrecht: Kluwer, 2001).

11   Bradley, *Aquinas on the Twofold Human Good.*

12   Herbert McCabe, 'Aquinas on good sense', *New Blackfriars* 67 (1986): 419–31.

13   M.C. Nussbaum, *The Fragility of Goodness: Luck and Ethics in Greek Tragedy and Philosophy* (Cambridge, UK: Cambridge University Press, 1986): chapter 10.

14   M.-D. Chenu, *Introduction à l'étude de Saint Thomas d'Aquin* (Paris: Vrin, 1950): 265; J. Tonneau, in *Initiation theologique vol. 3: Théologie morale* (Paris Cerf, 1952): 16–36: an excellent discussion.

15 John Mahoney, ' "The Church of the Spirit" in Aquinas', *Seeking the Spirit: Essays in Moral and Pastoral Theology* (London: Sheed and Ward, 1981), originally in *Heythrop Journal* 15 (1974): 18–36; Westberg, *Right Practical Reason.*

16 Since I have been assured by a convent-educated woman that, according to the nuns who taught her, Thomas denied that women have souls, it should be noted that he is absolutely clear that the decisive thing about being in God's image is that a human being has an intellectual nature, and women have this equally with men (ST 1.93.4).

17 Thomas is well aware that human beings can be brain damaged (cf. ST 1.84.7).

18 On Thomas on the Trinitarian image of God, see D. Juvenal Merriell, *To the Image of the Trinity: A Study in the Development of Aquinas' Teaching* (Toronto: Pontifical Institute of Medieval Studies, 1990); Ian A. McFarland, 'When time is of the essence: Aquinas and the *Imago Dei*', *New Blackfriars* 82 (2001): 208–23.

19 Roger Guindon, *Béatitude et théologie morale chez saint Thomas d'Aquin: origines – interpretation* (Ottawa: Editions de l'Université d'Ottawa, 1956).

20 Edward O'Connor, in St Thomas Aquinas *Summa Theologiae, vol. 24: Gifts and Beatitudes* (London: Eyre and Spottiswoode, 1974).

Chapter 8   Quarrels about Grace

1 Henri de Lubac, *Surnaturel: Etudes historiques* (Paris: Aubier, 1946): 700 copies were printed; 2nd edn. (Paris: Desclée de Brouwer, 1991); untranslated into English but see translations of his 1965 works, *The Mystery of the Supernatural* and *Augustinianism and Modern Theology* (London: Chapman, 1967 and 1969 respectively); for the most thorough analysis see special issue devoted to de Lubac's book, *Revue Thomiste* 101 (2001): 5–315.

2 When Thomas, like Augustine long before, speaks of the human creature's being *capax Dei* it must be remembered that *capacitas* here is understood as a purely passive receptivity, not being 'capable' in the modern sense of having the ability or competence to achieve something but in the pre-modern sense of being open to something one can receive only as a gift; see the clear account of this theologically fateful semantic shift in Jean-Luc Marion, *Cartesian Questions: Method and Metaphysics* (Chicago: University of Chicago Press, 1999): chapter 4.

3 In common parlance, of course, the 'supernatural' means miracles, ghosts, poltergeists, etc., phenomena by no means absent in Roman Catholic experience, but in theological jargon it is shorthand for whatever is bestowed by divine grace alone.

4 Aelred Squire, *Asking the Fathers* (London: SPCK, 1973): 15.

5 Third Council of Constantinople (680–81 AD); Norman Tanner, *Decrees of the Ecumenical Councils*, vol. 1 (London: Sheed and Ward, 1990): 128.

6   Thomas de Vio (1468–1534), better known as Cajetan from his birthplace Gaeta in Italy. De Lubac claims that Denys the Carthusian (1402–71), born at Ryckel in Belgium, one of the most prolific theologians of his time, preceded Cajetan in misreading Thomas Aquinas to fit with the naturalist and separatist philosophies of the Paduans; then Cajetan, followed by others, claimed that natural desire to see God existed only in the human being as elevated to a supernatural end and illuminated by revelation, and finally then Robert Bellarmine (1542–1621) came up with the hypothesis of the possibility of a purely natural last end – thus establishing the two-storey nature/grace model.

7   John of St Thomas (1589–1644), otherwise John Poinsot, born in Lisbon, a Dominican friar, sought to free Aquinas from the revisionary Thomism of Jesuits like Suárez; see J.N. Deely and M.D. Lenhart (eds.) *Semiotics* (New York: Plenum Press, 1981).

8   Réginald Garrigou-Lagrange (1877–1964), was a Dominican of Le Saulchoir originally but spent 50 years teaching in Rome; prolific author, explicitly in the tradition of Cajetan, Bañes, John of St Thomas and Billuart; utterly hostile to Suárezian Thomism and *la nouvelle théologie*; supervised doctoral research of the future Pope (see chapter 4, note 4) John Paul II.

9   George Tyrrell (1861–1909) born in Dublin, Evangelical Protestant upbringing, became a Catholic 1879 and a Jesuit 1880; he was excommunicated, as a Modernist, in 1907.

10 Antonin-Dalmace Sertillanges (1863–1948), Le Saulchoir Dominican, associated with a somewhat apophatic Thomism; wrote important commentaries on Thomas on creation (1928) and beatitude (1936).

11 Francisco Suárez (see chapter 4, note 4); the collective exposition of the Salmaticenses, discalced Carmelite friars at Salamanca, in the seventeenth century.

12 Joseph-Ernest Renan (1823–92), of Breton family, lost his faith while studying Hebrew in seminary, established himself as a scholar with his book on Averroes (1852); best known for his *Vie de Jésus* (1863): the finest picture of Jesus as 'charming and amiable Galilean preacher'.

13 Pierre Rousselot (1878–1915), Jesuit 1895; his two Sorbonne doctoral dissertations of 1908 appeared as *Intellectualisme de saint Thomas* and *Pour l'histoire du problème de l'amour au Moyen Age*.

14 Jansenism: derived from Cornelius Otto Jansen (1585–1638), associated with Louvain, whose posthumously published *Augustinus* (1640), condemned as heretical by the theologians at the Sorbonne (1649) and by Pope Innocent X (1653), was held to propagate the doctrines (1) that without a special grace from God it is impossible for human beings to keep God's commandments, and (2) that the operation of grace is irresistible; hence that human beings are governed either by natural or supernatural determinism. In effect, by maintaining that conduct according to natural law as grasped by natural reason is sinful unless ordered by the grace of supernatural faith, and denying that fallen human beings still have the natural resources to do good, Jansenism was regarded as crypto-Lutheran. See John Mahoney, *The*

Making of Moral Theology: A Study of the Roman Catholic Tradition (Oxford: Clarendon Press, 1987): 83–102, where he avers that Jansenism 'with its fierce loyalty to Augustine and its roots in Platonism' was a confrontation with the Jesuits who were 'attracted to the cool and rational, even humanist, optimism of Aquinas rooted in Aristotelianism' (p. 92 n. 76). It is not difficult to find evidence in the Roman Catholic Church today of movements one would not describe as humanist optimism.

15 Barth, *Church Dogmatics*, translated by G.W. Bromiley and T.F. Torrance (Edinburgh: T & T Clark, 1957–75). II/I, 411.

16 George Hunsinger, *How to Read Karl Barth: The Shape of his Theology* (Oxford: Oxford University Press, 1991): 145–7.

17 *Church Dogmatics*, IV/2: 498.

18 Hunsinger, *How to Read Karl Barth*, p. 273.

19 Bernard Quelquejeu, 'Naturalia manent integra', *Revue des Sciences Philosophiques et Théologiques* 94 (1965): 640–55.

20 In connection with whether, before the Fall, procreation would have been by sexual intercourse, Thomas concedes that many of the Doctors of the Church believed this could not have been so, considering 'the lust that besmirches copulation', citing Gregory of Nyssa for one. 'But this is not a reasonable position', Thomas contends: 'For everything that is natural to human beings is neither withdrawn from nor given to them by sin'. These *naturalia* include our genitalia; there is no reason to believe that these have not always been part of human nature. Incidentally, against some of his own contemporaries, including the Franciscan theologians Alexander of Hales and Bonaventure, who argued that, being tempered by reason, the pleasurable sensation of sexual intercourse before the Fall would have been less, Thomas contends on the contrary that, 'given the greater purity of human nature and bodily sensibility', the pleasure of sex would have been all the more intense (ST 1.98.3).

21 E.L. Mascall, *Via Media* (London: Longman, Green, 1956): 121–57.

22 Daphne Hampson, *Christian Contradictions: The Structures of Lutheran and Catholic Thought* (Cambridge, UK: Cambridge University Press, 2001): 122, 169–70.

23 John Milbank and Catherine Pickstock, *Truth in Aquinas* (London: Routledge, 2001): 93. Incidentally, this book has provoked almost ludicrously incompatible interpretations, ranging from contemptuous dismissal by Anthony Kenny (*TLS*, 5 October 2001, p. 14) to the claim by Stephen Webb, author of an important book on Barth, in a long and careful review, that it is 'one of the most important works in theology in many years' (*Reviews in Religion and Theology* 8 (2001): 319–25); the review by Adrian Pabst (*Revue Thomiste* 101 (2001): 475–9), not uncritical, regards the book as marking '*une importante percée dans les études thomistes*', indeed it is 'a very successful attempt to bring out the contemporary relevance of Thomas's positions for our (postmodern) questions, while circumventing the polemics between the diverse (neo)Thomist schools'.

24 John Milbank, *Theology and Social Theory* (Oxford: Blackwell, 1990): 219–20.

25 It has to be said that in his superb study *Justification: The Heart of the Christian Faith* (Edinburgh: T. and T. Clark, 2001), Eberhard Jüngel, the most distinguished living German Lutheran theologian, highlights what looks very much like a completely unbridgeable gap between Roman Catholic and Protestant forms of Christianity (as different as Sunnites and Shiites within Islam); once again, as John Webster notes in his introduction, the problem may be traced to Jüngel's 'competitive understanding of the relation of divine and human action, in which acts have properly to be assigned *either* to God *or* to creatures'.

Chapter 9   Deified Creaturehood

1 E.L. Mascall, *Via Media* (London: Longman, Green, 1956).
2 Aelred Squire, *Summer in the Seed* (London: SPCK, 1980): 119–21, chapter 10 passim.
3 R. Garrigou-Lagrange, *The Three Ages of the Interior Life*, vol. 1 (St Louis, MI: B. Herder, 1949): 50–1; (French original, 1938).
4 Myrrha Lot Borodine, 'Studies of the deification theme in Greek theology until the eleventh century' (1932–3), reprinted in *La déification de l'homme selon la doctrine des pères grecs*. (Paris: Cerf, 1970); commented on by Y.M.J. Congar, 'La déification clans la tradition spirituelle de l'Orient', *Vie Spirituelle* 43 (1935): 91–107.
5 *Dictionnaire de Spiritualité Ascetique et Mystique* (Paris: Beachesne, 1932) cols 1370–1459, virtually a monograph in one of the major expressions of French Catholic scholarship. The entry on divinization is in Fascicle 22–3 (1956).
6 The doctrine of the Trinity and the language of deiformity are much more overt in Bonaventure than in Thomas.
7 '*Deus non est permiscibilis subjecto ut forma, nec unibilis*', as Albert says (cited by Conus col. 1422).
8 A.M. Allchin, *The Dynamic of Tradition* (London: Darton, Longman, Todd 1981): 63–77.
9 Presbyterianism was legally established in 1690 but had little hold in the north-east of Scotland for many years after that date; a small but significant number of Episcopalians were 'quietists'. The writings of Jeanne Guyon (1648–1717) were quite influential in the first half of the eighteenth century in the same region – see G.D. Henderson, *Mystics of the North-East* (Aberdeen: Third Spalding Club, 1934), and *Religious Life in Seventeenth-century Scotland* (Cambridge: Cambridge University Press, 1937).
10 Robert W. Jenson, *Systematic Theology, vol. 1* (Oxford: Oxford University Press, 1997): 71. Emmanuel Hirsch was one of the theologians of the 'Deutsche Christen', the Lutherans who compromised with National Socialism, see Robert Ericksen, *Theologians under Hitler* (New Haven, CT: Yale University Press, 1985).
11 Jenson, *Systematic Theology*, vol. 2: 293 n. 17. For an introductory account of the Finnish interpretation see Tuomo Mannermaa, 'Theosis as a subject

of Finnish Luther research', *Pro Ecclesia* 4 (1995): 37–48; David S. Yeago, 'The Catholic Luther', in *The Catholicity of the Reformation*, edited by Carl Braaten and Robert Jenson (Grand Rapids, MI: Eerdmans, 1996): 13–34; Carl E. Braaten and Robert W. Jenson (eds), *Union with Christ: The New Finnish Interpretation of Luther* (Grand Rapids, MI: Eerdmans, 1998); Kurt E. Marquart, 'Luther and theosis', *Concordia Theological Quarterly* 64 (2000): 182–205; William T. Cavanaugh, 'A joint declaration? Justification as Theosis in Aquinas and Luther', *Heythrop Journal* 41 (2000): 265–80; and even more remarkably, David S. Yeago, 'Martin Luther on Grace, Law, and Moral Life: Prolegomena to an Ecumenical Discussion of *Veritatis Splendor*', *The Thomist* 62 (1998): 163–91, in which John Paul II and Luther have one and the same 'project', 'of integrating the moral and the mystical, and therefore of relocating the notion of divine law within the context of the perfection of nature by grace'.

12 R.J. Hennessy, St Thomas Aquinas *Summa Theologiae, vol. 48: The Incarnate Word* (London: Eyre and Spottiswoode, 1976): 13.

13 Cornelius Ernst, St Thomas Aquinas *Summa Theologiae*, vol. 30 (London: Eyre and Spottiswoode, 1972): 147.

14 Michael Green, *The Second Epistle General of Peter and the General Epistle of Jude: An Introduction and Commentary* (Leicester: Inter-Varsity Press, 1968, 2nd edn. 1987): 25–6, 73–5; 'This verse has also been a classic proof-text for the Greek patristic and Eastern Orthodox doctrine of the deification of man. This needs to be treated with great circumspection . . .'; Ernst Käsemann, 'An apologia for primitive Christian theology', in *Essays on New Testament Themes* (London: SCM Press, 1964): 169–95.

15 Malcolm Sidebottom, *James, Jude and 2 Peter*, in *New Century Bible* (London: Nelson, 1967: 106–7).

16 Richard J. Bauckham, *Word Biblical Commentary vol. 50: Jude, 2 Peter* (Waco, TX: Word Incorporated and Milton Keynes: Word (UK), 1983): 180–2.

17 On how Platonism was transformed by the Christian tradition see Andrew Louth, *The Origins of the Christian Mystical Tradition: From Plato to Denys* (Oxford: Clarendon Press, 1981) – an excellent account of Plato and Platonic tradition up to Plotinus, attending particularly to Philo – whose reading of the Bible was widely influential among the Fathers – and then through Origen, Gregory of Nyssa, Denys and Augustine.

18 Adolf Harnack, *History of Dogma*, vol. 6 (London: Williams and Nogent 1899): 279–80, 184–5.

19 A.N. Williams, *The Ground of Union: Deification in Aquinas and Palamas* (New York and Oxford: Oxford University Press, 1999): 34–101.

20 See also the two superb essays, A.N. Williams, 'Mystical theology redux: The pattern of Aquinas's *Summa Theologiae*', *Modern Theology* 13 (1997): 53–74; 'Deification in the *Summa Theologica*: A structural interpretation of the *prima pars*', *The Thomist* (1997): 219.

21 For the best collection of texts on the patristic doctrine of divinization by filial adoption, drawn from the biblical commentaries, see Thomas's *La Divinisation dans le Christ*, trans and commented by Luc-Thomas Somme

(Geneva: Ad Solem, 1998); backed up by Somme's book *Fils adoptifs de Dieu par Jésus Christ: La filiation divine par adoption dans la théologie de saint Thomas d'Aquin* (Paris: Vrin, 1997).

Chapter 10   Christ in the *Summa Theologiae*

1 *De articulis fidei et ecclesiae sacramentis, ad Archiepiscopum Panormitanum* (Rome: Commissio Leonina, 1979): vol. 42, 207–57.

2 Leonard Boyle, *The Setting of the Summa Theologiae of Saint Thomas* (Toronto: Pontifical Institute of Medieval Studies, 1982); for the alternative view, that the *Summa* was not for neophytes but a pedagogical work for very gifted students, future professors at the end of their philosophical and theological studies, see John I. Jenkins, *Knowledge and Faith in Thomas Aquinas* (Cambridge, UK: Cambridge University Press, 1997), another outstanding American contribution to the renewal of Thomistic scholarship, contending that, for Thomas, rational assent to the articles of faith is due to the influence of divine grace on one's cognitive powers, enabling one to apprehend these propositions as divinely revealed.

3 See his *responsio* to Baxianus of Lodi (Rome: Commissio Leonina, 1979): vol. 42, 321–4, 339–46.

4 We cannot go into one of the most contested interpretations of all, about what Thomas means by *sacra doctrina*: for Cajetan, John of St Thomas, and many modern interpreters, it means more or less what we mean today by 'theology'; since Yves Congar, 'Theologie', in *Dictionairre de Théologie Catholigue* (Paris: Letouzet et Ané, 1946), cols 374–92; James Weisheipl, 'The meaning of *Sacra Doctrina* in *Summa Theologiae* I, Q.1', *The Thomist* 38 (1974): 49–80; Albert Patfoot, '*Sacra Doctrina*, théologie et unité de la Ia pars', *Angelicum* 62 (1985): 306–19; Henry Donneaud, 'Insaissable *Sacra doctrina?*', *Revue Thomiste* 98 (1998): 179–224, among others; it should be clear that it means divine revelation issuing in Christian tradition.

5 Jean-Pierre Torrell, *St Thomas Aquinas, vol. 1 The Person and his Work* (Washington, DC: Catholic University of America Press, 1996): 89.

6 An excellent introduction to Thomas's Christology is provided by some of the studies in the magnificent collection edited by Kent Emery, Jr. and Joseph P. Wawrykov, *Christ Among the Medieval Dominicans* (Notre Dame, IN: University of Notre Dame Press, 1998): in particular, Joseph Goering on expositions of doctrine based on the articles of faith; Denise Bouthillier on the Christological themes in Thomas's commentary on Isaiah; Robert Wielockx on the hymn '*Adoro te devote*' (which he assumes was composed by Thomas); Joseph Wawrykov on Christ as Wisdom incarnate; Jean-Pierre Torrell on Christ in Thomas's 'spirituality'; and Ulrich Horst on Christ as the prototype of the Dominican friar.

7 The best discussion, if also extremely long and quite technical, is by Gilbert Narcisse, *Les Raisons de Dieu: Argument de convenance et esthétique théologique selon saint Thomas d'Aquin et Hans Urs von Balthasar* (Fribourg: Editions Universitaires, 1997).

8 The Council of Chalcedon (451), reaffirming earlier councils, declared Christ to be one person in two natures, the divine of the same substance (*homoousias*) as the Father, the human of the same substance as us, which are united unconfusedly, unchangeably, indivisibly, inseparably. Classically expounded by John of Damascus, *De Fide Orthodoxa*.

9 Jean-Pierre Torrell, *Le Christ en ses mystères; La vie et l'oeuvre de Jésus selon saint Thomas d'Aquin*, 2 vols (Paris: Desclée de Brouwer, 1999).

10 Aidan Nichols, 'St Thomas Aquinas on the Passion of Christ: A reading of *Summa Theologiae* IIIa, q.46', *Scottish Journal of Theology* 43 (1990): 447–59.

11 *De septem verbis Domini, opera omnia* (Naples, 1862): VI, 418 cited in St Thomas Aquinas *Summa Theologiae* vol 54 (London: Eyre and Spottiswoode): 188.

12 The classical study is Yves Congar, 'The idea of the Church in St Thomas Aquinas', in *The Mystery of the Church* (London: Geoffrey Chapman, 1960): 97–117; but see also John Mahoney, 'The "Church of the Spirit" in Aquinas', *The Heythrop Journal* 15 (1974): 18–36, and Avery Dulles, 'The Church according to Thomas Aquinas', in *A Church to Believe In* (New York: Crossroad, 1982): 149–69.

13 By far the best study in English of Thomas's Christology is by Matthew Levering, *Christ's Fulfillment of Torah and Temple: Salvation according to Thomas Aquinas* (Notre Dame, IN: University of Notre Dame Press, 2002), contending that Thomas's theology of salvation is thoroughly biblical, with Christ as perfect law and liturgy, placing the Cross in the historical context of God's covenant with Israel and the promise that those united to Christ become 'temples' of the Holy Spirit by sharing in his death and resurrection.

Chapter 11   God in the *Summa Theologiae*

1 Jürgen Moltmann, *The Trinity and the Kingdom of God: The Doctrine of God*, trans. M. Kohl (London: SCM Press, 1981): 16–17.

2 Karl Barth, *Church Dogmatics*, vols. II/1 (Edinburgh: T. and T. Clark, 1957): 329.

3 Colin E. Gunton, *The One, the Three and the Many: God, Creation and the Culture of Modernity* (Cambridge: Cambridge University Press, 1993): 138–42.

4 Wolfhart Pannenberg, *Systematic Theology*, vol. 1 (Edinburgh: T. and T. Clark, 1991): 181, 288 ff.

5 Karl Rahner, 'Remarks on the Dogmatic Treatise De Trinitate', in *Theological Investigations*, vol. 4 (London: Darton, Longman, Todd, 1966, original German 1960): 77 to 102; quotes in text pp. 78, 83–4. (Paradoxically, after all his polemics against the defective Trinitarianism of standard Roman Catholic theology 40 years ago, he says almost nothing about the Trinity in his 500-page long *Foundations of Christian Faith: An Introduction to the Idea of Christianity* (New York: Seabury 1978, original German 1976)).

Rahner trades on the great theological story, told by the French Jesuit scholar Théodore de Régnon (1831–93) in his four-volume history of the doctrine of the Trinity (1892–8): the Greeks put relationality first; for the Latins the divine being is a monadic substance. In *The Mystical Theology of the Eastern Church* (London: J. Clarke, 1957; French original, Paris: Aubier, 1944), Vladimir Lossky, relying on de Régnon, contends that, when the divine nature or essence assumes the first place in our exposition of Trinitarian dogma, 'the religious reality of God in Trinity is inevitably obscured in some measure and gives place to a certain philosophy of essence'. Worse still, 'all properly theocentric speculation runs the risk of considering the nature before the persons and becoming a mysticism of "the divine abyss", as in the *Gottheit* of Meister Eckhart; of becoming an impersonal apophaticism of the divine-nothingness prior to the Trinity'. Thus, Lossky thinks, Catholics 'return through Christianity to the mysticism of the Neo-Platonists' – Rahner's claim, in effect. De Régnon's main intellectual interest, incidentally, was in the metaphysics of causality. The first of his four volumes opens with a lengthy defence of anti-Cartesian epistemology; the second deals with Scholastic theologies of the Trinity (Thomas Aquinas and others), the third and fourth with Greek patristic theologies. For de Régnon, the medieval/Western emphasis on the one being of God and the patristic Greek emphasis on the Trinity are complementary. He says little about Augustine. It is hard to see why his work should ever have authorized the now standard account of the superiority of Greek patristic Trinitarianism over Latin scholastic essentialism (unitarianism). In the entry on de Régnon in the *Dictionnaire de Théologie Catholique* (Paris: Letouzet et Ané, 1937), Adhémar d'Alès (1861–1938), one of the major French scholars of the day, casts doubt, tactfully, on de Régnon's story. It is only with the splendid essays by Michel René Barnes that the story is properly examined: Michel René Barnes, 'De Régnon reconsidered', *Augustinian Studies* 26 (1995): 51–79; 'The use of Augustine in contemporary Trinitarian theology', *Theological Studies* 56 (1995): 237–51.

6 Rahner himself cites an array of pious books, by such authors as Columba Marmion (1858–1923) which sold in tens of thousands in the 1920s and 1930s. It is not credible that Catholics who simply went to Mass, perhaps with their missals, fortified by books such as Marmion's, never reading *de Deo uno* course books, were as unaffected by the Trinitarianism of the Catholic faith as Rahner maintains. At most, one might say, it would have been future clergy who acquired this defectively Trinitarian faith by the theology lectures they attended.

7 Hans Urs von Balthasar, *The Theology of Karl Barth: Exposition and Interpretation* (San Francisco: Ignatius Press, 1992; German original Cologne: J. Hegner, 1951): 263–6.

8 Henri de Lavalette, review in *Recherches de science religieuse* 50 (1962): 121–2.

9 *S. Ioannis Lectura, Super Evangelium* (Turin and Rome, Marietti, 1952), pars 1161, 2195.

10 *De articulis fidei et ecclesiae sacramenta* (Rome: Commissio Leonina): vol. 42, 245–57, no English translation.

11   Chenu, *Introduction à l'étude de Saint Thomas d'Aquin* (Paris: Vrin, 1950): 275.

12   Karl Barth extends this thought brilliantly (*Church Dogmatics*, vol. II/1 §27), resisting the 'magic of the ineffable One and All of the Greeks', turning analogical predication upside down, arguing that the biblical use of words in talking about God throws light on the everyday use and not the other way round; see the superb essay by Roger White, 'Notes on analogical predication and speaking about God', in *The Philosophical Frontiers of Christian Theology: Essays presented to D.M. MacKinnon*, edited by Brian Hebblethwaite and Stewart Sutherland (Cambridge, UK: Cambridge University Press, 1982): 197–226, quoting Barth's boutade: 'Only God has hands – not paws like ours'.

13   As is well known, the use of words or concepts analogically has given rise to one of the most contested of all questions in Thomist interpretation: all the way from Herbert McCabe's blithe dismissal of Thomas's 'alleged teaching on analogy' in the *Summa Theologiae*, vol 3, appendix 4 (London: Eyre and Spottiswoode, 1964) via Ralph McInerny's *Aquinas and Analogy* (Washington, DC: Catholic University of America Press, 1996), to the special issue of *Les Etudes Philosophiques* (July–December, 1989), including a massive study by Edouard Wéber of Thomas's use of analogy.

14   Usually Thomas regards 'He who is' as the name for God; here alone he suggests that the Tetragrammaton is superior, drawing on Moses ben Maimon; see the fundamental discussion by Armand Maurer, 'St Thomas on the sacred name "Tetragrammaton"', *Mediaeval Studies* 34 (1972): 275–86. 'I am who I am', or however the divine self-identification is to be translated, is, of course, the Tetragrammaton (YHYH) transposed into the first person.

15   Exodus 3:14 is cited here (ST 2.3 but also at ST1.13.11 and ST 2–2.174.6); while Exodus 3:6 'I am . . . the God of Abraham, the God of Isaac, and the God of Jacob' is cited once (ST 2–2.83.11).

16   *Patrologia Graeca* 94, 836.

17   Barth, *Church Dogmatics*, vol. II/1 §29: 324.

18   Beatitude is not a topic much discussed in English-language Christian theology; there is an excellent account by A. Gardeil in *Dictionnaire de Théologie Catholique* (Paris: Letouzet et Ané, 1932), cols 497–515, and by F. Nef and J.-Y. Lacoste in *Dictionnaire critique de théologie* (Paris Presses Universitaires Françaises, 1998): 148–53.

19   Barth, *Church Dogmatics*, vol. II/1: 283.

20   According to Thomas Gilby, in vol. 16 of *Summa Theologiae* (London: Eyre and Spottiswoode, 1969) the background to the question on divine bliss is, partly, 'a medieval tradition of Christian sufism' (p. 58fn): so far from the received account that it is worth a little attention (Gilby, after all, was the best known of the half dozen notable English Thomists, see Nichols, *Dominican Gallery* (Leominster: Gracewing, 1997). Sufism from Arabic for wool, means the quietistic devotional mysticism of (wool-clad) ascetics in second century Islam (before AD 800). The so-called *Theology of Aristotle*, translated into Arabic about AD 840, a main source of Sufism,

reappears in Latin as *Elementatio theologica,* material familiar to Thomas. Placing Thomas's *beatitudo* in the context of this Islamicized neo-Platonic Christian mysticism certainly offers a very different perspective from that of more familiar Aristotelian discussions of happiness. That there might be an Arab background to Thomas's concept of bliss was noted long ago by L. Gardet, 'Quelques aspects de la pensée avicennienne', *Revue Thomiste* 47 (1939): 537–75, 693–742, esp. 724–38 and again in L. Gardet and M.M. Anawati, *Introduction à la Theologie musulmane* (Paris: Vrin, 1948): 283–8.

21 Paul M. Collins, *Trinitarian Theology West and East: Karl Barth, the Cappadocian Fathers, and John Zizioulas* (Oxford: Oxford University Press, 2001): 120.

22 Readers of Rowan Williams's Aquinas Lecture will see how much the following paragraphs owe to it: 'What does love know? St Thomas on the Trinity', *New Blackfriars* 82 (2001): 260–72.

23 Thomas G. Weinandy, *Does God Change? The Word's Becoming in the Incarnation* (Petersham: St Bede's Publications, 1985) and especially *Does God Suffer?* (Notre Dame, IN: University of Notre Dame Press, 2000): 45–6 a remarkable attempt to reverse modern doctrines of the suffering God, arguing that the two-thousand year old tradition in which the impassibility of God was axiomatic, instead of being a surrender to the Parmenidean One (etc.), is actually the only way to maintain the uniqueness of the biblical sense of God as Creator, really distinct from, yet immanently active in, the created order.

24 T.F. Torrance, *The Christian Doctrine of God, One Being Three Persons* (Edinburgh: T. and T. Clark, 1996): 156–7, 165–6, 192.

25 See what Torrance calls the 'brilliant analytical argument for the recovery of the concept' by Eric Mascall, *The Triune God. An Ecumenical Study* (Worthing: Churchman, 1986).

26 See L.A. Kosman, 'Substance, being and energeia', in *Oxford Studies in Ancient Philosophy,* vol. 2 (Oxford: Oxford University Press, 1984): 121–49; a study of Aristotle but arguing that Thomas was
> right to see at the heart of Aristotle's ontology the claim that actuality is activity, and that being is therefore act; furthermore, if Aristotle had been addressed by a god with the words 'I am' he would have asked 'You are *what*?' (as Moses more or less did); the god might then have said 'Never mind, whatever I am, I am that'; Aristotle would have understood the divine being's self-description to Moses not as 'I am who am' but as 'I am what I am', and Aristotle would add: and that's the god's nature, to be what it is.

27 See Collins, *Trinitarian Theology West and East.*

28 David B. Burrell, *Aquinas, God and Action* (Notre Dame, IN: University of Notre Dame Press, 1979): 116.

29 Ibid., p. 54.

30 W.J. Hill, *The Three-Personed God* (Washington, DC: Catholic University of America Press, 1982): 260–4.

31 Balthasar, *The Theology of Karl Barth* (San Francisco: Ignatius Press, 1992): 341–3.

32 Maurice Blondel (1861–1949), French philosopher and devout Catholic, influenced Modernists as well as orthodox theologians such as Henri de Lubac and Hans Urs von Balthasar; Blondel saw the life of the human spirit as entirely directed to the beatific vision of God. See *L'Action: essai d'une critique de la vie et d'une science de la pratique* (Paris: Alcan, 1983), translated as *Action: Essay on a Critique of Life and a Science of Practice* (Notre Dame, IN: University of Notre Dame Press, 1984).

33 Herman Schell (1850–1906), see his *Katholische Dogmatik* (1889–93, re-issued Munich: Schöningh 1968–94); Romano Guardini (1885–1968), see, for example, his *Welt und Person: Versuche zur christlichen Lehre vom Menschen* (Würzburg: Werkbund-Verlag, 1939); and Michael Schmaus (1897–1993), whose *Katholische Dogmatik* (first published 1938 and expanded 1940) went through many editions: Balthasar quotes the fourth edition of 1949, vol 1, *Gott der Eine und Dreieinige*, p. 454.

34 Balthasar, plainly responding to Barth, claiming that mainstream Catholic theologians also regarded God as more like an event than an entity, kept returning to this topic: in *Das Endspiel*, the final volume of his *Theo-Drama*, published in 1983 (English translation San Francisco: Ignatius Press, 1998), he speaks of 'the triune process', insisting that we should never forget, when we think of God's being, that God exists in himself as an eternal essence or being which is an equally eternal 'happening' (his scare quotes); quoting remarks by Klaus Hemmerle, *Thesen zu einer Trinitarischen Ontologie* (Einsiedeln: Johannes Verlag, 1976), a remarkable theologian (and bishop) little known in the English-speaking world, to the effect that we should think of God primarily in terms of 'happening, action, consummation (*Geschehen, Vorgang, Vollzug*)'. Here, towards the end of his great work, Balthasar claims to be only 'following Aquinas', meaning by this that he too tries to build his theology on the articles of faith (Trinity; Incarnation, Cross and resurrection *pro nobis*; and sending of the Spirit to us in the Apostolic Church and the communion of saints); citing Thomas's 'celebrated prologue' to his commentary on the *Sentences* as evidence of his radically Trinitarian theology.

35 George Hunsinger, *How to Read Karl Barth* (Oxford: Oxford University Press, 1991): 30.

36 Robert W. Jenson, *Systematic Theology, vol. 1, The Triune God* (Oxford: Oxford University Press, 1997): 159–60, 207.

37 As regards the great debate between Barth and Erich Pryzwara about the theory of the analogy of being Jenson states that Barth misunderstood both Thomas and Pryzwara.

38 Jenson directs us to the 1944 German version of one of the fundamental works in the 'apophatic' Thomism associated with Le Saulchoir, first published in 1910, substantially available in English as *St Thomas Aquinas and his work* (London: Burnes, Oates and Washbourne, 1932) by A.-D. Sertillanges (1863–1948).

39   Barth, *Church Dogmatics*, vol. I/1.
40   Jenson, *Systematic Theology*, vol. 1: 225, 236, 21, 6.

Chapter 12   Conclusion

1   For example, in connection with arguments against a woman's presiding
    at the Eucharist, see Bernard Marliangeas, in *Clés pour une théologie du
    ministère: In persona Christi, in persona Ecclesiae* (Paris: Cerf, 1978; a
    dissertation at Le Saulchoir completed in 1964), showing that, while
    Thomas has something like the now dominant representationalist theory
    (priest as 'image of Christ', e.g. ST 3.82.3), the phrase '*in persona Christi*'
    is linked with what looks like a non-representationalist theory of the cele-
    brant's self-effacingly repeating Christ's words (e.g. ST 78.5). Thomas does
    not regard the eucharist as a nuptial mystery, with the celebrant as bride-
    groom and thus necessarily male – let alone anticipate Hans Urs von
    Balthasar's view, *Elucidations* (London: SPCK, 1975): 150

    > In its origin [the New Testament] presents to man and woman a
    > glorious picture of sexual integrity: the Son of God who has become
    > man and flesh, knowing from inside his Father's work and perfecting
    > it in the total self-giving of himself, not only in his spiritual but pre-
    > cisely also of his physical powers . . . What else is his eucharist but,
    > at a higher level, an endless act of fruitful outpouring of his whole
    > flesh, such as a man can only achieve for a moment with a limited
    > organ of his body?

2   Besides specialist journals of medieval scholarship it is possible to keep
    abreast by consulting such journals as *The Thomist* (Washington), *Revue
    thomiste* (Toulouse), and *Revue des sciences philosophiques et théologiques*
    (Paris).

3   Rogers, in *Thomas Aquinas and Karl Barth* (Notre Dame, IN: University of
    Notre Dame Press, 1995) has surely unsettled standard Barthian objections
    to 'natural theology'.

4   David Burrell demonstrates the importance of reading Thomas in conjunc-
    tion with Ibn Sina and Moses ben Maimon. See *Knowing the Unknowable
    God* (Notre Dame, IN: University of Notre Dame Press, 1986) and *Freedom
    and Creation in Three Traditions* (Notre Dame, IN: University of Notre
    Dame Press, 1993).

5   See Wayne J. Hankey, *God in Himself: Aquinas' Doctrine of God as
    Expounded in the Summa Theologiae* (Oxford: Oxford University Press,
    1987), and (difficult but fundamental) Edward Booth, *Aristotelian Aporetic
    Ontology in Islamic and Christian Thinkers* (Cambridge, UK: Cambridge
    University Press, 1983).

6   See Levering's *Christ's Fulfilment of Torah and Temple* (Notre Dame,
    IN: University of Notre Dame Press, 2002) for Thomas's Christology; for
    his doctrine of the Trinity see the splendid discussion in Thomas Weinandy,
    Does God Suffer? (Notre Dame, IN: University of Notre Dame Press,
    2000).

7 See Porter's *The Recovery of Virtue* (London: SPCK, 1990) and Pinckaers *The Source of Christian Ethics* (Washington, DC: Catholic University of America Press, 1995).

8 See Robert Pasnau, *Theories of Cognition in the Later Middle Ages* (Cambridge, UK: Cambridge University Press, 1997) and, more troublesome still, *Thomas Aquinas on Human nature: A Philosophical Study of Summa Theologiae 1a 75–89* (Cambridge, UK: Cambridge University Press, 2002).

9 Usefully discussed by Eric L. Mascall in his Edinburgh Gifford Lectures, *The Openness of Being* (London: Darton, Longman and Todd, 1971).

10 This gives rise to Karl Rahner's famous concept of the 'anonymous Christian'.

11 See Gilson's, *The Christian Philosophy of St Thomas Aquinas* (Notre Dame, IN: University of Notre Dame Press, 1994) and Grant *God and Reason in the Middle Ages* (Cambridge, UK: Cambridge University Press), a great book, arguing that the Age of Faith was already the Age of Reason, and that the 'culture of questions' in the medieval universities gave rise to the rational outlook of the Enlightenment.

12 See Clarke *Explorations in Metaphysics* (Notre Dame, IN: University of Notre Dame Press, 1994).

13 See Pinckaers, *The Source of Christian Ethics* and A.N. Williams *The Ground of Union* (Oxford: Oxford University Press, 1999).

14 In *God without Being* (Chicago: University of Chicago Press), Jean-Luc Marion comes remarkably close to suggesting that, by describing God as being rather than as self-communicating good, Thomas falls under the Heideggerian condemnation of making God an entity.

SELECT
BIBLIOGRAPHY

Aquinas, Thomas, *Summa contra Gentiles,* translated as *On the Truth of the Catholic Faith* by A.C. Pegis and others, 5 vols (New York: Doubleday, 1955–57, reprinted Notre Dame, IN: University of Notre Dame Press, 1975).

Aquinas, Thomas, *Summa Theologiae,* Latin and English, edited by T. Gilby and T.C. O'Brien, 60 vols (London: Eyre and Spottiswoode/ New York: McGraw Hill, 1964–74).

Aquinas, Thomas, *Summa Theologiae A Concise Translation,* by Timothy McDermott (London: Eyre and Spottiswoode, 1989).

Barron, Robert, *Thomas Aquinas: Spiritual Master* (New York: Crossroad, 1995).

Bowlin, John, *Contingency and Fortune in Aquinas's Ethics* (Cambridge, UK: Cambridge University Press, 1999).

Bradley, Denis J.M., *Aquinas on the Twofold Human Good: Reason and Human Happiness in Aquinas's Moral Science* (Washington, DC: Catholic University of America Press, 1996).

Burrell, David B., *Aquinas: God and Action* (Notre Dame, IN: University of Notre Dame Press, 1979).

Burrell, David B., *Knowing the Unknowable God: Ibn Sina, Maimonides, Aquinas* (Notre Dame, IN: University of Notre Dame Press, 1986).

Burrell, David B., *Freedom and Creation in Three Traditions* (Notre Dame, IN: University of Notre Dame Press, 1993).

Caputo, John D., *Heidegger and Aquinas: An Essay in Overcoming Metaphysics* (New York: Fordham University Press, 1982).

Cessario, Romanus, *Le Thomisme et les Thomistes* (Paris: Editions du Cerf, 1999).

Chenu, Marie-Dominique, *Toward Understanding Saint Thomas* (Chicago: Regnery, 1964).

Chesterton, G.K., *Saint Thomas Aquinas* (London: Hodder and Stoughton, 1933).

Clarke, W. Norris, *Explorations in Metaphysics: Being-God-Person* (Notre Dame, IN: University of Notre Dame Press, 1994).

Davies, Brian, *The Thought of Thomas Aquinas* (Oxford: Clarendon Press, 1992).

Elders, L., 'Thomas Aquinas and the Fathers of the Church', in Irena Backus (ed.) *The Reception of the Church Fathers in the West* (Leiden: Brill, 1997).

Emery, Kent, Jr., and Wawrykov, Joseph P. (eds), *Christ among the Medieval Dominicans* (Notre Dame, IN: University of Notre Dame Press, 1998).

Evans, G.R. (ed.), *The Medieval Theologians* (Oxford: Blackwell, 2001).

Finnis, John, *Aquinas: Moral, Political and Legal Theory* (Oxford: Oxford 1998).

Foster, Kenelm (ed.), *The Life of Saint Thomas Aquinas* (London: Longmans, Green, 1958).

Gilson, Etienne, *The Spirit of Medieval Philosophy* (London: Sheed and Ward, 1936).

Gilson, Etienne, *The Christian Philosophy of St Thomas Aquinas* (Notre Dame, IN: University of Notre Dame Press, 1994).

Grant, Edward, *God and Reason in the Middle Ages* (Cambridge, UK: Cambridge University Press, 2001).

Hall, P.M., *Narrative and Natural Law: An Interpretation of Thomistic Ethics* (Notre Dame, IN: University of Notre Dame Press, 1994).

Hankey, Wayne J., 'Making theology practical: Thomas Aquinas and the nineteenth century religious revival', *Dionysius* 9 (1985): 85–127.

Hennesey, James, 'Leo XIII's Thomistic Revival: A political and philosophical event', *Journal of Religion* 58 (Supplement 1978): 185–97.

Hibbs, Thomas S., *Dialectic and Narrative in Aquinas: An Interpretation of the Summa Contra Gentiles* (Notre Dame, IN: University of Notre Dame Press, 1995).

Hood, John Y.B., *Aquinas and the Jews* (Philadelphia: University of Pennsylvania Press, 1995).

Inglis, John, 'Philosophical autonomy and the historiography of medieval philosophy', *British Journal for the History of Philosophy* 5 (1997): 21–53.

Inglis, John, 'Emanation in historical context: Aquinas and the Dominican response to the Cathars', *Dionysius* XVII (1999): 95–128.

Inglis, John, *On Aquinas* (Belmont, CA: Wadsworth, 2002).

Jenkins, John I., *Knowledge and Faith in Thomas Aquinas* (Cambridge UK: Cambridge University Press, 1997).

Jordan, Mark D., *Ordering Wisdom: The Hierarchy of Philosophical Discourses in Aquinas* (Notre Dame, IN: University of Notre Dame Press, 1986).

Jordan, Mark D., *The Alleged Aristotelianism of Thomas Aquinas* (Toronto: Pontifical Institute of Medieval Studies, 1992).

Kenny, Anthony, *Aquinas* (Oxford: Oxford University Press, 1980).

Kenny, Anthony, *Aquinas on Mind* (London: Routledge, 1993).

Kretzmann, Norman, *The Metaphysics of Theism: Aquinas's Natural Theology in Summa Contra Gentiles I* (Oxford: Oxford University Press, 1997).

Kretzmann, Norman and Stump, Eleonore (eds), *The Cambridge Companion to the Philosophy of Aquinas* (Cambridge, UK: Cambridge University Press, 1993).

Leclercq, Jean, *The Love of Learning and the Desire for God: Study of Monastic Culture* (New York: Fordham University Press, 1978).

Levering, Matthew, *Christ's Fulfilment of Torah and Temple: Salvation According to Thomas Aquinas* (Notre Dame, IN: University of Notre Dame Press, 2002).

Libera, Alain de, 'Thomisme', *Encyclopédie Universelle, Les Notions Philosophiques* (Paris: Presses Universitaires de France, 1992).

Lisska, Anthony J., *Aquinas's Theory of Natural Law: An Analytic reconstruction* (Oxford: Clarendon Press, 1996).

Lonergan, Bernard, *Verbum: Word and Idea in Aquinas* (Notre Dame, IN: University of Notre Dame Press, 1967).

Louth, Andrew, *Denys the Areopagite* (London: Geoffrey Chapman, 1989).

McCool, Gerald A., *Catholic Theology in the Nineteenth Century: The Quest for a Unitary Method* (New York: Seabury Press, 1977).

McInerny, Ralph (ed.), *Thomas Aquinas: Selected Writings* (Harmondsworth: Penguin, 1998).

Martin, Christopher (ed.) *The Philosophy of Thomas Aquinas* (London: Routledge, 1988).

Marenbon, John, *Later Medieval Philosophy (1150–1350): An Introduction* (London: Routledge, 1991).

Marenbon, John (ed.), *Medieval Philosophy*, Routledge History of Philosophy, vol. III (London: Routledge, 1998).

Mascall, Eric L., *He Who Is: A Study in Traditional Theism* (London: Longman, Green, 1943, revised 1966).

Merriell, D. Juvenal, *To the Image of the Trinity: A Study in the Development of Aquinas' Teaching* (Toronto: Pontifical Institute of Medieval Studies, 1990).

Milbank, John and Pickstock, Catherine, *Truth in Aquinas* (London: Routledge, 2001).

Mulchahey, M. Michèle, *'First the Bow is Bent in Study': Dominican Education Before 1350* (Toronto: Pontifical Institute of Medieval Studies, 1998).

Nelson, Daniel Mark, *The Priority of Prudence: Virtue and Natural Law in Thomas Aquinas and the Implications for Modern Ethics* (University Park, PA: State University of Pennsylvania Press, 1992).

O'Meara, Thomas F., *Thomas Aquinas Theologian* (Notre Dame, IN: University of Notre Dame Press, 1997).

O'Rourke, Fran, *Pseudo-Dionysius and the Metaphysics of Aquinas* (Leiden: Brill, 1992).

Persson, Per Erik, *Sacra Doctrina: Reason and Revelation in Aquinas* (Oxford: Blackwell, 1970).

Piché, David, *La Condamnation parisienne de 1277* (Paris: Vrin, 1999).

Pinckaers, Servais, *The Sources of Christian Ethics* (Washington, DC: Catholic University of America Press, 1995).

Porter, Jean, *The Recovery of Virtue: The Relevance of Aquinas for Christian Ethics* (London: SPCK, 1990).

Porter, Jean, *Natural and Divine Law: Reclaiming the Tradition for Christian Ethics* (Grand Rapids, MI: Eerdmans, 1999).

Pouivet, Roger, *Après Wittgenstein, Saint Thomas* (Paris: PUF, 1997).

Preller, Victor, *Divine Science and the Science of God: A Reformulation of Thomas Aquinas* (Princeton, NJ: Princeton University Press, 1967).

Prouvost, Géry, *Thomas d'Aquin et les thomismes* (Paris: Cerf, 1996).

Rogers, Eugene F., Jr., *Thomas Aquinas and Karl Barth: Sacred Doctrine and the Natural Knowledge of God* (Notre Dame, IN: University of Notre Dame Press, 1995).

Runciman, Steven, *The Medieval Manichee: A Study of the Christian Dualist Heresy* (Cambridge, UK: Cambridge University Press, 1955).

Schoot, Henk J.M., *Christ the 'Name' of God: Thomas Aquinas on naming Christ* (Leuven: Peeters, 1993).

Smalley, B., *The Gospels in the Schools c.1100–c.1280* (London: Hambledon Press, 1985).

Tanner, Kathryn, *God and Creation in Christian Theology* (Oxford: Blackwell, 1988).

Torrell, Jean-Pierre, *Saint Thomas Aquinas, vol 1: The Person and his Work* (Washington, DC: Catholic University of America Press, 1996).

Tugwell, Simon (ed.), *Albert and Thomas: Selected Writings* (New York: Paulist Press, 1988).

Valkenberg, W.G.B.M., *Did Not Our Hearts Burn? Place and Function of Holy Scripture in the Theology of St Thomas Aquinas* (Utrecht: Thomas Institute, 1990).

Vos, Arvin, *Aquinas, Calvin and Contemporary Protestant Thought: A Critique of Protestant Views of the Thought of Thomas Aquinas* (Washington, DC: Christian University Press, 1985).

Wawrykov, Joseph P., *God's Grace and Human Action: 'Merit' in the Theology of Thomas Aquinas* (Notre Dame, IN: University of Notre Dame Press, 1996).

Weisheipl, James A., *Friar Thomas d'Aquino. His Life, Thought, and Works*, 2nd edn. (Washington, DC: Catholic University of America Press, 1983).

Westberg, Daniel, *Right Practical Reason: Aristotle, Action and Prudence in Aquinas* (Oxford: Clarendon Press, 1994).

Williams, A.N., *The Ground of Union: Deification in Aquinas and Palamas* (Oxford: Oxford University Press, 1999).

INDEX